Killing Tradition

Killing Tradition

Inside Hunting
and
Animal Rights Controversies

Simon J. Bronner

The University Press of Kentucky

Editorial and Sales Offices: The University Press of Kentucky
663 South Limestone Street, Lexington, Kentucky 40508-4008
www.kentuckypress.com

12 11 10 09 08   5 4 3 2 1

Library of Congress Cataloging-in-Publication Data

Bronner, Simon J.
  Killing tradition : inside hunting and animal rights controversies / Simon J.
Bronner.
    p. cm.
  Includes bibliographical references and index.
  ISBN 978-0-8131-2528-2 (hardcover : alk. paper)
  1. Animal rights—United States. 2. Hunting—United States. I. Title.
  HV4764.B76 2008
  179'.3—dc22   2008029789

This book is printed on acid-free recycled paper meeting
the requirements of the American National Standard
for Permanence in Paper for Printed Library Materials.

Manufactured in the United States of America.

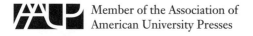 Member of the Association of
American University Presses

For Bert Wilson

Contents

Illustrations

Acknowledgments

My "field" for this project was mostly in the woods. I benefited from able guides navigating me through sometimes rough terrain and helping me see the forest for the trees. I started going to camp as an escape before it became fieldwork, but once the project took shape, the men at Camp Hunter and other haunts were wonderfully receptive to being studied. I am especially grateful to Glen Carnicelli for scouting hunting traditions on some unfamiliar ground and setting me on the right track.

Back in the halls of academe, and sometimes on the picket line, Jay Mechling taught me a great deal about the animal rights movement and the compelling issues of animal-human cultural relations. From his distant perch in California, he shared my excitement about the importance of events occurring in Hegins, Pennsylvania, and joined me in fieldwork there. I doubly owe him for passing along the suggestion of Jon Wagner, his colleague at the University of California at Davis, for the title of this book, which describes the Hegins scene and connects to the other examples I pursued. Gregory Sharrow of the Vermont Folklife Center shared his experience working on the "Deer Stories" radio series as I was working on the meanings of the hunting story. In New York State, Peter Voorheis passed along his knowledge as a hunter and a folklorist, and I value the time spent with him in his aptly named hometown of Friendship. At the University of Texas and various American Studies Association meetings, I benefited from discussions with Janet Davis, who helped me get a handle on the history and meaning of animal protection organizations. I also want to recognize the scholarly foundation for this work provided by C. Kurt Dewhurst and Marsha MacDowell at Michigan State University. They sent me packing to Presque Isle and the Upper Peninsula of Michigan, where I got more than my share of camp life.

Closer to home, Penn State colleague Ken Thigpen blazed a path for many workers in this field with outstanding films on deer camps and snake hunts. He kindly shared his findings with me and joined me at home and in conferences to discuss the idea of hunting culture. My contacts in the popular press were important to evaluate the media as an actor in the animal rights dramas I covered, and I am indebted to Cate Barron, managing editor of the *Harrisburg Patriot-News*, and Vicki Terwilliger, reporter for the *Pottsville Republican and Evening Herald*, for their assistance in my research into the journalism of animal rights protest. In Hegins, Bud Angst, Jennifer Miller, and Robert Tobash generously gave of their time to be interviewed and allowed me to mine their uncataloged papers on hunting and the town's pigeon shoot.

Back in the West, I gained wisdom from Bert Wilson every time I saw him at an American Folklore Society meeting or Fife Folklore Conference in Logan, Utah. He inspired me with his own hunting stories and historical photographs and moved me with his devotion to family and friendship as part of a fulfilling life. His impressive folkloristic legacy in Utah is carried on by other erudite professors who count hunting as a prime interest, such as Jacqueline Thursby and Eric Eliason.

As should be evident from the combination of folkloristics and psychology in this volume, I was influenced by the late Alan Dundes, who encouraged my work with what I came to call "contested traditions." As busy and productive a scholar as I have ever encountered, he made time to help me on both professional and personal levels. His analytic essays in *Interpreting Folklore* (1980), *Parsing through Customs* (1987), *The Cockfight* (1994), *From Game to War* (1997), and *The Meaning of Folklore* (which I edited in 2008) were truly affecting. Readers should note the differences in our approaches, however, especially my effort to be more ethnographic and behavioristic, taking into account symbolic perceptions and praxic enactments by different participants in traditional events, while also being aware of my intellectual debt to his symbolist and structural insights.

I could not have completed this book without the cooperation of advocates on both sides of the political aisle. Heidi Prescott, now senior vice president of the Humane Society of the United States, allowed me access to the papers and staff at the Fund for Animals and directed me to many valuable resources on the animal rights movement. She also kindly invited me to join meetings with her legal team after court hearings. Steve Hindi, founding president of Showing Animals Respect and Kindness (SHARK), and Doris Gitman, an animal rights activist who worked with Trans-Species Unlimited, also shared their time and information generously. Ingrid Newkirk of People for the Ethical Treatment of Animals (PETA) and her staff agreed to be interviewed and provided a number of useful materials. Melody Zullinger, executive director of the Pennsylvania Federation of Sportsmen's Clubs, and Mike Creamer, president of the Pennsylvania Deer Association, graciously responded to my many queries. Undoubtedly, they and their adversaries on the other side may not agree with my interpretations, but I hope they appreciate my earnest effort to give an inside-out view of the issues.

I am grateful to the Fulbright Program of the Council for International Exchange of Scholars for giving me a chance to carry my work across the Atlantic when I was awarded the Walt Whitman Distinguished Chair at Leiden University in the Netherlands. While there, I delivered a public lecture on animal rights at the behest of my gracious faculty host, Joke Kardux, and learned much from my audience. My research advanced thanks to resources extended by the Meertens Institute in Amsterdam and the collegiality of outstanding ethnologists and folklorists there, such as Peter Jan Margry, Marjolein Efting Dijkstra, Gerard Rooijakkers, Theo Meder, Irene Stengs, and Herman Roodenburg. In my investigation of hare coursing in the British Isles, I was aided by the Society for Folklife Studies, which provided funding for me to travel to Scotland. I am grateful to the society's energetic editor, Linda-May Ballard, and stalwart officers Gavin Sprott, Cozette Griffin-Kremer, Duncan Dornan, Elaine Edwards, Eddie Cass, and Jacqueline Simpson. I was also able to visit Oxford thanks to the efforts of Marcel Vellinga, Lindsay Asquith, and Paul Oliver, who provided me historical and ethnological insights on the British scene.

Some of the material in this book appeared previously in exploratory articles for academic journals. For this book, I substantially expanded, revised, and updated the essays and photographs to form connected chapters here. I want to thank the editors of the journals for valuable input at a critical stage of research: Elaine Lawless at the *Journal of American Folklore* (Hegins), Jacqueline Thursby and Sabina Magliocco at *Western Folklore* (deer camp), and Linda-May Ballard at *Folk Life* (hare coursing). My commentary on legal proceedings concerning the Hegins pigeon shoot has not been published previously, and I am grateful to Alison Dundes Renteln and Elliott Oring for their feedback on my presentation at the Western States Folklore Society meeting in Los Angeles. I also included perspectives on the hunting story that I first presented at the American Folklore Society meeting in Quebec City; there I benefited from the cross-cultural insights of Angus Gillespie, Greg Kelley, Jay Mechling (again), Wolfgang Mieder, and John P. Warren. Helpful to my revision was an opportunity to serve as commonwealth speaker for the Pennsylvania Council on the Humanities. It gave me the opportunity to address grassroots organizations across the expanse of the hunting culture and receive valuable comments on my ideas. Ronald L. Baker in the United States and Garry Marvin in England also helped with their careful reading of the manuscript and their astute observations.

I would be remiss if I did not mention the contribution of my marvelous colleagues in American Studies at Penn State–Harrisburg. Although working in different fields, Michael Barton, John Haddad, Charles Kupfer, and Yvonne Sims were always on the lookout for me. They were quick to provide clippings, references, and ideas relevant to my research and, even more importantly, created a stimulating learning environment. We are all supported by an amazing staff, especially Sue Etter and Cindy Leach, who keep us organized. Penn State also kindly granted me a sabbatical leave to complete my work in Hegins. Students working with me in this field were an inspiration, especially Julie Hurst on women hunters, Rachel Wolgemuth on pet cemeteries, and William G. Dugan on the Hegins pigeon shoot.

My wife, Sally, sent me off on my forays into the woods with encouraging smiles. Maybe I should have worried that she was overly agreeable to my departure. There was usually hell to pay upon my return, though. Yet she tolerated, and then understood, my immersion in this topic. We came to share much in the various connections we made to the research, whether it involved trying to get inside my son's head as he engaged in computer "shooting" games; reflecting on her maternal feeling for pets and my daughter's virtual adoption of Webkinz animals; shopping at Cabela's, Gander Mountain, and Bass Pro Shop (or *hunting* for bargains), which commodify the great outdoors; viewing *Animal Planet* or *Outdoor World* on television with a fresh perspective; going to the latest family movie with yet another besieged animal theme; or noticing campaign literature on sportsmen and guns in the heat of electoral politics. I knew I had hit the mark when she would arrive home and excitedly tell me, "I met someone you've got to talk to." The more we shared, the more I realized that the issues underlying the controversies I covered reach deeply into our lives, and yours.

Taking Aim

"We have been whaling in this town for centuries, so why shouldn't we continue?" Yoshinori Shoji, vice chairman of the Japan Small-Type Whaling Association, defensively addressed the reporter from the *Guardian* who had come to the tiny fishing village of Wadaura for the protest-filled opening of the 2007 whaling season (McCurry 2007). Aware that the protesters were declaring that the animals had rights, Shoji opined, "We have a right to decide what we eat" (Coleman 2007). Hearing his preparation of whale meat called an atrocity, he referred to it as tradition to justify its continuation. The community's hunts had been part of the town's social fabric for hundreds of years, and Shoji pointed out the family-owned boats and the customs passed down through many generations. Shoji was aware that world opinion was weighted against the whale hunters, but underscoring the cultural significance of whales to their folklife, he reminded reporters of the Japanese proposal for the International Whaling Commission to allow the hunting of minke whales by aboriginal people as a part of ceremonies or as a vital food source (Coleman 2007). The 1986 international ban on commercial whale hunting exempted the Baird beaked whale he had harpooned, but environmental groups, not satisfied with a partial ban, had stepped up their efforts to abolish all whale hunting and signal a new age for animal rights in the twenty-first century.

For many people, the Save the Whales campaign was their first awareness of avid animal protectionism. The public began to take notice during the mid-1960s, when biologist Paul Spong began experiments in the Vancouver Aquarium to communicate with killer whales and then develop what appeared to be a play relationship with them. Spong attributed anthropomorphic qualities of depression, pain, joy,

Japanese fishermen slaughter a Baird's beaked whale at Wada Port on June 21, 2007, in Chiba, Japan. Under the coastal whaling program, Japan is allowed to hunt only a limited number of whales every year, and Wadaura villages are permitted to hunt twenty-six whales during the season that begins June 20 and ends August 31. (Photo by Koichi Kamoshida/Getty Images)

and even music making to the animal. This discovery was coincident with *Flipper*, a movie (1963) and hit television series (1964–1967) that revolved around a dolphin's gratitude to a boy for saving it from being speared by heartless humans. The drama focused on the humans' decision of whether to keep or release the animal, but the movie showed that the animal made up its own mind. Nonetheless, it was a leap from sympathizing with apparently smiling dolphins to playing with formidable *killer* whales.

In 1968, Spong's stirring pronouncement that, as highly intelligent social beings, the killer whales in Vancouver should be freed from captivity received wide media attention. Inspired by his call, a fledgling environmental activist group named Greenpeace, formed to protest nuclear tests in the Pacific, made news when its vessel the *Phyllis Cormack* confronted a Soviet whaling ship sixty miles off the coast of Eureka, California. Greenpeace positioned an inflatable Zodiac between the harpoon and a targeted whale, but the gunner fired anyway. The filmed record of the activists risking their lives to protect whales from commercial interests generated worldwide interest in a post–civil rights direct-action movement. Before the end of the century, the social bonding attributed to killer whales became the basis for another boy-animal buddy movie portraying fishermen as the bad guys when Hollywood's *Free Willy* (1993) and several sequels concluding with *The Rescue* (1997) made a splash at the box office.

A stirring protest song called "Save the Whales," released as a single by American rock performer Country Joe McDonald in 1975 and covered by the legendary counterculture band the Grateful Dead, became an anthem for environmental activists. Its lyrics reflected on the "good old days" of sail and bemoaned the "modern ship and a modern crew with sonar scopes and explodin' harpoons / A mechanical boat made outta steel, a floating machine built to kill the whales" (McDonald 1994). In this repeatedly performed song, McDonald connected whale hunting and animal abuse to the corrupting force of commercial mass culture:

> There're lots of whales in the deep blue sea, we kill them for the
>   company
> We drag 'em 'longside and chop 'em in two and melt 'em down
>   and sell 'em to you
> There hardly is a sailor alive who can keep the tears from his eyes
> As he remembers the good old days when there were no whales to
>   save
> Thank the Russians and Japanese for scouring the deep blue seas
> Looking for ivory and perfume and plastic toys and pet food.

For discontented youth at the time who believed "the times they are a-changin'," as Bob Dylan heralded, the Vietnam War was over, but all was not right with the world. Modernization, globalization, and incorporation did not seem to bring the social and environmental progress they yearned and fought for. Looking back at the abstracted old traditions "when my grandpa was a boy," McDonald intimated that things were no better now, for "after six months out at sea, it's nothin' but death and misery." The song wondered aloud what had happened to the high hopes for peace and harmony of his Woodstock generation. The song could be interpreted as dispirited, an alarm that people would not wake up to the dawn of the age of Aquarius, or it could be seen as a rallying cry to launch a campaign for a new universalist morality, beginning with the rescue of majestic, peaceful whales from destructive machine power and commercial exploitation (Kemmerer 2004a).

Moved by the plight of the hunted whale, a California teenager and her mother founded a marine preservationist and educational organization in 1977 and called it, you guessed it, Save the Whales. Subsequently, the value-laden phrase entered folk speech in variations and parodies as a modern shibboleth and a marker of dewy-eyed liberal sentiment. In response to a flood of goods such as board and computer games, tote bags, neckties, earrings, note cards, shirts, stuffed animals, adopt-a-whale kits, and key chains emblazoned with "SAVE THE WHALES," comic T-shirts sported the phrase "SAVE THE MALES," a backlash campaign implying that animal rights was a hyped bleeding-heart, feminist cause, and all the more annoying for it (Burke and Black 1997). To add insult to the feminist sentiment, bumper stickers were quickly fashioned with messages such as "SCREW THE WHALES, SAVE THE BIMBOS" and "SAVE THE WHALES, HARPOON A FAT CHICK." Building on the Save the Whales momentum, animal protection organizations promoted spin-offs such as "save the dolphins" (Animal Welfare Institute), "save the seals" (World Animal Foundation), and "save the polar bear" (Greenpeace, Project Thin Ice).

Proponents of whale protection used the campaign to address larger problems of modernity, as they viewed it, with its encouragement of cutthroat social competitiveness and industrial capitalist exploitation. One pillar of the campaign's edifice was the protest of unnecessary human depletion of natural resources with the powerful tools and profit motives of industrial capitalism; another was the violence done to gorgeous beings who represented human aspirations of family bonding and social harmony (Heller 2007; Roberts 1990; Roman 2006). Thus the artwork for the Save the Whales campaign often included idyllic scenes of the noble creatures leisurely swimming in family groups or majestically, playfully rising above the water with no worries about machine-propelled harpoons. To underscore this social reform message, games brandishing the "Save the Whales" label advertised that they were cooperative rather than competitive. Ken and Jannice Kolsbun, who developed their Save the Whales board game in 1978 as part of a wider line of cooperative games, boast that it has been their most popular. Players move metallic whales with names around the board. As the Kolsbuns relate, "Here in the spirit of kinship with Nature, players work together to 'save' 8 great whales: Bowhead, Fin, Blue, Gray, Humpback, Right, Sperm and Orca. Meanwhile, oil spills, radioactive waste and catcher ships are moving these great whales toward extinction—just as in real life. Players earn 'survival points' and make group decisions to save the whales. Misjudgments or a string of bad luck may cause the ship to catch a whale—always a sad event" (Cooperative Games 2008). A computer game adaptation developed by Steve Beck in 1983 puts the responsibility for protection in the hands of the player who controls a submarine and must prevent harpoons and nets fired from a smoke-billowing tanker on the surface from harming the cute, multicolored whales. If the sinister tanker is not enough to combat, the player also has to watch for the dreaded radioactive flotsam that crawls across the screen in an obvious signal of modern technology gone awry (Video Game Critic 2008).

The "Save the Whales" slogan, emblematic of animal rights advocacy reported in various media as either earnestly compassionate or absurd, is turned on its head in cartoons showing whales holding up a protest sign declaring "SAVE THE HUMANS." The parodies betoken misplaced human concern for animals when many supposedly more serious problems run rampant. Yet animal rights activists insist that ending animal cruelty and exploitation is the path to ultimate solutions. They fervently believe that a better world is attainable by attacking the deep roots of injustice, discrimination, and violence in humans' mistreatment of animals. And what more visible symbol for the persecuted animal than the whale? Its gargantuan size is reduced to small cubes of consumable meat by the avaricious humans whom they dwarf. It exhibits the human, family quality of a mother feeding her young with milk from mammary glands. Whale sightings are anxiously awaited at lookout points as glorious, breathtaking moments. Schoolchildren hear the dulcet sounds of whales interpreted as songs and are taught that whales, too, have hair, on obligatory trips to natural history museums. They recall with a frown Captain Ahab's crazed obsession with destroying the white whale in Herman Melville's *Moby-Dick*. But whales are not always gentle in people's imagination. After all, how many remember that Ahab's monstrous whale took his leg and reduced his ship to splinters? Or whales may bring to mind that nagging biblical imagery of Jonah in the "belly of the beast" (Jonah 1:17) and the comparison of Pharaoh to a whale or monster in the seas (Ezekiel 32:2). Animal welfare organizations such as the Compassionate Action Institute reach out to children to emphasize the human qualities of animals and establish them as our friends and companions. Its Web site with the pacifist message of *pleasebekind.com* explains, "Whales are mammals just like us. They give birth to live babies which they nurse. Even though they live in the water, they need to breathe air. The blowholes on their backs are like our nostrils. Whales use their flippers for more than just swimming. One mother whale was seen slapping her baby with her flipper to teach him to stay away from a ship. Baby whales are called calves. Whale calves' aunts often babysit for them when their mothers have to go somewhere" (Compassionate Action Institute 2000–2002). The point is that although the animal rights movement mounted a broad frontal attack on objectionable practices involving a variety of animals, the anthropomorphic symbolism of the whale made the Save the Whales campaign, and subsequent ones in which animals were depicted as viciously "hunted down," especially memorable.

For the present, the essential ethical principle for animal rights activists is that people do to one another what they do to animals, and they complain that what is happening to whales and other creatures is despicable. Not everyone is convinced, especially if one believes that animals can benefit humans by providing such basics as medicine, shelter, and food. Also voiced is cynicism among racialized groups who are not about to share their victimhood with animals. In fact, they may even be repelled by the comparison. More than twenty years after Country Joe McDonald's landmark song, for instance, popular black ghetto rapper Shyheim sardonically sang "Save the whales, save the whales, Free Willy . . . save anything, nobody cares" in his edgy CD *Manchild* (1999). But obviously a lot of people do care enough to risk their lives to stop the hunt.

If many seemed jaded by all the fuss over saving animals while ghettos grew and wars waged, the *Guardian*'s graphic coverage of the opening of whaling season was hard to ignore. Set beside a grisly image of a giant, hacked-up whale's head lying in a mammoth-sized pool of blood, Greenpeace's advertisement blared a message that was more aggressive than a simple call for mobilized defense: "Defend the Whales, Invest in Their Future." The gruesome image of a mutilated creature often described as "peaceful," "majestic," and "biblical" by environmentalists produced strong negative reactions from readers—perhaps intensified by the attitude of the hunters. As bearers of a venerated skill passed down from one generation to another, the villagers seemed unfazed by the protesters' shouts or the gore and stench as they methodically went about their ritual cutting of blubber, much as their ancestors had. For families in Wadaura, butchering the whale offered meat for food and a livelihood. If anti-hunters "think that is wrong, I fail to understand them," Shoji opined. The headline for the story summed up his fellow villagers' retort to whale hunting's foes: "Killing Whales Is Our Tradition." If so, animal rights groups responded by redoubling their efforts to kill that tradition.

Is tradition a justification or a ruse for the killing of animals? Are the supposedly "humane" deaths of these creatures and the benefits accruing to humankind mitigating factors? Does the fact that hunting provides a livelihood exculpate the villagers? Does the commercial aspect of hunting make it more reprehensible or tolerable? Is it significant that, as a custom, hunting or the use of animals is integrally woven into the fabric of culture? Does it make a difference whether the animal in question is a cockroach, rat, snake, pigeon, turkey, pig, or hare? What if the group being protested was your community or your family, rather than an exotic, primitive slice of the past across an ocean? What happens to ethical considerations when hunting is used for recreational or gaming purposes rather than sustenance? Why are such heated passions aroused in the debate over killing traditions—whether to perpetuate or abolish hunting heritage?

These questions raised by the battle over killing tradition force us to reflect on our fundamental ethical beliefs and their implications for the conduct of society, past and future. Beyond the signal example of the Save the Whales campaign, other controversies in heartland settings closer to home have challenged culturally based assumptions about the social and physical relations of animals to humans, definitions of violence and cruelty, the rights of animals or human communities to engage in activities that may be deemed objectionable by a large part of society, and governmental responsibilities for environmental—and economic—protection. Although the issues involved in each controversy are varied, I find a common thread in the repeated dispute over the meaning of tradition as a guiding principle in animal-human relations for a rapidly modernizing society. Animal rights indeed must be taken seriously alongside other social movements geared toward initiating change (Beers 2006; Jasper and Nelkin 1992; Kean 1998). There is no doubt that the animal rights movement has had a profound impact in terms of protecting animals from cruelty and making people more sensitive to the exploitation of animals for entertainment purposes and commercial gain. What has been widely accepted as unethical in the use of animals for scientific experimentation, media productions, food processing, and fashion since the late twentieth century has become institutionalized in the ubiquitous label, "no animals were harmed in the making of this product."

But my argument is that most people have a harder time assenting to the unconditional elimination of time-honored practices that provide social capital or human benefit through the idea of tradition in an increasingly individualistic, fragmented society. Hunting and gaming are prime examples of activities that are viewed as important to cultural maintenance, and therein lies the rub, for those societies in which animal rights are rising as an issue typically claim progressive egalitarian goals of curbing abuse and exploitative practices. The two sides appear difficult to reconcile when their perceptions of each other are so skewed. Animal rights activists send out an alarm whenever men shoot guns, especially when they are negatively stereotyped as "slob hunters" associated with beer-guzzling killers and unscrupulous poachers. Or hunters are cast in the image of vexatious rocker Ted Nugent, who announces his libertarian hunting credo as "whack 'em and stack 'em" and preparation for war (World 2000; Nugent 2000).

The frequently mentioned link between military strength and hunting in Hollywood films such as *The Deer Hunter* or British imperial tracts is problematic if people are to feel safe. During the throes of the First World War, Henry Salt of the Humanitarian League made a distinction between hunter and soldier: "We conclude, then, that Sport, considered as a school for War, is doubly to be condemned, inasmuch as, while it breeds the aggressive and cruel spirit of militarism, it does *not furnish* that practical military training which is essential to successful warfare. Sport may make a man a savage; it does not make him a soldier" (1915, 154–55). The U.S. Army today disagrees, as evidenced by its advertisements in hunting magazines. In the October 2007 *Field and Stream*, the army took out a full-page ad featuring the testimony of soldier Kyle Robbins that begins, "Nothing prepared me for the military better than being an outdoorsman. . . . Hunting and fishing gave me the confidence, discipline and pride that allowed me to stay strong and steady through all situations." At hunting shows, the army's exhibits present the soldier as another type of outdoorsman. The army would prefer to replace Salt's characterization of sport making a man "savage" with Robbins's list of values gained from hunting: "Loyalty, Duty, Respect, Selfless Service, Honor, Integrity, and Personal Courage" (Robbins 2007). These attributes are summed up in the army's slogan "Army Strong." Yet for all the rhetoric, one is hard-pressed to find any mention of guns—or killing.

At the same time, a heroic counterimage exudes nostalgia for American pioneer heritage (or ancient regal tradition in Britain) and feelings for community. In many homes and hunting lodges from the nineteenth century to the present, romantic portrayals of hardy New World adventurers taking aim at deer for their sustenance or showing their mettle in a fight to the death with a fierce buck grace many a wall. As orange-clad hunters step out into the woods for the annual ritual of buck season, do they imagine themselves blazing a frontier trail, as depicted in this art? Narratives abound, particularly in the United States, regarding hunting's relation to the founding mythology of America. Two that are especially prominent concern the conquest of the land and the establishment of freedom for newly arrived settlers. There is James Fenimore Cooper's Deerslayer character, a precursor of the western hero, who exhibits rugged self-sufficiency with his trusty hunting rifle in tow. Pioneer trailblazer Daniel Boone, too, was revered as a hunter who dared to expand beyond the original thirteen colonies to Native American hunting grounds and open the way west to settlement. A contrast is replayed in many Revolutionary War reenactments between the victorious ragtag, individualistic Americans armed with their hunting rifles and the stiff, lockstepped British in backwoods settings such as forested King's Mountain, North Carolina, a 1780 battle that supposedly turned the tide in the War for Independence.

One can hear this longing for the rugged individual of yore on the seas as well as in the woods. In Country Joe McDonald's song, he finds discord between the hardy sailor of adventurous tradition and the corporate whaler of motorized modernity, killing by oceanwide proportions in anything but a fair fight. The same characters despised as

"The Life of a Hunter. 'Catching a Tartar.'" This Currier and Ives print (1861) illustrates combat between male foes. The hunter appears to be thrown back as the buck is about to launch a penetrating blow with his antlers.

slobs and murderers can be glorified as spunky ring-tailed roarers and trailblazing scouts that schoolchildren are taught to admire and idolize. This dilemma causes psychological conflict for many people, reflecting how their ethics respond to a mercurial world accelerating at breakneck speed, and they find inconsistency in conventional sources of ethical construction in religion, education, popular culture, and politics. Postmodern promoters of hunting and fishing incorporate these activities—or sports—into the healthful world of the outdoors, an antidote to the corporate routine and social restraint of a climate-controlled machine civilization. When hunting in the *great* outdoors, they underscore, one feels alive and free.

The master controversy is how this feeling of humanity set against nature is achieved. At a stage of civilization when people do not need to hunt to survive, animal rights activists argue, killing animals is not imperative, and in evolutionary terms, it is backward and barbarous. The objection is to activities in which the death of animals is turned into "sport" or "recreation" for human amusement. Countering the image of hunting as mindless massacre (or even an animal holocaust, in extreme depictions), sportsmen and outdoorsmen point out the pragmatic aspects of their pursuit. They are ecologists, after all, preserving nature's balance by controlling animal populations, protecting forests, and eradicating pests. The rhetoric of sport facilitates this task and rewards mastery of the endangered life skills of relating to the wild, they say. They have a time-honored set of ethics, they point out, encapsulated in the idea of "fair chase," or the notion that animals are given a sporting chance and humans are willing to put themselves in danger for the enlivening thrill of the hunt. They cite an important social ethic, too: that is, hunting is steeped in tradition that encourages family bonding and cultural identity, which are especially important in a postmodern world that threatens to disintegrate those ties. That hunting is in decline is not really surprising, outdoorsmen emphasize, but they would refute the idea that this reduction represents progress. They point to the dwindling of wilderness, more home-bound pursuits, loss of filial piety, and modernization as taking a toll on the valuation of hunting. But advocates claim that hunting is more necessary than ever socially, if not for survival. From my vantage of understanding modern culture, what I find newsworthy is not that hunting has declined but that it has persisted as well and long as it has. And I ask in this book why that is, in light of the dramatic shift in the environment and society. I observe the ready acceptance of animal protection in the wake of the Save the Whales campaign, but the prospect of eradicating hunting and sporting events, with their associations of heritage and tradition, makes people pause and, in many cases, resist. My explanation of the conflict hinges on the key word *tradition* used by both sides. I probe the way symbols and rituals are formed, enacted, gendered, and reshaped in animal rights controversies to deal with foundational traditions that appear to simultaneously destroy and regenerate life.

In the twenty-first century, the cry to save the whales does not come from radical scientists or countercultural singers as much as Hollywood celebrities, giving the cause popular culture chicness. As the International Whaling Commission (IWC) met in 2007, members heard from vocal protesters that nothing short of a complete abolition of commercial whaling would do. Lest the public think that the battle had been won back in the 1980s with a partial whaling ban, the Whaleman

Foundation used the occasion of the IWC meeting to launch "Save the Whales Again," with stars of the small and big screens as spokespersons. At a press conference, youthful actor Hayden Panettiere, from the hit television show *Heroes*, took a T-shirt emblazoned with "SAVE THE CHEERLEADER," referring to her endangered character, and replaced *cheerleader* with *whales*. Later, she took to the streets in Anchorage, Alaska, in the "Big Blue March," along with people dressed as blue whales and lots of children for whom saving the whales would, according to protesters, make the world they inherit more ethical and peaceful. Not to be pegged as merely a pretty-faced talking head, on October 30, 2007, Panettiere joined other activists on surfboards in Japan to interfere with a dolphin hunt. Maybe to offset actor Charlton Heston, forever known as Hollywood's Moses in *The Ten Commandments* (1956) and as the face of the National Rifle Association (NRA), the likes of Irish actor Pierce Brosnan, famous for playing debonair secret agent James Bond, and *Baywatch* veteran Alexandra Paul lent their familiar profiles to the Save the Whales campaign, alongside causes advocating gun control, nuclear disarmament, and environmental protection.

At this point, readers are probably asking themselves on which side of the whale-sized divide I stand. To be sure, most tracts on hunting and animal rights controversies are devoted to a polemical position. Rather than take a side, though, my purpose is to get *inside* the issue, to probe its significance as part of culture at this moment in history, to get inside people's heads to explain their way of thinking and their worldview. I want to know why different outlooks on animal-human relations sometimes escalate into fisticuffs. In this book, I present the idea that the radically contrastive symbolism of animals and humans' relations with them has affected the ability to communicate about a normative ethics for modern society. As the whaling example indicates, I find the matter of tradition paramount in relation to the idea of modernity. Yet as the expressive songs and images show, both sides have a problem with modernity, and each side accuses the other of being out of step with the needs of contemporary life. The rest of us are left to figure out what lessons to take into our lives and teach our children.

To be sure, animal liberation philosophers talk about ways of not just abolishing old, cruel traditions but also instituting new ones geared toward an egalitarian mind-set opposed to "speciesism" (Kemmerer 2004b; Luke 2007; Ryder 1989). The polarized nature of the discourse on hunting heritage and animal rights is an important part of my story. Lots of socially constructed binaries exist—between old and new, past and present, men and women, rural and urban—and I plan to interpret and, to a certain extent, disrupt them by getting beneath the rhetoric to the fears and hopes that drive the oppositions. By taking an inside view, I want to investigate how people perceive these concepts and apply them to their ethics and cultural practices.

My orientation and much of my evidence come from folkloristics, which combines the ethnography of cultural scenes with symbolic, rhetorical readings of collected texts of stories, objects, and customs. This approach is appropriate to a study of tradition, since folklore studies have the scholarly distinction of contributing cross-cultural perspectives on tradition as both concept and expression (Bronner 1998, 2000a). But in the mode of thematic studies of animals and nations, I also bring historical, sociological, and political work into the mix to deal with animal rights as a social movement and hunting and animal protection in public policy (see Beers 2006; Herman 2001b; Isaac 1980; Kean 1998). As my earlier discussion of commercial songs and movies shows, I use the content of, and responses to, popular culture and literary sources to talk about a public imagination that influences people's attitudes about animals, hunters, and animal rights. I keep watch for visual and material sources as well as verbal ones to view symbol building in more than one dimension. If that accounts for my interdisciplinary methodology and data, my interpretation looks for the sources of behavior and expression in cognition. I turn to psychology to explain why people involved in the contested traditions see the events so differently. I understand that many of the meanings I uncover are outside the awareness of participants; as a result of the often disturbing issues of taking life in hunting or assuming an antagonistic position for animal rights, people project their wishes, conflicts, and values into the socially sanctioned outlet of lore. The meanings are situated within the historical, social, and geographic settings of contested traditions, and based on my experiences in America, Europe, and Japan, I have endeavored to show how these controversies are connected and differentiated in various places.

My academic position is that not enough humanistic scholarship has been devoted to hunting, although it is considered, even by its foes, to be one of humankind's oldest and most pervasive traditions. Undoubtedly, the tendency to exalt fine art and exotic or elite culture in humanities has distracted many intellectuals from pursuing the apparently vernacular practices of ordinary folks in the rough woods to assess the ethical foundations of society. Even among the disciplinary edifices that give critical attention to everyday life—such as anthropology, sociology, and history, not to mention folkloristics and other cultural studies—the consideration of hunting customs and policies has been limited. There is certainly no lack of slick publications for followers of hunting and nature, most of which relate stories of wilderness adventure, venerate animals and describe their personas, or offer tips and gear for being successful "out there." And for every hunting publication, there is an anti-hunting tract or newsletter. Yet I think there is room for critical approaches that pose in an accessible way the ultimate question of humankind's relationship to animals as models for social and environmental relationships.

Within the scholarship on hunting, folklore has not been adequately tapped as a source, probably because hunters—often considered a temporary folk group—have been underappreciated compared to ethnic, regional, and age subcultures. Another consideration is that the traditions of hunting and animal contests have been obscured by scholarly scrutiny from the outside in. By that, I mean hunting has been generalized into statistical profiles and historical chronologies. I include that useful material in my contextualization of human-animal relations, but I have found that participating in the scenes of protest and listening to the stories people tell have given me a qualitative view that is more inside out. This is a message that folklorist Alan Dundes, who broke fresh ground with his provocative psychological theses on the meaning of cockfights, bullfights, and combat sports, often iterated (Dundes 1987b, 1994, 1997). Folklore is crucial to a knowledge of human experience, he observed, because "as autobiographical ethnography" it permits a view "from the inside-out rather than from the outside-in" (1975, xi). That is, the advantage of folklore as a form of metacommunication is that it conveys what people think in their own words and actions, and what they say, make, or sing in texts and gestures expresses what they might not be able to express in everyday conversation. Dundes evinced that in folklore, more than in other forms of human evidence, "one finds a people's own unselfconscious picture of themselves," and that is a position I hope to advance here (1975, xi).

In this book, I test his theses about the need for men to prove their manhood by means of combative play in which rivals, whether human or animal, are feminized and anxieties about manliness are projected to symbolic cultural practices. In focusing tightly on gaming traditions in all-male groups, however, Dundes and others have failed to extend the analysis to groups' use of the contest to conduct their cultural scenes and construct their ethical systems. Noting that symbolist approaches seek a singular meaning for the text of an event, I have called for "semiotic layering" to get at the sources of conflict by locating the different symbolic perceptions of the same event experienced by various participants (Bronner 2005a). Especially because the hunting and animal rights movements have both changed as a result of the confrontation between them, I consider it important to know what they see when they process, for example, a boy with blood smeared on his face after his first deer kill, a pigeon put out of its misery by having its neck wrung, or the excited cries of gamblers as panting greyhounds are "slipped" to catch pesky hares called "pussies." Indeed, pro- and anti-hunters relate different narratives about the same event that reveal their fundamental beliefs and worldviews and influence their varied attempts to impose their ethics and values as the cultural norm. I also go beyond the usual range of narrative evidence found in folklore studies to include traditions in building, tools, illustration, and photography.

The meaning of animals as pest or pet, wild game or protected species, entertainment or sustenance, is subject to cultural variation that reflects and affects ethical attitudes. Even if a minority of the population participates in these events as shooters or protesters, the social and political issues reverberate through the society and form a foundational dialectic on humanity as well as modernity. This is especially true in a new millennium declared to be enigmatically *postmodern*, when a discourse on the compatibility of tradition in modernity appears to be crucial to balancing the individualistic benefits of freedom and rights with the social need for community and identity based on a collective heritage. Having tradition that provides a sense of cultural guidance, historical roots, and social belonging remains important, but the question is which traditions become ingrained in the fabric of life. It is not enough to shallowly justify hunting as something that has always been done or, on the other side, to vilify hunting as an irrational vestige of barbaric rituals. Hunting and sporting events involving animals have persisted for a reason. The fact remains that people make choices about the traditions they enact and symbolize—and canonize as culturally central or metaphorical—and I want to answer the question "What were they thinking?" for both sides.

One perspective that I apply is to extend the ethnography of cultural practices to a philosophy of *praxis*, such as when I refer to a hunting praxis in addition to a hunting ritual or custom. This usage is intended to draw attention to the symbolic qualities of acts that have social and cultural significance. Hunting as practice is the pursuit of animals with weapons. But what about video games with names such as "Buck Hunter Pro" that allow one to shoot an animal on the screen and notch a "kill"? Is that hunting? And what about people who do not go out into the woods and stalk prey as a killing tradition but avow that they are going hunting for bargains at the mall, urge the hunting down of Osama bin Laden, or go to the library to hunt for information? They choose the rhetoric of hunting to convey a cognitive concept that others in their context can understand and associate with various images inculcated through tradition. The rhetoric reveals their thinking and translates it into symbolic behavior. I have worked with praxis theory since publishing *Grasping Things* (1986) and *Following Tradition* (1998), where I noted the Aristotelian roots of the idea of activities that mark one's political and ethical life. For cultural studies, praxis is significant as an activity in which the doing—the processes involved and the conditions present—is paramount, rather than solely the end result. I am intrigued by hunting as praxis because of the idea that the act of "going out hunting" or "going to the shoot" as a mode of behavior is more important than the outcome. Philosopher Richard Bernstein summarized the interpretive possibilities well when he wrote that attention to praxis encourages "understanding of the ways in which men *are* what they *do*, of how their social *praxis* shapes and is shaped by the complex web of historical institutions and practices within which they function and work" (1971, 306). I would add that praxis takes on importance when the underlying, often unstated values and beliefs connoted by what they do are challenged or revised in a process of cultural construction.

One becomes well aware of praxis in debates on whether the process of hunting animals constitutes pursuing, killing, murdering, or harvesting. In controversies, people are forced to articulate the meaning of their actions and relate them in language to fundamental values and beliefs. In the creation of binary oppositions typical of controversies, we are pushed to comprehend the sources of difference and connection in polemical stands and determine whether resolution is possible. Controversies intrude on the existence we take for granted and impel us to reflect on what we do by contemplating what would happen if we no longer did it that way. This is no study of continuities passed unthinkingly from generation to generation; instead, it faces up to the discontinuities, disparities, and paradoxes of our customs. The cultural scenes of contested traditions therefore provide critical opportunities to analyze the dynamics of cultural behavior. Although humanities has been mostly concerned with artistic products, attention to praxis underscores the impact of process and its conceptualization, especially when it takes on the quality of representing cognition, worldview, and identity. In the examples presented in this book, the praxis and rhetoric of hunting, shooting, and coursing take on those qualities.

To get inside the dynamics of tradition and modernity in relation to the cultural struggle between animal rights and hunting heritage advocates, I present three case studies of key controversies occurring in the last two decades. My purpose is to analyze in depth representative cultural scenes that can be applied to other situations, rather than provide a broad survey of the animal rights campaign. The first cultural scene is in the deer camps of Pennsylvania, a leading location for what has been called America's hunting culture. I look at the rhetoric and strategy of the anti-hunting campaign that has directed its wrath against the images of "barbarism" in the all-male gatherings at deer camp. Deer as a subject is significant because it is the most widely targeted prey among hunters associated with American pioneer heritage; yet in the popular imagination, modern assaults on Bambi and other furry, saucer-eyed characters evoke feelings of guilt or an urge to protect (Hummel 1994, 117–33). Against the background of this divided set of loyalties and antagonisms, I examine the symbols and functions of deer camp traditions as perceived by hunters and their opponents, particularly the long-standing controversy over "blooding." Narrators from different sides relate the blood smear tradition as either horrible infanticide or beneficent coming of age, and I seek to find meaning in these oppositional perceptions and the way they have been communicated to the public.

Discussion of the totemistic images of blood and tradition continues in the second chapter. Chronicles of the animal rights movement often mention the protest of the public pigeon shoot at Hegins, Pennsylvania, during the 1990s as the key battle to end what the movement derisively calls "blood sports" (Blechman 2006, 73–99; Luke 2007, 231–33; Phelps 2007, 243–49). Having spent time working in the sleepy hamlet before the dispute erupted, I did not imagine then that it would garner international notoriety. But that is exactly what happened when global media covered mass protests and direct action on the fields where shooters took aim at live pigeons released from small boxes. It quickly became clear that the stakes in the pigeon shoot were high. For the animal rights movement, organizations tried to take their cause to the heartland, where they found fewer supporters for their anti-experimentation and animal protection offensive than they had in the cities. For pigeon shoot organizers, defending the pigeon shoot meant making an appeal to the public at large about a community's right, following tradition, to be different. Unlike Wadaura, a foreign, distant village to which Americans could hardly relate, Hegins emerged as ancestral small-town America, the heart of traditional values where farmers toil and animals graze. And instead of majestic, anthropomorphic whales on the open seas, the animal in question was the familiar pigeon—drawing derision as a repulsive rat with wings or exaltation as a gentle dove of peace.

The case of the pigeon shoot relates to a host of cognate events linked by the use of contests to control what are perceived to be pests, including rattlesnake roundups, prairie dog shoots, and bunny bops (see Adams 2000, 50; McCormick 1996; Van Putten and Miller 1999, 1113–15). Even if not domesticated as pets, animal rights activists ask, aren't these feral creatures still worthy of protection as living beings? Don't they deserve sympathy when they are shown being clubbed, battered, and bagged as the perpetrators smile over their prey? Under most animal cruelty statutes, causing protracted pain in an animal constitutes abuse and cruelty, but causing a quick death by shooting a nonendangered species probably does not. Arguments arise over the pain that animals suffer and the rights of humans to derive enjoyment from animals in traditions such as county fairs, rodeos, circuses, and horse races. The law gets murkier when conflicts arise between the animal rites communities claim for their identity and the rights animals can expect under the law (Renteln 2004, 94–113). And that is an important part of my coverage of the Hegins pigeon shoot, as courts addressed the question of whether tradition is a defense for the perpetuation of this community custom.

I close with an example of an animal rights dispute that threatened to topple a nation. I look at the practices and protests that led to the revolutionary passage of the Hunting Act of 2004 in the United Kingdom. For Americans acculturated to deer hunting as the metaphor for pioneer adventure in the woods, the passions raised by calls in the British Isles to ban hare coursing and foxhunting across hill and dale may seem alien. But that is exactly the interpretive point. As I show, the controversies have a long history that is very British and complicates the relations of city and country, tenant and landowner, hound and hare. Yet they also relate to broader conflicting desires for a gloried past that signals belonging and a hopeful future promising peace and social progress. The mighty reverberations of the sea change in animal-human practices in the United Kingdom reach west to the United States and east to the rest of Europe. Much of the global coverage focused on the apparently bizarrely polarized stands on whether hares and foxes can be chased by hounds. I explain, and rationalize, the positions by pointing out how coursing as a praxis brought out into the open the festering national conflicts over the value of countryside heritage.

I am often asked how I took up hunting, coursing, and shooting as a subject of inquiry. I know that what the interrogator really wants to know is whether I have experienced the killing tradition. In other studies I have done of woodcarvers, old-time musicians, and navy men, the issue of my participation rarely came up, although some of my interpretations were also highly charged (Bronner 1987, 1996a, 2006a). I can say that the roots of the present study actually go back to my graduate student days, when I attended church picnics in southern Indiana featuring the unusual fare of homemade turtle soup. I made inquiries and followed the trail of the turtle hunters, who I found were marginalized in the community despite the fact that the soup was a matter of local pride. No busloads of protesters descended on the picnics, but there was ambivalence among residents that I tried to explain in an essay entitled "The Paradox of Pride and Loathing, and Other Problems" (1983). Few people I talked to actually liked the taste of turtle meat, and even fewer enjoyed the work required to hunt, butcher, and prepare the turtles. I could posit historical reasons for their introduction into the diet. The area had always been predominantly Catholic,

Butchering a turtle for soup, Huntingburg, Indiana. (Photo by Simon Bronner)

and the Catholic Church's prohibition against eating meat on Fridays did not extend to the eating of turtle flesh. In a region where home butchering and wild game hunting were common, harking back to the days of pioneer settlement in this remote location, the gathering of turtles did not seem as unusual as it did in other "domesticated" environments. In the face of regional agrarian decline, turtle soup was a reminder, in residents' minds, of better, hardier days. Symbolically, turtle soup was a comfort food steeped in tradition, even though these people might be aware that in some cities, turtle soup had highfalutin ties to haughty French cuisine, while elsewhere, the notion of eating a slimy reptile found in rotten swamps was repulsive. Of course, it did not help rhetorically that "turtle soup" could occasionally be heard as slang for diarrhea and that the new generation of children questioned the consumption of animals they regarded as cute pets. Some residents resolved the conflict by pointing out that the preparation of turtle soup provided a distinction for an area that was often overlooked in regional development and lacked tourist cachet.

Residents also made sure that they did not have to confront chunks of the turtle floating in the soup, using a host of ingredients blended together to mask the animal's presence and gamy taste. Others invoked tradition, as Shoji did for the consumption of whales, by saying, "Hell, I've always eaten it," and pointing out that churches sponsored turtle soup feasts. Turtle soup made in the churches involved intense socializing that could compensate for some of the ambivalent feelings about consuming turtles. Another way to deal with cognitive dissonance was to create distance between the messy hunting and butchering of the turtles and the preparation of the soup, which became clean and wholesome in contrast (Bronner 1986, 161–78). After this career-changing experience, I continued to explore in every place I worked the significance of animal-human relations to cognitive patterns, ambivalence toward traditions, and the dynamics of tradition and modernity. Even though I had not traveled to southern Indiana to investigate animals (I was working on ethnic material culture), I quickly realized that the creatures pervaded human relations in symbol, act, and thought.

Sources for dealing with the problematics of expressive culture involving animal-human relations in cultural studies were emerging at the time, although there was no separate field for it and few psychological models of explanation (Aftandilian 2007; Bronner 1983; Dizard 1994; Dorson 1982a; Gillespie and Mechling 1987; Hummel 1994; Mechling 1989; Mieder 1993; Newall 1971). To encourage far-flung workers in this area, the groundbreaking international journal *Society and Animals* was launched in 1993, and an "Animals and Society" section of the American Studies Association was formed in 2003 (Shapiro 1993; Nibert 2003). These were positive developments, although the ethnographers among us could not help but notice the avoidance of the rhetoric of culture, despite the fact that, for many critics, the driving question was how hunting with its historic associations fit into modern culture.

If people were tired of hearing about saving whales in the new millennium, other headline-grabbing animal rights issues kept up the public discourse. These included passage of the Animal Enterprise Terrorism Act in 2006, targeting animal rights protesters; NFL quarterback Michael Vick's conviction on dogfighting charges; campaigns to abolish "canned hunts" or hunting preserves in several states; the announcement of a boycott of Canadian seafood by animal rights groups to stop seal hunts (a spin-off of the Save the Whales campaign called "Protect Seals"); legislative votes to ban cockfighting in Louisiana and bear hunting in New Jersey in 2007; and PETA's call for the end of race-track betting after the horse Eight Belles had to be euthanized at the conclusion of the 2008 Kentucky Derby. As journalists sought scholarly authorities to call, they usually found more political than cultural commentary, although they often referred to animal rights controversies as figuring prominently in "culture wars." Something was afoot. And it was about time.

If that was my scholarly route, what about my personal journey? I did not go to hunting camp as a child, but after moving to Pennsylvania as a young adult, I became friends with people who owned camps, and I was invited out to the woods for recreation and socializing. I have tried my hand at hunting, but I do not call myself a hunter. I have shot guns and as an adolescent earned a marksman medal. I eat meat not only from the supermarket but also from the wild; I have tasted gamy bear and venison from Mississippi to Maine. I have reluctantly had pets. My bedside reading consists of *Field and Stream* and *Animals Voice Magazine*—an unusual combination, judging from the libraries of pro- and anti-hunters I have visited. At home as well as in the field, I have endeavored to see animals and the controversies surrounding them from different vantages.

Living in a wooded area, wild as well as domesticated animals cross my property. One incident got our neighborhood roiled. It involved a black bear that came down off the mountain and wandered into some backyards. My neighbor who does call himself a hunter grabbed his gun and took aim, but the bear ran away before he could get off a shot. An animal control officer came by and warned my neighbor that he could not shoot the animal. "What if he comes on my porch? What if he threatens us?" The officer stood firm. Tempers flared as home owners, many of whom were also hunters, gathered. That confrontation caused a buzz about the legal limits of human actions to protect self and property against animals in this suburban borderland between wild and domestic life. The neighbors gathered in the street voiced different opinions about who was in more danger—animals or people—in the wake of modern development and the more noticeable influence of the animal rights movement.

I find that the debate over whether humans are justified in killing animals is really a commentary on the struggle to build a civil society and a consciousness of the changing environment. On a macro level, animal rights groups have initiated a debate about the need for war and violence to gain social control; they also engage the public in the issue of the shrinking natural environment and how it is maintained. Both sides agree that the environment is a good thing but differ on how it should be managed. The debate is also about how human relations can be improved, embedding arguments over whether traditional patriarchy is responsible for either a strong sense of family values extended to society or a social hierarchy that results in the mistreatment of minorities and children. Another divide has occurred between rural and urban life, particularly as societies on both sides of the Atlantic have grappled with the implications of a shift in socioeconomic emphasis from rural to urban culture. Politicians take photo opportunities while out hunting to show their toughness and ability to lead; screenwriters and the popular press, meanwhile, have constructed the redneck, hunt-loving, rural alpha male as a comical foil to the suave, civilized urbanite (Cambell, Bell, and Finney 2006, 3–8). Animal rights rhetoric builds on this constructed uneasiness with rural patriarchy and its imagery of bigoted yahoos brandishing guns and kicking animals and people around, à la the movie *Deliverance* (1972). Animal rights appeals as a youth cause can be heard in popular music, with bands like Goldfinger producing new anthems and videos such as "Free Me" (2002), with biting lyrics: "So free me / I just wanna feel what life should be / I just want enough space to turn around / And face the truth / So free me." Lead singer John Feldmann introduces the video, featured on PETA-TV and YouTube, with the explanation, "I love animals." He tells viewers that he supports veganism to prevent the abuse of animals and that he wrote the song after seeing chickens being brought to a slaughterhouse and feeling "helpless that I couldn't save any of their lives" ("Goldfinger" 2007).

On the other side, country music lyrics are wont to heap scorn on the depravity of urban life and its association with the political correctness of wacky fashionable social causes. They revel in the "good ol' boy" ethic of honoring family, hunting, and raising hell. Is that merely nostalgia cloaked in humor for a bygone time and place? Hank Williams Jr., in a signature song released in 1981, offered an anthem in the title "A Country Boy Can Survive." More than waxing poetic on country life, the popular singer threw down the gauntlet in the divide between urban and rural values:

Because you can't starve us out
And you can't make us run
Cause one of 'em old boys raisin' ole shotgun
And we say grace and we say Ma'am
And if you ain't into that we don't give a damn.

"You" in the song is the urban power elite, and he tells them that he can do things they cannot: "We can skin a buck and run a trout-line." He contrasts his raising with that of his New York City friend: "My grandpa taught me how to live off the land / And his taught him to be a businessman." The meaning is hardly subtle: country life and hunting are wholesome, character-building pursuits related to the sanctity of family and tradition. In this imagery, urbanites are tainted with the dog-eat-dog life of chasing money, and not being on the land, they can hardly appreciate nature. Rather than retreating into the woods, many songs following Williams's credo shout with bravado. In the twenty-first century, country singer Trace Adkins had a monster hit with "Ladies Love Country Boys" (2007), relating the story of a woman from an urban "subdivision" of "uptown, ball gown, hand-me-down royalty" who falls head over heels, naturally, for a country boy with "camouflage britches" riding in the "middle of a pickup truck, blaring Hank Jr., yelling, 'Turn it Up!'"

Adkins's reference to a subdivision is a twenty-first-century reminder of the areas between city and country, where the boundaries in music or geography are not so clear and the interests of commuters and sportsmen, not to mention people and wild game, often collide. Hunters view suburban and retail development as swallowing up woods and hunting grounds, while residents with manicured lawns get spooked by the sound of gunfire in the distance. Increasingly, as both farm and inner-city populations decline, suburbia with its betwixt and between landscape is home to the weekend and vacation hunter as well as the animal welfare worker and is therefore a target for both animal rights and hunting rights groups seeking recruits.

With animal rights campaigns making headlines and national candidates forced to take stands or represent related images (photographed in a cowboy hat or hunting gear), the debate is also political and ethical. It raises questions about dictating what people are allowed to eat, wear, and do and, at a fundamental level, about the meaning of "rights," especially with "animal rights" squaring off against "hunters' rights" in various polemics. To be sure, parodies may dismiss animal rights as being about lowly creatures rather than being about people, but increasingly, communities care about what happens to animals because they feel a connection to them. As I will argue, attitudes toward animals are wrapped in parental, gendered views of childhood and the environment, and to an extent, the increased visibility of animal-human issues is a sign of the perceived loss of stable family and community identities. Years after turtle soup stimulated my thinking as well as my taste buds, I am attracted to animal-human topics that make a connection between public policy and cultural issues. In this case, political wrangling has intensified because the changing modern context of egalitarianism, libertarianism, and pacifism has transformed what was previously viewed in hunting tradition as an ephemeral enactment of heritage into a test of civil rights and the potential for peace. In sum, at stake in hunting and animal rights controversies is the very definition of humanity.

CHAPTER 1

Ritual and Controversy
at Deer Camp

Many places in America are both venerated and vilified as hunting havens—Pennsylvania, Texas, Michigan, Wisconsin, and Missouri among them. They rise to the top of national surveys recording the number of hunters licensed. In terms of the percentage of total population participating in hunting, other places with hardy backcountry reputations figure prominently in the picture of hunting in America. In the Wild West badlands of Montana, North Dakota, and South Dakota, for instance, between 15 and 19 percent of the residents hunt. Arkansas, Maine, and West Virginia claim 14 percent—a sharp contrast to the urbanized locales of California, Connecticut, Massachusetts, and New Jersey, where only 1 percent hunt. In short, hunters are located in every state but are culturally concentrated in several regions that conjure the image of a frontier rich in flora and fauna. From the Rockies to the Appalachians, if publicity is to be believed, going out hunting liberates folks from their routines and lets them get back to nature; it is hailed or cursed as a vitalizing force in modern society, particularly for men. It is associated with an untethered spirit of ruggedness, a hardy mettle required for venturing into the wilderness.

Beyond the statistics are places where hunting as the pursuit of game is etched into the notion of national heritage. Kentucky and Tennessee do not have the largest numbers of hunters, but their backwoods figure in the popular imagination as home to frontier bear-shooters and pathbreakers. These states have promoted the heroic legendry of the likes of Daniel Boone and Davy Crockett as hunter-frontiersmen in

27

historic sites and literature. The names of Boone and Crockett epito-mize a hunter-frontiersman spirit that supposedly is basic to a founding American character, as evidenced by the reverence given to the Boone and Crockett Club formed by Theodore Roosevelt in 1887. Alarmed by the accelerating pace of mass industrialization, Roosevelt and others such as George Bird Grinnell, folklorist and editor of *Forest and Stream* magazine, worried that America's wild hunting grounds were endan-gered along with the country's pioneer culture. The conservationist organization is known today for maintaining big-game records, and as its Web site declares, it works on the one hand at "preserving our hunt-ing heritage" and on the other at combating the threat "that someday we might lose our hunting privileges and our wildlife populations for future generations."

Pennsylvania shares in this pioneer boosterism by drawing tourists to the rough-hewn Daniel Boone Homestead near Reading. The story it tells portrays Boone as a trailblazer, and modern-day visitors can ap-preciate the life of eighteenth-century pioneers by walking through the site's sylvan environment. One can go fishing in Daniel Boone Lake and see demonstrations of the Pennsylvania or Kentucky hunting rifles that distinguished the American frontiersmen and supposedly tamed the wilderness. In the modern age, Pennsylvania can also boast that it issues more hunting and fishing licenses than any other state in the nation. It has been home since 2003 to Cabela's in Hamburg, the larg-est outdoor goods and hunting supply store in the country, with over a quarter million square feet of space. In popular culture, the forested landscape of Pennsylvania was noticeable as the backdrop for *The Deer Hunter* (1978), which won the Academy Award for best picture. At the same time, Pennsylvania is depicted in song and story as a sym-bol of mass industrialization—its rise and fall—from the steel mills of Pittsburgh to the anthracite coalfields south of Scranton. It thus raises sometimes conflicting images of American resources and their claim on national heritage.

If it is a prominent hunting haven, Pennsylvania also commands attention in any study of human-animal relations because it is tucked among headquarters for the largest animal protection organizations in the world: the American Society for the Prevention of Cruelty to Ani-mals (ASPCA) in New York City, the Fund for Animals in neighboring Maryland, and People for the Ethical Treatment of Animals (PETA) in

Virginia. The Fund for Animals has a lobbyist devoted to animal rights issues in Pennsylvania, countered time and again by representatives of the Pennsylvania Federation of Sportsmen's Clubs (PFSC), who announce, via the organization's Web site, that they work to ensure that hunters' "rights and interests are protected."

Thus Pennsylvania has emerged as a major battleground over the value of America's hunting heritage. "Deer camp" is a central cultural symbol that different sides hold up as the best and worst impulses in humans. For sportsmen, it is a time-honored tradition involving the idyllic commune with nature and family bonding. Away from machine civilization, according to this view, one can truly feel alive in the great outdoors and relate to the founding narratives of the country in the frontier experience. For animal rights organizations, camp-based hunting, raising images of a macho military campaign, is one of society's root evils. It is a scourge that nurtures killing and violence. Though they despise recreational hunting nationwide, their sights are symbolically set on Pennsylvania as the head and heart of American hunting culture. If the honor of tradition can be subverted there, the thinking goes, then anything is possible. With more than a million hunters out in force during buck season, though, they have their work cut out for them.

The opening of buck season is predictable in Pennsylvania. It arrives on the Monday after Thanksgiving, and just in case one forgets, school closings and splashy front-page coverage in newspapers serve as reminders. Its occurrence after the ritual celebration of nature's bounty, America's abundance, pioneer heritage, patriarchal family, and a good amount of meat-eating is not lost on reporters, merchants, or hunters (Donnelly 1999; Schneck 2001a). More hunting licenses are issued for this "antlered" deer season than for any other, and stores that issue licenses fill the major dailies with full-page advertisements. Following a festive family feast, then, and buoyed by ample commercial and social encouragement to ritually return to the woods for hunting, many men are especially inclined to extend the social spirit of the season at what they affectionately call deer camp.

Camp may be a cabin one owns and invites friends or family to share, a rental unit, or an organizationally held structure for which one pays dues for maintenance (Carpenter 1999; Maas 1999; Edwards 1985; Lefes 1953, 55–57). Camp is the common destination, because

Storytelling at Camp Hunter, Mifflin County, Pennsylvania. (Photo by Simon Bronner)

going hunting usually involves taking a "hunting trip" (defined by the U.S. Fish and Wildlife Service as venturing at least twenty-five miles from one's residence) rather than hunting at home (Center 1998, 8). In the wooded locations known for holding deer in the north-central part of the state, communities of camps form, with supporting institutions of taverns and stores, even though the camps are used only a few weeks out of the year. The traditional camp is not comparable to a second home, because more than likely it lacks the modern conveniences of indoor plumbing and electricity. Heat is probably supplied by a stove or fireplace, light and cooking with propane gas. The camp name implies a remote location, probably in Pennsylvania's wooded highlands in the central and western parts of the state. It also suggests a shared living situation, probably with all the residents being men, who assuredly lack for privacy during the experience. Hunting lore gives homage to camp with tales of embarrassing moments: wandering to the outhouse in the snow and getting caught with one's pants down, or the noises emanating from sleeping buddies at night in a structure without interior walls.

By the Fish and Wildlife Service's count, 92 percent of all hunters in the state are men (U.S. Department 2003). Although the large majority of hunters in Pennsylvania camps are state residents (86 percent), these sites attract hunters from throughout the United States. The result is that Pennsylvania usually leads the nation in the number of deer licenses issued and the number of days hunting (U.S. Department 1993, 53; Steele 1998). In fact, Pennsylvania is one of the few states where the number of people participating in hunting actually increased between 1996 and 2001 (U.S. Department 1998, 2003), although there is general concern about the decline in numbers in both the state and the nation since then—reportedly around 4 percent between 2001 and 2006. Yet this decline in hunting activity has not necessarily meant disapproval. One scientific survey by Responsive Management Inc. in 2007 reported that 78 percent of Americans support hunting as an outdoor activity, up from 73 percent in 1995. Eighty percent of respondents indicated that "hunting has a legitimate place in modern society." Meanwhile, the percentage of Americans who say they disapprove of hunting declined from 22 percent in 1995 to 16 percent in 2007 (Moyer 2007). What is going on?

At the third annual Governor's Hunting Heritage conference held in Hershey, Pennsylvania, as the new millennium dawned, the need to create a positive image for hunting weighed heavily on the minds of attendees. They freely shared anecdotes about the competition for potential youthful hunters from the entertainment world and organized sports. They worried that older hunters were not handing down their traditions to youth. Some believed that the reconstitution of hunting as the original "extreme sport" (or X-sport) would tap into the teenage rage for the intense dirt, danger, and sweat of motocross and BMX. Others argued for hunting's modern role as a form of environmentalism to increase public support, if not increase the ranks of hunters. Hunting could also be presented as socially conscious, with programs to donate venison to food banks and encourage and empower women to become involved. At the same time, the refrain from animal rights group could be heard: the decline of hunting was a natural evolution that needed to be accelerated. There was little difference from the rhetoric of cruelty and barbarism pronounced by Henry Salt at the beginning of the last century: "In a civilised community, where the services of the hunter are no longer required, blood-sports are simply an anachronism, a relic of savagery which time will gradually remove; and the appeal against them is not to the interested parties whose practices are arraigned—not to the belated Nimrods who find a pleasure in killing—but to that force of public opinion which put down bear-baiting, and which will in like manner put down the kindred sports (for all these barbarities are essentially akin) which are defended by similar sophistries" (Salt 1915, vii).

Hunters as a group constitute about 5 percent of the American population, but many more people are involved in a public debate about their place in society. The only other area to show growth in the number of hunters is the West–South-central region (U.S. Department 1993, table B-2). The middle Atlantic region has held steady at around 6 percent of the total population since the Fish and Wildlife Service began its national surveys in 1955. The height of participation in the middle Atlantic region was 1975, when 6.9 percent of the population hunted. Nationally, participation in hunting diminished from a high of 11.2 percent in 1960 to 5 percent in 2006. Involvement in hunting nationally also peaked in 1975, when more than 17 million residents over the age of twelve participated (U.S. Department 1993, table B-2). The Fish and Wildlife Service estimated that in 2001, the number of hunters in the United States over the age of sixteen was 13 million. In Pennsylvania, the number of deer killed is rising, even if the number of hunters is steady or declining. In 2003, hunters killed—or "took," using the Pennsylvania Game Commission's terminology—142,270 antlered deer. The year before, the harvest set an all-time record for the state at more than half a million deer, and records were set in the two previous years as well.

One factor in the perception of hunting is its integration into the American holiday season. By the time Thanksgiving is over in Pennsylvania, preparations are already being made for the big hunt on the first day of buck season. Many camps welcome their members on Friday or Saturday with a ceremonial dinner—and a hardy dinner it is, typically consisting of fat venison or beef steaks and oversized baked potatoes, washed down with generous amounts of beer. A highlight of the evening is joining in narratives of hunting exploits and comical misadventures of the past year, as well as those from previous seasons that are repeated year after year. Much as the men in these camps celebrate this continuity from one generation to the next, there is a growing awareness of change. Even though hunting remains a popular activity in Pennsylvania involving more than a million participants, the belief is pervasive that fewer young people are involved in hunting now than were a generation ago.

The Pennsylvania Game Commission reports that the number of junior license buyers (ages twelve to fifteen) dramatically declined 40 percent from 1976 through 1999 (Kittrell 2003, A1; Fegely 1999, 164). As a result of the introduction of a combination license for young hunters and organized efforts to promote hunting among youth, the number of licenses rose by 5.5 percent from the 1999–2000 to the 2002–2003 season, but the total of 103,606 was still well below the levels of the mid-1970s. *Field and Stream* conducted a national hunting survey in 2003 and found that 19 percent of hunters have children aged eighteen or younger who do not hunt, and a whopping 58 percent do not have children in that age range; only 22 percent reported having children who go hunting. These figures suggest a decline in the vertical transmission of hunting to the younger generation or an aging hunter population (*Field and Stream* 2004). My main point, from the perspective of folk belief, is that hunters have the *perception* that fewer young people are interested in hunting and that commercial culture is to blame. The front-page headline of central Pennsylvania's major daily on the opening day of antlered deer season indicates this attitude: "Combo Permit Seems to Limit Lure of Malls, Video Games" (Kittrell 2003).[1]

The perception by senior hunters that youths—enervated by mass culture and its affinity for animal rights sensitivity—are not engaged with hunting has significance beyond the future vitality of hunting. For most of these men, hunting is associated with a coming-of-age experience and the patrilineal transmission of tradition. Indeed, most hunters report learning how to hunt from their fathers; others learned from friends in their own age group (Jackson and Norton 1987, 42). The Fish and Wildlife Service reports that 42 percent of all hunters, representing the largest figure in the survey, began hunting when they were twelve to fifteen years old, and another 28 percent started between six and eleven (U.S. Department 1993, 95; see also Herman 2001a).[2] At the beginning of the twenty-first century, the average age of hunters obtaining licenses was forty-two, compared with thirty-five in 1970 (Kittrell 2003).

The disruption of its transmission to youth is not the only perceived threat to hunting's future popularity. Often reported as the primary concern is the shrinking wildlife habitat, often blamed on urban sprawl and commercial development (*Field and Stream* 2004). Hunters are also acutely aware of threats to their practice from the growing animal rights movement, which would like to ban hunting altogether (Muth and Jamison 2000). They additionally feel pressure from anti-gun lobbies that want to limit firearms circulating in society, especially for recreation (*Field and Stream* 2004). When hunters were asked by *Field and Stream* magazine whether they had been confronted with anti-hunting sentiments directly, 56 percent replied that they had. Even if these anti-hunting movements did not exist, older hunters would still voice the folk belief that youth today are "soft" or "spoiled," unwilling to face the often harsh, manliness-testing conditions of hunting, and distracted from the family tradition of hunting by mass media or institutional, especially school-related, activities. It is common to hear that hunting demands an intensive commitment that many contemporary adolescents are not willing to make. Although the role of hunter is not a primary identity for most of these men, during the time spent in camp, that identity is centralized by the total immersion in the hunting life.

I vividly recall one conversation after Friday night dinner at the appropriately named Camp Hunter in central Pennsylvania.[3] It began with one of the members asking another, "Where's your son?" He replied, "Watching TV" and then added under his breath, "that lazy ass." "Too rough out here for him?" someone followed. "Oh, he likes his comfort," the father of the boy remarked, and another hunter teased him that his son would rather be with his girlfriend than with his father. Much as hunting is categorized as sport or recreation, the implication was that doing it right involves sacrifice. Socially, maybe teen boys do not appreciate family ties or the company of men, they sighed. The men were convinced they knew why young people do not hunt: they are not up to it. And they conveyed a sense of wonder that youth even have a choice. In their raising, going to camp was an obligation, a calling repeated after every Thanksgiving, sure as the turkey on the table. I interjected a question they hear more often now than in their younger days: "So why do you hunt?" A cascade of stock answers flowed: connecting with nature and the wild, the thrill of the hunt, getting away from everyday routine (and their wives). They knew it was not about providing food anymore, and one of the more vocal members got to the "heart of the matter": "When we were younger, we looked forward to the kill, the big shot, but I tell you now it's about the rituals and the traditions of camp; it's about being with these guys. And lately, we've been more into our rituals and traditions because they've been more important to us." Pointing to a board behind him displaying cut shirt-tails from the 1950s to the present, framed by a buck's head on top and photographs of the group gathered at deer camp, he said, "This is why we hunt," and the other men nodded their assent.

What did that mean, exactly? What was the role of camp in all this? Why were rituals and traditions more important to them now? What was the significance of the cut shirttails displayed on the wall? What were the rituals and traditions that encapsulated the experience for them—as men, as sportsmen, as fathers, as Pennsylvanians? And as fathers, did they feel that they had to compete with their sons' girl-friends for their sons' affections, or did they feel that the competition was between them and their sons coming into manhood? Overarch-ing these questions is the interpretation of the cultural experience of hunting. It is significant matter, I contend, because of the perspective it gives on all-male groups and the way human-animal relations, par-ticularly in ritual combat, provide symbolic expressions of social and psychological processes, including the reaffirmation of manliness. In the pro- and anti-hunting debates, the redefinition of manliness for modern life is often at issue, with hunters striving to show they are not the brutish demons that popular culture and animal rights orga-nizations have portrayed. They want to appear sensitive to the natural environment, family men spending quality time with their sons, proud of America's heritage steeped in hunting pioneers. Yet the consistency of these images with rituals bordering on hazing that mark camp often have to be explained to a public influenced by images of hunting as a barbaric behavior promoted by animal rights organizations—and Hol-lywood movies. For many Americans, the hunter cannot live down the stigma of stalking innocent Bambi, even if in days of yore he was Little Red Riding Hood's rescuer.

When hunters depart for camp, they initiate a move out of the domestic environment into the wild. Along with this border crossing comes a behavioral expectation, social integration, and cultural scene set apart from everyday modern life. The move therefore should draw out a discussion of its function as an escape from and reflection of mod-ern society. One notable distinction is the "high-context" communica-tion of deer camp, where participants develop close connections over many years and many aspects of cultural behavior are unstated because members know what to do (Hall 1976). In such situations, symbols and functions of behavior are unquestioned because they are ingrained in the context. Participants at deer camp are well aware of the rituals because of how much they differ from the practice of modern life. One notable difference is that camp is about killing, and rituals of blood and guts are designed to move from the peaceful world of home to the pursuit of prey at camp. They recognize the move from low-context modernity to high-context camp with a set of rituals steeped in the group members' knowledge of themselves. Hunting itself is ritualized behavior, set off from the ordinary world and repeated seasonally with social ceremony; consequently, its rituals serve as cultural synecdoche for the whole experience (see Hufford 1992, 42–78; Wegner 1984, 171–95; Burkert 1996).

Hence, my approach to the problem of uncovering the cultural experience of hunting is to interpret the rituals most commonly recognized by deer camp participants: shirttail cutting (for a missed shot at a buck), storytelling (or, as hunters sometimes quip, "lying"), blood smearing (on one's face after a kill), blood drinking, and the "hunter's dish" (eating of the deer's heart and liver by the person who shot it). To explain the meaning of these activities, I take into account the way different groups perceive the symbolism of the events and communicate that to others. Each one of the rituals mentioned often relates to a constellation of beliefs and customs that are mentioned in interviews: "buck fever" (missing a shot because of psychosomatic symptoms), lucky objects (e.g., a rabbit's foot), refraining from shaving, the last bite (feeding the deer grass after the kill), cutting the throat to bleed the animal, cutting the tarsal glands to prevent the meat from being ruined, observing the dangerous behavior of bucks, narrating stories of "ghost" bucks, relating the aphrodisiacal powers of the antlers, taking a "trophy" (usually the tail), snapping the obligatory photograph with the hung buck, and so on. Many camps have other rituals particular to their group, but I have found that the aforementioned rituals are the most pervasive in camps; for most hunters, their practice defines the traditional camp. Considering the objective of going to camp to bag a buck—that is, making a kill—the rituals of camp are replete with references to the stakes of life and death, and I have organized the following discussion of rituals and traditions as responses to risk and anxiety under their thematic references to sparing life and taking life.

The U.S. Fish and Wildlife surveys mentioned earlier, for example, provide valuable demographic data and show that deer are the most common prey of hunters, but they do not give information on the social settings for the practice. Such surveys are methodologically limited because they gather recollections from individuals in the modern setting rather than from the group members as they interact with one another. An all-too-rare survey of the social experience of hunting conducted for *Deer and Deer Hunting* revealed that most hunters prefer hunting with family members or in small groups of three to nine individuals. Reflecting the importance of grouping was the high rating of "companionship with friends" as one of the satisfactions obtained from hunting. Even higher on the scale was "escape from routine," underscoring the perception of hunting as a distinct, immersive context countering contemporary mass culture. Not surprisingly, "provision of food" and "solitude" ranked much lower as satisfactions derived from hunting (Jackson and Norton 1987). Unfortunately, the role of cultural practices or rituals did not enter into the study, and folklorists, sociologists, and anthropologists have not contributed broadly to an ethnographic database, despite the fact that hunting is one of America's long-standing traditions.[4]

A few folkloristic collections have mentioned these rituals but left them unanalyzed. The blood smear is found in collections taken from oral tradition by William Koch (1965, 166) from Kansas and Anthon S. Cannon (1984, 281) in Utah; the hunter's dish is mentioned in Newbell Niles Puckett's compendium of Ohio beliefs (Hand, Casetta, and Thiederman 1981, 2:1020). Jane Beck (1992, 126) quickly summarizes the blood smear and cut shirttail in Vermont as a boy's rite of passage; James Swan (1995, 136; 1999, 124–25) agrees but attributes sacred, mythical undertones to the "initiation." John Boyle's note in *Folklore* (1969) identifies the blood smear as a Eurasian hunting ritual, but Swan and others have identified examples globally. In the United States, antebellum writer William Elliott (1859, 173–74) described a hunter who "bathed his face with the blood of his victim," followed by the assertion, as if it went without saying, "This, you must know, is *hunter's law* with us, on the killing of a first deer." The shirttail ritual, meanwhile, appears to be concentrated in North American deer camps. Although historical and ethnographic chronicles that detail the cultural practices of deer camp are generally lacking beyond romantic nature writing, there is evidence of a long, wide lineage for the rituals of the American deer camp (Faulkner 1994, 114; Marks 1991, 21, 129, 140; Huffman 1997, 60, 96–99; 2001, 190–93; "Camp" 2003). They are often framed rhetorically as part of the *time-honored family tradition* of hunting, as journalists discover when they do their obligatory interviews for the opening of hunting season (Steele 1998; Donnelly 1999; Schneck 1999, 2001a).

Because the practices under consideration have been variously identified as initiations, customs, and rites, I should explain my analytical focus on ritual. Ritual applies because the practices draw attention to themselves as events that are typically repeatable, structured, expressive, performed, and intentionally symbolic (Rappaport 1992, 249; 1996). Examined as a process, the practices suggest that the act of ritualization condenses and symbolizes relationships; ritualization is central to the communicative dimension of social life (Bell 1992, 197–223; Shepard 1973, 196; Beattie 1966, 65; Leach 1968, 13:524). Following this emphasis on ritual involving symbolic action and embodying social contract, Roy Rappaport asserts that ritual is the "fundamental social act upon which human society is founded" (1992, 254). My point is that participants in the hunting camp socialize around ritual and ritualize the social, symbolizing the conflicts between life and death as well as the relationships of masculinity to modernity; this is the essence of the cultural experience out in the wild, but the meanings of ritualization and socialization are typically outside their awareness in a high-context situation.

Although *custom* is an activity performed with regularity, and the term could be applied to activities at camp, it is commonly, as Richard Sweterlitsch has noted, "a vast aggregate of human behavior" that is usually described as part of the ordinary routine in people's lives (1997, 1:168). Ritual breaks everyday routine, creates a different space and time, and establishes an *extra*ordinary action or symbol as routine (see Abrahams 1986). In so doing, it holds social attention as well as signaling an expressive moment. The initiation is a type of ritual, to be sure, with special reference to a transition of status. Rites constitute another subset of ritual that implies religious or magical functions (Pentikäinen 1997, 2:734–35). In the analysis of hunting, use of rites connotes a sacred or magical connection to sacrifice and transformation, while ritual as a symbolic form expressively embodying social contract brings into view sociopsychologically interpretable behavior (Pentikäinen 1997, 2:735; Bell 1997, 61–90; Girard 1996; Burkert 1996; Turner 1967, 1969). Because rituals are performative and encapsulate values and symbols inherent in the group, they have attracted the scrutiny of groups protesting hunting. Whereas shirttail cutting may be perceived by outsiders as a strange frivolity suggesting childish horseplay, insiders speak about it as socially significant and memorable. Blooding, as discussed later, is more contentious a matter and one in which the perceptions of symbols are even further apart.

Deer camp participants commonly refer to the practices as "traditions" or collectively as "traditions and rituals" to underscore their continuity with the past (Various 1999; Donnell and Lamar 1987, 32). In their rhetoric, it is important to communicate that these practices persist despite rapid change outside this natural world in modern, commercial society. As traditions, they are also linked to the familiarity of a small group, often connected by familial ties to founders of the camp. Many camp names, in fact, derive from their founders; for example, according to narratives known to present-day members, Camp Hunter is located on land staked out for hunting by a pair of brothers named Hunter. Overall, the oral references to "traditions and rituals" I heard at camp connect generations and distinguish the hunters' identity.

Ritual in deer camp is enlivened by an air of play. This fusion is a contrast to the usual practice of deer hunting, which involves long periods of quietly waiting alone in a tree stand. Back at camp, as one account delicately put it, "a highly spirited atmosphere of camaraderie" or revelry takes hold. This description was accompanied by an illustration of a hunter at camp hitting a crouched man on the rear end with a paddle while a group of hunters roared in laughter (Huffman 2001, 193). Characteristic of all-male groups, the interactions at camp usually involve a great deal of teasing, joking, swearing, playful insulting, and pranking (Spradley and Mann 1975, 87–100; Mitchell 1985; Bronner 2005b). Among the activities prevalent at camps are card playing, throwing darts, gambling, drinking, joke telling, and looking at pornographic and outdoor magazines (Hanna 1986). Despite the therapeutic image of hunting as recreation and escape, its risk taking, specialized skills, and regulations mark it as sport for many men. It is culturally framed by hunters, therefore, as ritualized play and suggests a fictive stage on which symbols, anxieties, and fantasies are enacted. Its contrast with the scientific management of hunting by government adds to many hunters' resolve to create a social environment that they control culturally to match the freedom, and the pioneer image, implied by being in the wild. Indeed, the Game Commission contextualizes hunting as environmental control and uses the ecological rhetoric of "harvesting" to refer to the killing that occurs during hunting season. The formal bureaucracy is further distanced from the folk culture of the camps by its licensing requirements and enforcement of hunting limits and its significant punishment for poaching (see Frye 2006; Ives 1988; Dahles 1991).

With the stakes of hunting rhetorically set in terms of life and death, the hunt follows some patterns of "deep play" as highly risky and symbolic, as suggested by Clifford Geertz (1994) and Jeremy Bentham (1882) and elaborated by Alan Dundes (1994). The rhetorical construction of hunting as serious, or even dangerous, because it involves guns and violence and as playful because it is recreational and social creates a dramatic tension, and cultural ambiguity, enacted in ritualized events. At another level, the high stakes at deer camp involve intimacy among men in close, communal quarters, and this also involves grave risks, expressed in and compensated by ritualized play. The stakes that make an event ritually "deep," according to Geertz and Dundes, relate to the high degree of "metaphorical refocusing" through fantasy. In other words, the ritual, which frames an activity as special, contains symbols that are recognized as highly value laden. An *extra*ordinary event signifying the meaning of the ordinary that cannot be realized in everyday expression, such as a cockfight that involves ritualized male combat with animals, presents texts to be read closely and interpreted. For Geertz, the reading results in a relation to social structure; for Dundes, it involves a psychological reading of masculine formation. In the deer camp, it is a set of events, connected as ritualized play and narrative and manifested visually and materially, that forms a complex whole of the cultural experience (see Armstrong 1971; Dorson 1982b; Morgan 1998, 152–80). Often separated cognitively for adults, ritual and play in a setting that involves risk, such as the deer camp, feed each other symbolically; ritual provides ordered performance, while play offers disordered irreality (Sutton-Smith 1997, 166–72). Added to this ambiguity is the setting of the wild as a liberating primal state that distorts identities and invites reconstruction, particularly of the relations between dominance and submission, humans and animals (Dahles 1993; Dizard 1999, 2003).

Sparing Life: Shirttail Cutting and Buck Fever

Shooting deer is often done in solitude, with the hunter positioned in a tree stand. Some camps arrange for deer drives, in which the men walk as a group and scare deer toward a shooter in a stand.[5] Other hunters take positions on high ground and may take a partner or two, especially if a father goes into the woods with his sons. It is important to keep a good distance from other hunters in the group, and to know their positions, to avoid accidentally shooting them. When shots ring out, they can be heard widely, and the expectation is that a shot results in a hit. If a hunter is observed missing a clear shot at a deer or is suspected of it, the result can be a ritual cutting of his shirttail by his campmates. The typical hunter's garb of flannel shirts, with their long tails, is akin to an occupational uniform. The accused hunter often initially resists being

Shirttail cutting at Ten-Point Deer Camp, Mississippi. To add to the shooter's humiliation, his wife was called in to cut the shirt. (Photo courtesy of Mississippi Department of Archives and History)

a voluntary participant in the ritual, since it implies his humiliation and failure. Lacking a buck is forgiven if a good shot is not possible or if the deer do not come to the hunter's position, but missing a shot is not. The usual ritual, then, is for a gang of campmates to hold the hunter while his shirttail is cut off. Afterward, hunters hang the tail on the wall, often inscribing it with the date and the name of the wearer. The offender feels social pressure from his campmates to wear his cut shirt as long as possible, preferably until the end of the day, although stories about the event last much longer.

Sometimes campmates attach comments or short poems to the cut fragment. The results are often gathered and mounted on a framed board and hung below a buck's head. The Camp Hunter board had shirttails hung from 1955 to the 2002 season, but only a few were dated from the 1970s. The dates of the fragments were concentrated in the 1950s to 1960s and 1980s to 1990s. This pattern bears out the opinion that the "traditions were part of camp and then came back in." In 1955, a roster of fourteen men was included on the board, along with notations about the assigned cook, one man who made a kill, and one who missed two shots. Alongside was the score of the Army-Navy football game that year. A "toast" was scratched into the board for that year: "May their wives accept the affection of their husbands for this institution." A. R. Hayes, one of the original members, had his shirttail pinned a few times, as did George Thompson, but more than thirty other tails were from one-time offenders. Some of them added information about whether the miss was "on the run" or "standing." Other inscriptions included "Valley Skunk Racing Society," a comical reference to an imaginary organization for performers who "stink"; "10 point—sent it over," drawing attention to a prize buck that got away; "Honesty does not pay," indicating that the hunter had confessed his sin; and "3 shots," publicizing a particularly poor effort. One elaborated that the reluctant participant in the ritual had been convinced by ten of his campmates in solidarity to give up the shirttail. Only once was the presence of a woman indicated, on December 1, 1964: as if to double the bad shot's embarrassment, the camp fellows sent for his wife to cut his shirt. During the last few years, the cutting ritual has been reserved for new hunters. As one of the camp members said in 2003, "We want them to know that they need to work into the camp, to show them we've been around and it counts for something."[6] Relating the ritual as a kind of social control, and distorting the boundaries between animals and humans in the wild, he added, "They're like little bucks who need to be put in their place."

Ethnographer Stuart A. Marks provides an example of how ritual and play can be elaborated in an account of the opening of buck season on October 15, 1979, in a North Carolina camp. In this rod and gun club hunt, a "hunt master" is in charge, unlike the egalitarian camps I attended in Pennsylvania. Rank-and-file "standers" signify club members assigned to be shooters at a particular stand, while "drivers" force the deer toward them. Organizationally, the club has a hierarchy expressed through the structural frame of a court scene in a ritualized play:

> While the carcasses are flayed into six sections each, the hunt master assembles the standers for the last time. He calls for his shirt-cutting knife, an eighteen-inch machete, and demands order in his court. He asks those who missed to assemble in a line. One culprit remains out of the lineup. When his name is called, he yells "he's just left " and is then dragged by his buddies into the line.
>
> Six shirttails are to be cut this afternoon. For each offender, the hunt master asks how he pleads. "Guilty" is the usual reply. The first shirttail is cut by Ronnie, who is anxious to perform since the offender cut his shirt last season. Ronnie folds and cuts a broad strip from the offender's undershirt. The next offender pleads "not sure." The hunt master allows him to consult a "lawyer." When his friend steps forward to take his picture, the offender says, "I want a real lawyer, not a half-assed one." His shirttail is cut high. Mister Goober, who in the morning let a buck slip, is summoned. While threatening to cut his shirttail, the hunt master sentences him to two years suspended verdict. (Marks 1991, 149)

In this mock trial, the person faces a kangaroo court of peers. Marks observes that punishment is not doled out equally: "The amount of shirttail removed and hung in the clubhouse is contingent upon the offender's reputation." If the defendant has a lofty reputation for marksmanship or if he is known as a prankster or joker, "the jury may demand everything except the collar" (Marks 1991, 140).

Marks interprets the shirttail ritual as one of many deer-hunting traditions that establish social boundaries of a male-bonded community differentiated from the world of women. He recognizes the special significance of rituals for buck hunting, since the buck hunter is "the epitome of a masculine mystique" constructed from the pursuit of the buck as an especially masculine animal—a "patriarch" and "monarch," as he is often referred to with his crown of antlers (Marks 1991, 161). But following a Geertzian social structural model that views ritual as having the function of bonding as well as differentiating a community, he fails to note the symbols that make this particular ritualization meaningful for the unstated understanding of masculinity.

What, after all, is so humiliating, and metaphorical, about having one's shirttail cut? The answer relates to the man's anxieties about his exposed anatomy and the process that he endures reminding him of the social necessity of scoring a hit. When the shirttail is cut by a gang of men, the buttocks are exposed, suggesting that he is prone to homoerotic attack (see Dundes 1987a). In an Alabama camp described by Rich Donnell and May Lamar (1987, 28), the attack is symbolized by a paddling on the rear end with two dozen hunters looking on. "I ain't got to get my ass whipped," the man protested, and each smack drew "a round of laughter" from two dozen "jovial onlookers." At some camps, the shirttail of the unsuccessful hunter is hung on the meat pole reserved for a killed buck, further implying violation by naked exposure (Mione 1991). Added to the symbolism is the act of cutting, which leaves the shirt ineffective and the man therefore symbolically castrated. Thus the offender is humiliated because he is being emasculated or feminized.

This metaphorical refocusing raises the question of why the hunter's offense merits this ritualization. By symbolically castrating him, his campmates are reminding him of the consequences of his impotence in the face of the buck. In the drama of the hunt, configured as a male combat ritual between two physically imposing and therefore sexually potent forces, the man needs to muster his phallic gun as a sign of prowess against the horned buck. Missing the shot undermines the phallic power of the gun for his fellows, since it is the main extension of the man and has potent symbolism when loaded. One visual reminder of the symbolic equivalent of gun and phallus is achieved through humor: T-shirts show a male hunter urinating in the woods with a gun leaning against a tree next to him. In the distance a buck strolls by. The caption reads, "DAMN! THE THINGS YOU SEE WHEN YOU HAVE THE WRONG GUN IN YOUR HAND."

In the shirttail ritual is a reaffirmation of the campmates' potency and manliness; in the visualization of the ritual on the wall is the displacement of anxiety about performance in combat with a playful construction of dominance over others. Another visual reminder at Camp Hunter, this one positively reinforcing, is across the room—a relief map of the area marking places where members have made kills. On top of the board is an imposing mounted buck's head emphasizing the prominent antlers. On the walls are photographs emphasizing the successful kill; the photographs deemed worthy of display are those that show the hunter, gun in hand, with the gutted deer hanging upside down. The communicative dimension of this environment and ritualization is to repress sentiment for the animal; the hunt needs to be about emerging victorious from combat. Lest the missed shot appear to be the sparing of a life out of feminine sympathy, the ritual pins the blame on a lack of male potency and expresses it as a lack of manly aggression. This ritual is reserved for combat against the buck, since it is more acceptable to spare the life of a doe. As Natty Bumpo says in James Fenimore Cooper's *The Deerslayer* (1963 [1841], 13), "there's little manhood in killing a doe," and that sentiment is still prevalent among hunters. A teasing comment made by the oldest member of Camp Berish near Lewistown, Pennsylvania, to his young, reluctant son-in-law before opening day of antlered deer season bears this sentiment out: "You're probably going to shoot a doe on opening day; you have no pride." Taking umbrage at the remark, the son-in-law retorted, "Unlike you, Tom, I don't have to kill an animal to prove my manhood."

The use of the shirttail-cutting ritual for new hunters, usually adolescents, is consistent with the symbolism of male potency in combat with the buck and the punishment of feminization. In a social setting usually consisting of father figures who worry about their performance, or potency, in sexually tinged combat, the "young buck" in the camp can be threatening to the ego because he has youth and vigor on his side. A boastful proverb frequently heard at camps is, "The older the buck, the stiffer (or harder) the horn," while youth may be described as "hearty as a buck" (see Mieder 1992, 73; Whiting 1977, 47). The ritual reinforces the age- or experience-based hierarchy of the camp by converting the new hunter's youthful vitality to impotency in a ritual that infantilizes as well as feminizes. The offense of missing a shot, or displaying impotence, is more punishable in youth because of the expectation of energetic performance and the need to socialize the young hunter into the culture. The linkage of childishness and femininity is common as a form of submission, such as the rhetorical use of "girl" to represent grown women. Cutting the shirttail emphasizes its absence from the article of clothing; imagining the shirttail as even longer than it is, it can represent the long frock worn by both boys and girls during infancy as late as the 1950s (Calvert 1992, 109; Randolph 1976, 58; Riney-Kehrberg 2005, 120–21). The frock conveyed childish asexuality following from an image of childlike innocence and purity (Calvert 1992, 109).

Folklore collector Vance Randolph relates a story he heard in the Ozarks about "shirttail boys" that underscores the competition of the coming-of-age youth with the father, as well as the humorous image of a man with his shirttail exposed:

One time a stranger come out to old man Kerr's place on Shanker Branch, to see about buying some hogs. There were two little boys a-setting on the gallery, and they didn't have a stitch on except their homemade shirts. Pretty near all little boys wore long shirts in them days, without no pants. When a youngster was about twelve years old, the folks give him his first pair of jeans. Well, the stranger knowed all about that, and he never paid no attention to them little shirttail boys. But when him and old man Kerr went to look at the hogs, there was a full-growed man out there, and he didn't have nothing on but a shirt neither. The big fellow was setting on a stump, with his long hairy legs a-sticking out, and he looked like one of these here tarantulers. The stranger never had seen no shirttail boy that big before, and he thought it was mighty funny, but he knowed better than to laugh. So he just kept on a-talking about hogs with old man Kerr, and never let on like he seen anything out of the way. After the hog-buying was done, though, he stopped one of the little boys out of the gate, and asked who was the big fellow without no pants on. "Looks like he's kind of old, for a shirttail boy," says the stranger. "Oh, that's my brother Lem," the boy says, grinning like a young possum. "Lem's got kind of stuck up since he went to business-college in Springfield, and this morning he done something at the table that hurt Aunt Ethel's feelings. So paw just hauled off and knocked him back fifteen years." (Randolph 1952, 93–94)

In another story relating to shirttail boys, the fatherly attempt to repress the boy's potency is implied when "the old man" at the dinner table submits that it is finally time to "put pants on" his twelve-year-old shirttail boy because "that's the second time he's crawled up there and drug his tallywhacker through the butter" (Randolph 1976, 57–58).

In the initiatory representation of the shirttail as childhood frock, the cutting implies that it is time to step up, to "put pants on" the initiate, even as he is reminded of his novice state. This paradox of transition or liminality is typical of initiation rituals, particularly as rites of passage into all-male groups, which often mark ridicule and achievement with some kind of cutting ceremony (Myerhoff 1982; Turner 1969, 94–130; 1967, 93–111). For many young American boys, this ceremony may be the first haircut, often administered on the boy's first birthday by his parents to signify the leaving behind of infancy, and often remembered by saving a lock of hair. Among basketball players, cutting can be used to ridicule the defeated team as well as to claim a prize. It is a common ritual for each player on the winning team to cut a piece of the net and hold it up as a prize of conquest. The prize is not only a reminder of scoring through the hoop but also a castration of the other team, equivalent to holding up the cut tail or genitals of a hunter's kill.

The paradox of being ritually vigorous and impotent at the same time is how the ritual of shirttail cutting draws attention to itself and to the competitive anxieties in the group. Further evidence of this symbolism is found in aviation, the other major pursuit that engages in a shirttail ritual. As in hunting, there is ganging behavior around the initiate who undertakes a risky, male-dominated enterprise, although in this case, it seemingly recognizes success rather than failure. As one aviator recalled, "When a student had made sufficient progress so that he could handle a plane alone, the fellows ganged up on him and cut a two-inch square from his shirt. This was labeled and dated as a trophy to hang on the office wall. Eventually there were fifty or more hanging there. My older son made his solo flight on his sixteenth birthday which was the legal age to secure a state license" (Weimer 1993). Upon com-

Cutting off a deer's tail as a trophy at a Michigan hunting camp.

pletion of military flight training, one is likely to be dunked in water rather than have a shirttail cut, suggesting a baptismal rebirth and integration into the tight-knit unit (Harms 1999). In small-plane aviation, the novice does not perform as a member of a unit, but rather individually; he gains an identity that, metaphorically, involves a penetrating extension of the body. The shirttail ritual for the male-dominated world of private plane aviation is similar to the ritual in hunting, in that it recognizes the initiate's acceptance into the group but involves his operating independently; it also draws out his shortcomings. It is not fully integrative, because prospective pilots still must achieve the next stage of certification, and as many as half of them do not make it. It is a dubious achievement, according to pilot Fred Harms, because as a "new guy," one is easy to spot on the ramp as someone who is apt to make mistakes (1999).

Another cognate of shirttail cutting that sheds light on its symbolism comes from masculine-centered military lore in the form of the shavetail. Recorded in the United States since the nineteenth century, and especially during wartime, *shavetail* is a derisive term for a young second lieutenant who is presumably inexperienced in combat, even though he is an officer. A shavetail, according to one linguistic source, is "the lowest creature in whom authority was vested" (Keeley 1930, 374). Most slang dictionaries trace its origin to a custom of shaving the tails of untrained mules for easy identification (Dickson 2004, 32; Hall 2002, 885; Wentworth and Flexner 1967, 464). Linguist Mary Paxton Keeley's fieldwork-based article "A. E .F. English" assertively links the term to a West Point tradition of a senior getting his coattail shaved off when he donned the uniform of a second lieutenant (1930, 374), and a wartime military publication notes that newly commissioned officers from the ranks, who were called shavetails, had their shirttails cut (War Department 1943, 4; see also Dukes 2005, 4).

What is the connection between shirttails and mule tails? Further, what is the linkage between the freshly minted lieutenant and the rituals of cutting shirttails and shaving mule tails? Most sources offer a literal interpretation: the lieutenant, like the mule, is young, unbroken, or untried. He may be scientifically bred or formally educated, but he has not been tested in the field, that is, initiated according to tradition. In other contexts, the officer's persona is one of a young, naive tenderfoot or an unreliable fish out of water, but he is usually not ascribed the mule's classic attribute of stubbornness. What is it about the mule or shirt that makes *shavetail* a derisive or, in Keeley's observation, a "profane" term? Unwilling to go beyond the literal reading of the mule origin, lexicographers Harold Wentworth and Stuart Berg Flexner in their *Dictionary of American Slang* criticize Keeley, who made the shirttail connection, for not taking into account earlier meanings of the word in the mule corps (1967, 464). Yet they overlook uses of the term as early as 1832, prior to the mule corps references, to describe a backcountry Munchausen character, suggesting that the shavetail was one who told tall tales or was too big for his britches (Morrison 1952, 231). These characteristics are often attributed today to participants in hunting as well as military camps (Bethke 1981, 38–54; Hunt 1918; Shoemaker 1992, 40–70).

Keeley should be credited, though, with providing a vital clue to the symbolic connection between mules and shirts when she confesses in the opening of her article that "a man should have made this article." She was not deprecating her linguistic skills but observing that, culturally, the language and customs of military men had "obscene or profane" significance under conditions of combat stress and social male intimacy. Other allusions to this masculine social context that can be compared to the deer camps are abundant in military literature and other settings in which all-male groups are cooped up somewhere, isolated from home (Camp and Hartman 1937, 74; Hunt 1918, 136–41; Simons 1933, 31). Berton Braley, for example, penned some verses under the title "The Shavetail" in his book *Buddy Ballads: Songs of the A.E.F.* (1919, 72–73). He laments that although he loves his men, "They view me as sort of a joke"; he wants to be "Bud," or a buddy, "to that bunch," but he is demeaned as a "Louie, that's all" (derisive slang for a lieutenant, which may be humorous to the ranks in part because of the connection to the British loo, or lavatory). He longingly notes that they appear so "big-limbed and strong," and they feminize him as inconsequential and inexperienced. Part of the feminization is because of the lieutenant's role as a maidservant "second" or "assistant" to the patriarchal master or captain. There is no third lieutenant, suggesting that the second lieutenant is perpetually dominated.

During Keeley's fieldwork among the American Expeditionary Force in World War I, she recorded one instance when the ranks came up with a term for a category lower than a shavetail. She refers to the folk circulation of the term *dovetail* for new officers who had not yet been commissioned and therefore had not bonded to any group. While offering documentation of the related terms, she writes of her bafflement as to why *dove* replaced *shave*. She speculates that the men were equating the dove with meekness, but in keeping with the "razzing spirit" (in her words) of combat forces, the scorn of the dove is its feminine association, evident in its cooing and nonaggression (the dove of peace). Along these lines, Lieutenant Jeffery Fleece observes that *shavetail* drew attention to a young officer's inadequacy in the context of shooting wars, when, as he says, "war was thrilling" (1946, 71). Dudley C. Gould in his memoir *You Tremble Body* notes that his men called him a shavetail because of his lack of shooting experience, suggesting impotence (1999, 56). The term also stuck, he intimates, because of a scatological reference to exposure of the buttocks that connects impotence with an infantile anal stage. Fear had caused him to lose control during combat, evoking the folk imagery of "scaring the shit out of me"; in his words, he "felt a looseness of the asshole" (1999, 56). Sometimes in oral tradition, in fact, *shavetail* becomes an adjective to describe *asshole* (Castle 2006). This is the implication in slang combinations such as *shavetail rocket,* a term for an unguided, solid-propellant projectile that often sputters and splatters (White Sands 2008). Perhaps the connection of the shavetail to the mule as an ass is meant to characterize being anal as being feminine, or impotent as a man. One detail of the mule metaphor that I have not found mentioned in slang dictionaries, for instance, is that mules are usually sterile. The ranks view themselves as burly and manly, whereas the young lieutenants, because they supposedly do not exert themselves by getting down in the trenches, are often accused of being thin and effeminate. For example, in the World War II humor tract *It's a Cinch, Private Finch!* one of the yarns describes a burly "Old Army Man" who has been "in every battle since Blenheim . . . [and] has nine hashmarks, three wound strips, and more medals than you can shake a shavetail at" (Stein and Brown 1943). This wording substitutes *shavetail* for *stick,* suggesting that the shavetail is not well endowed physically or experienced in battle. Following this line of thinking, the comparison to the shaved mule tail is appropriate because of the body shaving associated with women, and phallically, the tail is conspicuously thin compared with that of other equines. Adding to the feminization of the tail is the tassel or tuft left at the end. In a metaphor for maturation, when the tuft grows out, the mule will graduate to being called a "bell sharp," meaning that the pack animal will take its place among the other mules at the ringing of the bell (Essin 1997, 95–96). The shaving of hair as feminine also comes up in the contemporary usage of *shavetail* for shaved female pudenda (Urban Dictionary 2008). The feminine symbolism of *tail* is also apparent in hunting T-shirts that depict a comely, scantily clad woman below mottoes such as "HUNTING FOR TAIL" and "HUNT WHITE TAIL AND LET THE MOON [FEMALE BUTTOCKS] SHINE."

Cutting the shirttail is, following this symbolism, exposure of the buttocks to feminize the victim by showing his inability to shoot. Another anxiety concerning the failure to land a shot in deer camp lore is folklorized as "buck fever." It is an ailment, hunters avow, manifesting as the inability to perform when confronted by a deer. Commonly reported symptoms are a kind of paralyzing shock making it impossible to fire the gun, palpitations or the "shakes" and "sweats," temporary blindness, double vision or loss of focus, or even blackouts. Many hunters relate the folk belief that it is a disease of new hunters. Another belief about buck fever is recorded by folklorist William Koch in Kansas:

"You always miss your first shot in deer season because you have 'buck fever'" (1965, 166). Sportsman Robert Wegner describes the symptoms as follows: "Your heart speeds up, your temples pound, and your arms and legs weaken" (1987, 243). Many stories use buck fever to explain why bucks got away or to account for the shooting of men and cows by hunters (Hruska 1999, 109–12). It is presented as a mysterious malady or a function of inexperience. Implicit in the narratives is the idea that the illness is inexplicable, adding to hunting's mystique as an intense experience and a separate reality. Writers give clinical accounts such as "nervous shock" and "a temporary block . . . between the straining mind and the willing but uncontrolled muscular system" (Wegner 1987, 245). Psychological analyses remark on the conflict between taking a life, especially that of a male animal to which the hunter relates, and the fear of inadequacy (Wegner 1987, 243).

From a philosophical perspective, José Ortega y Gasset reflects in *Meditations on Hunting*, "Every good hunter is uneasy in the depths of his conscience when faced with the death he is about to inflict on the enchanting animal." The ambivalence of the hunter is emphasized in his commentary: "He does not have the final and firm conviction that his conduct is correct. But neither, it should be understood, is he certain of the opposite. Finding himself in an ambivalent situation which he has often wanted to clear up, he thinks about this issue without ever obtaining the sought-after evidence. I believe that this has always happened to man, with varying degrees of intensity according to the nature of the prey—ferocious or harmless—and with one or another variation in the aspect of uneasiness" (Ortega 1995, 98). Expressing a belief in buck fever may be an admission of this ambivalence, implying a need for ritual immersion in the world of the camp to regain confidence.

It is common for hunters to use buck fever as an excuse for missing a shot when facing the prospect of the shirttail ritual or even paddling. This defense risks evoking the retort that the fever is typical of a juvenile or a girl, and the shirttail ritual reinforces the belittling symbolism. Narratives about someone else's buck fever are easier to relate than confessions of one's own because the first-person account suggests performance anxiety. The inability to fire the gun and control one's body signifies a lack of aggression related to male sexual prowess, which is ritually tested in combat with another male opponent that needs to be feminized and infantilized. The symbolism of affliction in ritual, as anthropologist Victor Turner points out in a study of hunting cults in Africa, conveys the prophecy that initial misfortune is followed by success (1967, 143). Closer to home, hunting gear supplier Cabela's mounted an advertising campaign in 2007 showing three worn-out, gun-toting hunters at dusk with the caption, "Everyone has their own idea of a successful day." The implication was that struggle paid off and that satisfaction can differ from the sedentary, sterile corporate view in mass culture. Therefore, the psychosomatic malady applies to coming-of-age experiences in which taking a life is seen as a social necessity. From the socially understood illness is derived a ritual regeneration. The belief that the first shot of the season will be accompanied by buck fever is a rehearsal of coming-of-age; its attribution to novices recognizes hunters as a group of men with a distinct identity and specialized, potent skills and aggressive demeanors associated with maturity; in short, the ritual emphasizes hunters as a manly lot.

The question remains, however, why the shooting of a buck involves more ritualization than the killing of other animals does. After all, the fever is specifically attributed to the inability to shoot at a buck rather than other common game such as bears, rabbits, and turkeys. The fear of inadequacy represented by buck fever may be more than a conflict between the power to spare a life and the power to take one. It may also be a fear of revenge, especially by adolescent hunters, who must be aware of the image of the buck as a father figure. When spotting deer, hunters believe that the sighting of a doe means that a protective, patriarchal buck will soon pass by (Cannon 1984, 2:1020). As the respected "patriarch," "king," and "monarch" of the woods in folk speech, the buck takes on a paternal role, in contrast to the supposedly gentle, submissive doe. In popular culture, T-shirts show bucks in commanding, manly positions, such as the image of a stern buck with a weight lifter's muscular torso below the message: "DEER HUNTING: IT'S NOT AN ATTITUDE, IT'S WHO I AM" (Arkansas 2008). It follows, then, that hunting is an adolescent coming-of-age experience not just because the father commonly teaches it to his son but also because it involves the symbolic killing and replacement of the father. In killing the buck, the hunter acquires his strength, but not without unease.

Referring to buck fever as "signs of an anxiety attack," psychologist Richard Sterba postulates deer hunting as unconscious patricide. He gives the example of a patient who was an excellent hunter but developed buck fever for the first time in his life when he went hunting shortly after his father's death. Sterba concludes that "the actual death of his father had mobilized his oedipal guilt feelings to such an extent that he was incapable of committing another father murder in the form of shooting a deer" (1947, 425). As with other psychoanalytical interpretations taken from clinical cases of abnormal conditions and applied to normative culture, one must be cautious in formulating an immediate link. Yet as Sterba points out, the buck is a "typical father symbol, with its proud and showy antlers as his male characteristic" (1947, 423). He suggests that the custom of hunting big animals in groups implies the need to compensate for anxiety over symbolic patricide by showing strength in male numbers (Sterba 1947, 423).

Buck fever invites comparison with the couvade, in which the husband of a pregnant woman displays psychosomatic symptoms of labor. In his survey of couvade rituals, psychoanalyst Theodor Reik found that it was commonly observed with the birth of the first son, and he postulated that the symptoms originated from an unconscious fear of retaliation by the son as the incarnation of the grandfather. Reik gives an anthropological example of children among the Borans, who are sent away to be reared by hunters until they mature and are then returned to their families (Reik [1931], 87). The symptoms of the couvade are often interpreted as an expression of sympathy for the woman and a compensation for the man's inability to give birth. In either case, the behavior is perceived as feminized or even infantilized if the father is actually imitating the baby rather than the woman giving birth (Dundes 1987b, 156). Given the belief that "the child is father of the man," the pains and sweats of the couvade are ritualized so that the man can move into his new role. In buck fever, too, the boy is giving life and is apparently feminized not only because he does not shoot, and therefore fails to act aggressively and potently, but also because he has not symbolically matured by asserting himself rather than submitting to the fatherly buck.

Taking Life: Smearing Blood, Eating Testicles, Telling Lies

If the shirttail ritual is often applied to a miss by a new hunter, even greater ritualized emphasis is placed on the first kill. The most frequently reported rituals involve smearing blood from the deer on one's face, drinking the blood of the animal, and washing in its blood—often summarized as rituals of "blooding." The new hunter is often aided by other hunters, who celebrate the kill as his entrance into the identity of hunter. These practices are not limited to the killing of the first deer, as James Swan notes in his descriptions of blooding in initiation rituals for buffalo and moose (1999, 124–28). Swan, like many hunters, imagines the ritual as being connected to primitive man and postulates sacred meanings. "Many hunting rituals involve painting one's body with blood, or drinking the blood of the animals, as it is believed that this conveys the spirit of the animal to the hunter," he writes. The blood is especially symbolic, he notes, because it is the seat of life, soul, and spirit; it is sacred and powerful. According to Swan, such rituals contribute to deer camps' function as "today's versions of the secret societies of tribal hunting cultures, the social groups that men have formed for thousands of years to support the ethics of the hunt and adulthood as well as to have a good time" (Swan 1995, 136, 38).

Swan's view is that the hunt is important as an initiation into adulthood because it is a positive form of aggression, thereby providing a social framework for the use of "powerful instinctual energies" (Swan 1995, 136). Hunting, according to this argument, is a basic instinct; it is as natural for man to hunt as it is for deer to roam the woods. Its symbols reenact man's dominion over, and commune with, nature. The implication is that to repress this instinct, as animal rights organizations do, tampers with the natural order, and no good can come of that. Swan constructs an opposition between the bliss of nature evident in the hunting context of the woods and the artificial, technological corporate modernity of animal rights groups, and he implies that, unchecked, this modernity will swallow up nature. The foreboding message is that in the battle for hunting, the fate of the environment as a spiritual resource hangs in the balance.

Animal rights organizations counter that the basic human instinct— at least in the modern age, which should be characterized by progress over destruction of the environment and people—is to care for animals (Prescott 1995). In this view, hunters are relics or representatives of a reactionary minority who, through lobbies such as the National Rifle Association, seek to impose masculinist, patriarchal practices that are out of step with the norms of a society seeking safety and peace. The different stances on instinct are difficult to prove, of course, and they stand as important tenets of faith for both sides that contribute to their apparently irreconcilable differences and worldviews. In answer to the issue of promoting peace, for example, hunting advocates point out that shooting in the woods acts as a safety valve for aggressive instincts and therefore preserves civil society, whereas animal rights advocates underscore that hunting nurtures stalking and killing and results in a desensitization to violence.

For culture critic Barbara Ehrenreich, transformative rituals positively reinforce the act of killing rather than reflect a positive basic instinct, and no more transformative ritual exists than blooding. She argues that blooding is evidence of "our species' long prehistoric sojourn as hunters of animals," and in hunting lies the origin of the centrality of war and violence in human society. "It is the taste for meat and the willingness to kill for it that supposedly distinguish us from other primates, making us both smart and cruel, sociable and domineering, eager for the kill and capable of sharing it," she writes (Ehrenreich 1997, 21). And hunting as a sign of social control is customarily a man's

Adolescent's face smeared with the blood of his first deer, Ten-Point Deer Camp, Mississippi. (Photo courtesy of Mississippi Department of Archives and History)

domain. Conflict over taking life is resolved by creating religious rituals of blood sacrifice with animals, she asserts (Ehrenreich 1997, 26–29). The sacred ritualization of killing is deemed necessary if the animal is to be slaughtered and the meat is to be eaten (Ehrenreich 1997, 33). In this hierarchy, as the biblical story of Abraham's sacrifice of Isaac shows, there may be an insecurity that dominating elders or gods will firmly distinguish between children and animals. In the Bible story, a horned ram replaces Isaac on the altar at the last minute (see Ehrenreich 1997, 34). One way to alleviate this uncertainty is to have the boy do the killing and mark a transference of blood from an animal in a similar social stratum.

John Boyle's survey of British versions of blooding, which appear to be related to American traditions, cites historical precedents for blooding as an initiation of a young hunter.[7] In addition to the transference of the animal's skill to the young hunter, the act of an experienced hunter applying the blood implied that his wisdom would also be given to the youth. Boyle speculates on the influence of ancient war practices on the ritual, such as the Irish draining the blood of their dead enemies and smearing their faces with it (1969, 16). In his cultural history of hunting, Charles Bergman expands this analysis by noting that blood is one of the chief symbols of manliness, and hunters' language is full of references to blood ties, bloodlines, and bloodlust. "The young hunter becomes a man," he writes, "when, from the entrails of the prey, he is 'blooded' by an older male" (Bergman 1996, 293). In this perspective, blood is especially appropriate for a young hunter's coming-of-age because it is so private and intimate. Transferred from animal to boy, the blood elevates the strength—and therefore the maturity, in a patriarchal way of thinking—of the boy. Bergman editorializes, however, that "this is a terrible model of intimacy—the private spilled—and publicly displayed as spectacle. The internal is violated. The price for male strength has been intimacy" (1996, 293).

Sigmund Freud, though, postulated that blood rituals involving animals represent sacrifices of a father figure—and a rejection of women—that strengthen fraternal intimacy among members of a clan. From Freud's viewpoint, as expressed in *Totem and Taboo*, members of a clan take on the characteristics of an animal designated as a totem (Freud 1919, 3–4). The totem can be imagined as dangerous and feared and then, through ceremonies, rendered harmless and ed-

Enjoying a meal with a dead deer. (Postcard illustration)

ible (Freud 1919, 3). The question for Freud was why drinking, spilling, and smearing blood—taboo in everyday life—would be tolerated in these special circumstances. In spite of the dread that protects the life of the animal considered kin, it becomes necessary to kill it from time to time in solemn conclave and to divide its flesh and blood among the members of the clan (Freud 1919, 230). Freud's interest was in rationalizing through psychology the rituals of exotic cultures deemed strangely "primitive" by elites in Western industrialized countries. He did not examine deer camps or hunting groups in those countries but did mention blood drinking from a slain animal among the Bedouins: "the victim, a camel, was bound and laid upon a rough altar of stones; the leader of the tribe made the participants walk three times around the altar to the accompaniment of song, inflicted the first wound upon the animal and greedily drank the spurting blood" (Freud 1919, 241). Such examples led Freud to connect the custom of sacrifice in an all-male group with a reenactment of parricide so that members can grow by suspending the obligation to obey the father. Slaying a dangerous animal, Freud thought, is thrilling because it commemorates "the triumph over the father" (1919, 241). The " benefits of this deed," Freud posited, "included the appropriation of the father's properties" (1919, 242).

Hunter posing with a buck's head in his groin. This photo was conspicuously displayed in the hunter's photo album and circulated among the men at deer camp.

The significance of the blood, according to a Freudian viewpoint, is not only in the dramatization of a son's replacement of the father; it is also a declaration that the blood spilled or smeared by one hunter is common blood for the clan. Blood rituals, Freud surmised, provide "solidarity of life within the clan," simulating the relationship of brothers and thus ensuring "that no one of them is to be treated by the other as they all treated the father" (1919, 242). Indeed, brotherhood is often mentioned as the bond among members of deer camp, and the symbolism of the deer kill is crafted so that the buck as a father image cannot represent members of the camp fraternity. Something that Freud did not account for is the symbolic shift as animals are killed and ritualized to compensate for the guilt of destruction. Before the kill, hunters' talk about the buck emphasizes its patriarchal qualities; upon its death, it becomes feminized by references to its big rack (breasts) and attractive tail (buttocks) and by the removal of its genitals. The shift is framed in T-shirts sold in catalogs catering to hunters. Images of scantily clad women are accompanied by slogans such as "WHAT DO HUNTERS LIKE TO SEE ON DEER AND WOMEN—BIG RACKS"; "DEER HUNTING: FIND ONE WITH A BIG RACK AND MOUNT IT"; "HUNTERS LIKE WHITE TAILS AND BIG RACKS"; and "HUNTERS HAVE BIG GUNS AND MAGNUM LOADS" (Arkansas 2008).

Probably because of the association between blooding and childhood, it has been a focus of protest against hunting practices. In fact, it has been held up by animal rights groups as a symbol of the way hunting fosters bloodlust and even child abuse. Henry Salt writing for the Humanitarian League complained that "of all practices connected with 'sport' none are more loathsome than those known as 'blooding,' whether it be the 'blooding' of children, which consists in a sort of gruesome parody of the rite of baptism, or the 'blooding' of hounds—viz., the turning out of some decrepit animal to be pulled down by the pack, by way of stimulating their blood-lust" (1915, 155). In chapter 2 I explain the symbolic equivalence of boys and hounds as small, supposedly faithful companions who are raised and trained in a patriarchal cultural system. Of relevance here is the outrage expressed because the ritual is perceived to be a baptism into antisocial violence. Signifying blooding as baptism gives rise to the image of an innocent infant incorporated into an ethical community as well as being blessed by God. The implication, though, is an opposition of holy water and devilish blood, with the latter obviously representing the corruption or violation of minors.

Salt exclaimed, for example, "But what a ceremony in a civilised age! One would have thought that twentieth-century sportsmen, even if they would not spare the . . . [animal], might spare their own children!" (1915, 156). Animal rights supporters I talked to described blooding with revulsion because they view the smearing of blood as defilement rather than honor. To them, it appears to be a signal of death, whereas the child should represent life. In this light, one can understand this comment: "When they should be given milk, they're drinking blood. How awful is that?" It is as if the child is murdered rather than the animal. As famed writer George Bernard Shaw commented in an anti–blood sport tract, "Just as the murder of a child is more shocking than the murder of an adult (because, I suppose, the child is so helpless and the breach of social faith therefore so unconscionable), the murder of an animal is an abuse of man's advantage over animals" (1915).

Hunters I talk to think of blooding as a custom for adolescents and young adults rather than as an infant rite. They might mention its coming-of-age representation of the warrior-hero venerated and narrated in hunting culture. They usually stop there and dig no deeper. There is a sense that if they gave too much thought to the meaning of blooding, it would take away from its function in camp life. Cognitively, the important point is that the ritual has been conducted for many generations, and hunting camps are maintaining it as a tradition. They are therefore a link in a chain that will continue after they are gone, and the ritual provides identity and visibility to hunting culture. Through tradition, hunting is transformed from an activity or procedure to a way of life and a worldview. The connection of the private and intimate ritual of blooding to coming-of-age is not elaborated beyond its drawing attention to itself, or else the image of the naive teen metaphorically losing his virginity through the kill is purposely or unconsciously avoided.

Before I explain in more detail the ritual symbolism of blooding, there is more to say about the milk-blood-water equivalence assumed in anti-hunting perceptions of blooding. Relevant to accusations about hunters' bloodlust and bloodthirstiness is the psychology in European-American culture of vampire figures and their bloodlust for young victims. I propose that there is an unstated connection between this psychology and animal rights groups' narrative construction of the predatory hunter engaged in a "blood sport," suggesting the act of killing for lustful pleasure. It sheds light, I believe, on both anti-hunters' repulsion to blooding and pro-hunters' attraction to it.

When I showed photographs of blood-smeared boys to people who were not familiar with hunting culture, their overwhelming response was to liken the image to vampirism. The important detail that evoked this allusion was the blood around the mouth. Whether this was influenced by the recent spate of vampire films and books or Halloween celebrations is hard to say. Regardless, picking up on the perceived linkage, I find a significant association between the infantilization of blood-smeared teens in animal rights discourse and the common traits and functions of the vampire in oral tradition. For one, many people associate the ghoulish male revenant with the drinking of blood, which is also a ritual related to the function of the blood smear at camp. Young hunters who have made their first kill often mark the milestone by drinking the animal's blood. The idea that the dry and therefore sickly vampire needs wet blood to live fits into a cognitive association of dryness with death and wetness with life (Dundes 1998, 163–64). Sucking or drinking blood from an animal or other being therefore draws out life, and the smear of blood around the mouth underscores the consumptive way the victim's life has been sacrificed for the vampire's rejuvenation. Indeed, there is evidence that the word *vampire* owes its origin in the Greek root *pi*, meaning "to drink" (Afanas'ev 1976, 164; Dundes 1998, 162).

Of significance to the perception of vampirism is that the blood-thirsty revenant often pursues young family members as victims, and the oral contact is often portrayed as both an angry bite and an erotic sucking of blood from the neck or chest. Significant to symbolist interpretations of the vampire is his occasional drinking of milk in addition to blood. Vampires supposedly take milk away from nursing mothers and cows, leaving their human and animal prey barren and dry (Jones 1971, 119). As symbols of life, blood and milk have a rejuvenating power. Both are associated with the chest as the location of life-giving nourishment: the heart and the breast. Nonetheless, the vampire's habit of extracting these liquids from family members through biting and sucking has baffled literary critics because of its combination of incestuous and infanticidal tendencies. Folklorist Alan Dundes thought he had found a key to unlock the puzzle by citing the Freudian idea that a child's death wishes directed toward a parent or other rival are projected to a guilty conscience, resulting in a fear that the dead parental figure will return to exact vengeance (Dundes 1998, 166; Jones 1971, 112). This made Dundes think that "the mixture of love and hate towards the parental figures is symbolized by sucking (love) and biting (hate), actions taken by vampires towards the living" (1998, 166). He posited a projective inversion in which "the lost object (the deceased love one) will return to take revenge by means of sucking or biting. . . . Instead of infants sucking from adult breasts, adults suckle from children's breasts" (1998, 167–69). The vampire, even if he is male, emulates the original life-giving and partly erotic sucking of breast-feeding but also shows revengeful anger in the aggressive act of biting.

Among the many scholars analyzing how the vampire legend has captivated the Euro-American psyche, Dundes has, to my mind, given the most compelling explanation of why the vampire is viewed as both fearsome and attractive. But what does that have to do with the blood smear? My quick answer is that the accusations tossed at hunters—that they are bloodthirsty, seek to satisfy bloodlust, and corrupt or even abuse children—evoke vampire images because of the family dynamics connoted by the youth begrimed with blood. There is also the Euro-American predisposition to view the woods as a mysterious, dangerous place and the perception of hunters as predators. The image of the vampire takes away the violation of the boy having shot the animal; the corruption of the boy is emphasized in his being transformed by a consumptive act. The bloody mouth represents tearing into flesh, reinforced by the protests against meat eating by animal rights advocates and playfully underscored in slogans on hunters' T-shirts: "PETA: PEOPLE EATING TASTY ANIMALS" and "SCREW PETA" (with an image of a man eating a big, juicy steak).

Another link that Dundes did not take into consideration makes the image of vampirism particularly evocative in a discussion of wildlife. This is the prevalent vampire-related belief in revenants shape-shifting into animals or preying on animals. As a result of having its flesh and blood consumed, the hunted animal does the revenant's bidding. An example in American lore is the fabled "hellhound" made famous by Robert Johnson in a blues song in which the deathly creature pursues humans (Lincoln 1979). Other beliefs involve a strange smell reportedly not unlike the odor emanating from the deer's tarsal glands, which are cut by hunters after the kill. Related to this belief is the idea that pigeons "are not good unless they have all their blood drained from them right after being killed, so the accepted way of killing pigeons was to bite their throats." The custom was for two men to "work together, one would pull the pigeon from under the net, bite it and throw it down, the other would make a mark for each pigeon thrown down" (Lounsberry 1946). In the discourse of anti-hunting, these images converge to reinforce the charge of bestiality against hunters. Whereas the hunted deer represents infantile innocence and vitality in the anti-hunter's worldview, the hunter turned bloodthirsty vampire brings death by viciously sapping the animal dry.

What about the family dynamic in the narrative complex of blooding? Where is the guilty conscience for death wishes or the fear of parental revenge? The difference in the blooding context is that roles are reversed from the Eurocentric vampire narrative. Sure, the blood smeared on a youthful face may give the impression of a bloodthirsty predator, characteristic of a vampire, but this is a cherubic face rather than the ghoulish countenance of a dry, withered figure in need of rejuvenation through the acquisition of body fluids. The image is doubly reprehensible, though, because the bloodied youngster is both killer and deceased. The boy becomes scary as a beast capable of matricide. Unlike the vampire narrative, which allows some parental bond and even an erotic attraction, the bloodied face gives the impression that the youth is simultaneously a victim of infanticide and a bestial savage. The killing beast thus subverts the image of the innocent, feminized, milk-drinking animal that an affinity for animal rights is supposed to promote. Instead of ambivalence toward parents being worked out in a kind of dream fantasy, blooding washes the hunting scene in nightmare (Jones 1971).

The tradition of ritual blood drinking after one's first kill only adds to the ghoulish qualities of hunting, in the eyes of protesters. At one blood-drinking ritual at a deer camp in central Pennsylvania, the young hunter looked at the glass with great trepidation while his campmates encouraged him with calls of "bottom's up" and "you're a man now." Recognizing that imbibing the liquid would test his moxie, since it was considered disgusting by polite society, the young man was at first reluctant but then showed his bravado by announcing the taste to be a mixture of red wine and beer. He expressed surprise at the warmth of the blood, in contrast to the cold gusts blowing around his face, but that only added to the mystique of the drink. "Why are we doing this?"

he naively asked. An older member of the party answered in the rhetoric of oral tradition: "I was told it restored life in the deer's soul because its blood was now circulating again in a living creature" (Guerriero 1994, 2–3). At another camp, an older member explained that blood drinking was akin to a primitive ritual initiating a warrior, thereby emphasizing his manliness. At Camp Hunter, whereas the blood smear announced the kill and set the initiate apart, the blood drinking was seen as a sign of membership in the group marked by its experienced male adult status. One member of the party added that he was now loosened from his domesticated home and bound to the primal, manly instincts of the wild. The praxis of smearing even more than drinking, though, evoked comments about primitivist carnivorous characteristics, probably because of the connection between smearing and infantile fecal play (Dundes 1966). Smearing blood is thus embraced in the ritual as intentionally repulsive and simultaneously compelling, worthy of gaining status by drawing attention to maturation and individuation.

Drinking blood and using the testicles, tail, and penis of a slaughtered animal to affirm manliness are also reported in an ethnography of bull butchering. Yolanda K. Snyder observes that many butchers drank blood because "they claimed it gave them strength and that there were a lot of vitamins in it." She finds in this ritual play an elevation of the man's carnivorous status in an occupation that requires taking life: "John Bachman said that 'Bones drank it down and everybody was standin' there watchin' and he smiled and the blood was runnin' down between his teeth and his mouth just looked like, you know, all messed up inside and this was a gory look" (Snyder 1987, 8). The bull, like the buck, is considered dangerous and hypermasculine, if not patriarchal.

The ritualization of blood smearing is epitomized by the common practice of having an older member of the camp cut the deer's throat and smear the blood on the young hunter (Koch 1965, 166; Huffman 1997, 99). An initiation is implied by the older member preparing the youth for presentation to the group, marking his immersion in the hunt. In the commentary accompanying his family's photographic record of a deer camp in the Mississippi Delta, Alan Huffman notes that "modern viewers may be repulsed," particularly by shots of the ceremonial smearing of blood. He explains that "the hunters of Ten Point saw these traditions as honest responses to the natural world" (Huffman 1997, 98). Repeating them for the sake of continuing tradition in a changing world seemed to him a justification in itself. Although he understood that it appeared "basically savage," he also considered it an "act of humility" and a rite of passage into the "fraternity of the hunt." As an example, he cites abundant photographs of hunters who have "ganged up on the initiate, and the scene might be mistaken for a bloody wrestling match if not for the smiles on everyone's faces" (Huffman 1997, 98). The combination of ritual and play suggests important cultural functions for what folklorist Michael Owen Jones calls "disgusting behavior": building a sense of bravado through the allure of the forbidden, creating group solidarity by separating from conventions of normative culture, and humiliating oneself to gain sanctity and acceptance (2000, 59–60). In Ehrenreich's analysis (1997), it is a celebration of violence, and a root of war, because it teaches that vanquishing an opponent is regenerative, even redemptive.

But limiting Ehrenreich's interpretation is the fact that expressions of aggression and disgust are not restricted to coming-of-age, and I offer a close, inside look at the significance of retrieving blood from a *male* buck by a maturing boy. I suggest that blooding represents the boy's loss of virginity by usurping female sexual powers and activities, especially at a time when the aroused boy feels that females are not available to him (Dundes 1997, 40). Males combine symbols of female maturation, evidenced by menstruation, with defloration of the female. In fact, in adolescent humor such as the "what's grosser than gross" jokes (e.g., "finding a tampon at the bottom of the tomato juice can," "two vampires fighting over a bloody tampon"), menstruation is often defined by males as "disgusting," while also noting that it is an enviable source of power or a visible sign of maturation (Bronner 1985; 1988, 131–32; see also Dundes 2002a, 92). Menstrual blood flows through the hymen, or "maidenhead," and rupturing it is believed to be a sign of the loss of virginity. Males even cite a humorous proverb to indicate the connection: "Old enough to bleed, old enough to breed." A related example from the military—another male-dominated group acculturating its members to pursuit with guns—is instructive. Among paratrooper units, new soldiers are recognized, or shamed, by giving them red helmets inscribed with the word *cherry* or decorated with a picture of a cherry, indicating a virginal girl. After a paratrooper's first jump, he has "popped his cherry," a reference to the female hymen being penetrated. Or a new soldier may be forced to carry a cherry pie on the jump, resulting in a gooey red mess smeared on his face, thereby indicating his loss of virginity as if he were a female (Bronner 2005b, 14–15).

The common association of blooding with a boy's coming-of-age is thus related to gaining sexual potency, and in hunting, the kill marks the boy's initiation into manhood. The initiatory praxis appears to be another instance of what Dundes and Bruno Bettelheim hypothesize as usurpation of female sexual powers deriving from male envy of the female organs (Dundes 1978, 102; Bettelheim 1962, 45). Whether envy or appropriation, the male uses the sexual-aggressive symbolism of blood to visibly mark the change from novice youth to adult male hunter. The ritual is not so bizarre when one takes into account the male recognition that coming-of-age is more publicly recognized in ceremony, and more physically recognizable, for females, especially in contemporary American culture. As Ray Raphael (1988) concludes from his study of rites of passage, relative to other cultures, there is a notable *lack of public transitions* for the adolescent male in America, even though his need to dramatize maturity and manliness is arguably more acute than the female's because of social expectations and physical insecurities.

In the light of blood smearing as a metaphorical loss of virginity using female symbols, the basis of the teasing conversation at Camp Hunter described earlier becomes clearer. The boy sitting out hunting camp is reason for derision of the father, who is supposedly responsible for ushering in his son's maturation. The implication is that the boy is drawn away from camp by the lure of sex and mass culture. Since having sex with females is apparently available to him as a means of passing into adulthood, he does not need the rituals and traditions of camp intended to simulate the loss of virginity through combat with males and maturation by the symbolic replacement of the father. The domestication and feminization of the low-context mass culture, and specifically the passive action of watching television, are antithetical to the high-context folk culture of the camp, which stresses aggression and male bonding. The folk speech accusation hurled at the boy—that he is a "lazy ass"—underscores his passivity with homoerotic or feminized undertones, thus emphasizing the manly virility of the men in camp and their process of initiating a boy into tradition as well as manhood.

Taking a bite out of the dead buck's liver at the time of the kill, or cooking the heart, kidneys, and testes in a special dish given to the successful hunter, is related to blooding in its symbolic consumption and domination of the animal. The organs are cooked ritually on the day of the kill (Hanna 1986, 4). Newbell Niles Puckett heard the term "hunter's dish" used for the special preparation: "Certain game or parts of game can only be eaten by the person who shot them. The heart and liver of all horned animals is the hunter's dish, and should be eaten by the hunter. The rest of the people may eat the other parts of the deer or other horned animals" (Hand, Casetta, and Thiederman 1981, 2:1020). The consumption of these organs from a "horned animal" is important, I maintain; it goes beyond the taking of life in the blood smear to encompass the very consumption of the patriarchal animal. Literally, one is eating the guts and therefore gaining guts—slang for bravery. Eating the liver immediately after the kill is considered disgusting by many moderns because the liver—an organ that filters waste—is symbolically unclean and attached to excrement. But as the legends of "Liver-Eating Johnson" and accounts of snakes attaching to a person's liver attest, consumption of the liver is considered a particularly carnivorous, triumphant act (Hand 1961, 106–7). It is therefore a manly act because of its distaste and the suggestion of phallic penetration into the body cavity (see Jones 2000, 59; Adams 2000, 50–73; Freud 1994, 6–8). Like the external antlers, which may be cut and kept, signifying a symbolic castration, the liver marks the internal emasculation of the buck (see Dundes 1997, 30). Indeed, some camps feature a liver dinner as a measure "of our success during the first two days of the season" (Edwards 1985, 29). For anti-hunters, the ritual of eating the liver, heart, and testes is only more evidence of deer camp as a site of barbarism, with a symbolic connection to cannibalism. But for pro-hunters, the dish is a badge of honor signaling triumph in the wild. More so, it enacts a hierarchy with men in command, in contrast to the egalitarian rhetoric of speciesism. Trijicon, a gun scope manufacturer, tapped into this hierarchical thinking when it ran full-page ads in hunting magazines in 2008 announcing, "You're at the top of the food chain, so enjoy the view." Understanding the hunter's anxiety about the *wild* animal's advantage over the domesticated man, the ad copy read, "A trophy elk may outsee you, out-smell you and out-hear you, but with the new Trijicon Accupoint the advantage is yours to enjoy" (Trijicon 2008). Yet anti-hunters believe that humans always have, and exploit, their advantage.

If the heart represents the animal's center and is a sign of courage and aggression, the testicles mark his sexual potency. It is not coincidental that eating the testicles, like drinking blood, is a use of distaste to show male bravado—or "having balls," as it would be expressed in folk speech. Often surrounded by an air of play, the boy's consumption of the testicles may be done with the father supervising. As one deer camp directive stated: "Any boy shooting his first buck will, at that evening's dinner, be given the choice of eating either the right or left testicle of the buck. Cook will serve 2 hush puppies of not less than 3 inches diameter each to the boy. After a suitable silence, the boy's father or guardian will say, 'Hell, I'll make it easy for you, son,' and consume one hush puppy whole. He will then smack his lips and declare, 'Now that's a good testicle'" (Camp 2003).[8] This patriarchal scene has a parallel in the British tradition of "breaking the stag," in which the highest-ranking nobleman received the testicles and other highly relished tidbits (Cartmill 1993, 64). Although the boy may be disgusted at the thought of eating the testicle, he may be encouraged by its aphrodisiacal qualities. The other implication is that he will grow into or replace his father. If not eaten, the genitals may be hung, as Sterba reports in Michigan "as a trophy, on a tree on the road nearby the place where the buck was killed" (1947, 424). The accompanying belief is that if the genitals are not cut, the meat will go bad, suggesting that the kill is not effective. The antlers or the entire head may be kept as a trophy, marking a symbolic castration; the tail may also be kept, apparently as a sign of feminizing the male opponent in victory. Puckett even recorded a belief that if the hunter fails to take the deer's tail as a trophy, he will have bad luck (Hand, Casetta, and Thiederman 1981, 2:1020). The implication is that if he is not aggressive and dominating, he will not succeed in the hunt. The hunter asserts his manliness by taking a life and thereby acquiring animal qualities that help a boy grow into a man or a man become more manly.

These maturational images raised in ritual are ones of exaggeration. This hyperbole delights hunters, who view the wild as an accentuated context that forces one to be stronger and more alive in response to the feminizing influences of modern society. It chagrins animal rights advocates, who see a confirmation of the atavistic qualities of modern consumptive culture. One location to see this conflict is the hunting story: for one side, it celebrates the transgressive quality of going out hunting, while for the other, it brags about destruction and is thus despicable. Hunting lends itself to narrated exaggeration in the popular imagination, and popularly, the hunting tale is equated with the tall tale—an outrageous lie presented as life as usual. Bass Pro Shops, a superstore aimed at outdoor types, capitalizes on this image by emblazoning over its doors the come-on, "WELCOME FISHERMEN, HUNTERS AND OTHER LIARS."

The hunting story is inscribed in public imagination but lost in folkloristic chronicles. Perhaps part of the problem is the structure of narrative indexes that organize knowledge by nationality, characters (e.g., animals, ogres, the dead, the wise and the foolish), or events and actions (e.g., tests, marvels, rewards and punishments, magic). Yet some themes that cut across categories are recognized as folk materials. For example, Stith Thompson's standard reference, the *Motif-Index of Folk-Literature* (1975), devotes sections to sex, religion, and drunkenness as deserving their own range of motifs because presumably they inspire narrative commentary. One might also surmise that such categories involve conflicts and guilt, leading to symbolization in narrative. The door may seem to be open for other activities related to narrative creation, but El-Shamy and Garry's *Archetypes and Motifs in Folklore and Literature* (2005) does not have a single entry on hunting in the index. Likewise, Thomas Green's *Folklore: An Encyclopedia of Beliefs, Customs, Tales, Music, and Art* (1997) and Mary Ellen Brown and Bruce Rosenberg's *Encyclopedia of Folklore and Literature* (1998) omit hunting. The classic *Funk and Wagnall's Standard Dictionary of Folklore, Mythology, and Legend* lists hunting in relation to magic and as the subject of an English-Scottish border ballad considered "one of the finest ballads in English," but there is no speculation on why hunting would be so central to these beliefs and narrative genres (Leach 1949, 1:511). One would expect more elaboration on hunting as a central narrative theme, given the many references to it in public imagination. The small allowance for hunting in the context of expressive genres in the *Standard Dictionary* provides a clue to the unease associated with hunting as a folkloristic topic; for intellectuals who acknowledge it at all, it is easier to embed it, and thereby marginalize it, beside the preferred romantic themes of love and salvation rather than treating hunting as a fundamental human action.

An exception is Americanist Jan Harold Brunvand, who includes an entry on hunting written by Mary Hufford in his *American Folklore: An*

Encyclopedia (1996), reflecting Brunvand's goal of covering topics that relate to Americans' sense of their own heritage. Hufford echoes my point that hunting as a subject in traditional discourse is abundant and notes that it has barely been given "serious attention." Hypothesizing the significance of hunting in narrative based on her fieldwork with fox hunters in New Jersey, she observes that "hunters constitute their quarry and assign meaning to the zoological distance they traverse through empathy, pitting their mental acuity and physical stamina against the intelligence or guile of a most worthy adversary" (Hufford 1996, 379–81; see also Hufford 1992). The interpretation she offers, if obtusely stated, is that hunting for some people is constructed culturally as sport out of the perceived tension in society concerning animal-human relations. That is a reasonable observation, but it does not explain why hunting assigns meaning in a special way and why hunting is perceived variously by nonhunters.

The strategy of "constituting" is, in Hufford's view, crucial to an understanding of hunters' attraction to the spinning of yarns, judging by her repetition of the rhetoric of constituting: "Through narrative, hunters constitute a world in which they appear as characters who exercise sportsmanship and fellowship (or whose exercise of sportsmanship is vigorously debated by those present at the storytelling)." She correctly contextualizes the world of hunting as a man's world and ties the preponderance of "lies," or tall tales, to this world's location "at the margins of everyday life." Thus, "the sociality of hunting conjures a prankish milieu in which men trick each other" (1996, 381). But as with the mock shirttail-cutting trial discussed earlier, the consequence of sociability is confused with the cause of the action. Yes, it is primarily a man's world, often isolated from normative society, but when considering the symbolic interaction of pranking, it is often overlooked that hunting is usually a private, even secret world. The pranking, therefore, carries meaning not as frivolous play but as a significant contribution to the transgressive, maturational experience of hunting. As Dundes has pointed out, pranks "occur most often to individuals *who are placed in some kind of new situation or status. The key word is new*" (Dundes 1989a, 104). Pranks are played on novices and are markers of a change in status or situation. An assumption in enacting the joke, and later talking about it in the play frame of an oft-repeated story, is that the novice is not only new but also weak. The prank toughens him up, moves him up, and leads him away from the comfort of home and mother to join the fraternal group.

By virtue of pranks being called "practical jokes," a narrated sequence is implied, usually involving an audience, that is deemed humorous. Dundes structures them as "(1) Deceit proposed by prankster, (2) Deception accepted by dupe, and (3) Revelation of deception" (1989a, 104). Tall tales and practical jokes are related structurally as forms of deceit, or undetected lying. An example relevant to the context of hunting is the prevalent tradition of the "snipe hunt" narrative, in which a dupe is told that the group is going to hunt snipe (described as an elusive bird, which it is, or a furry rodent) at night. The novice is encouraged to join the group in a social activity that, he is emphatically told, has gone on for many generations, thus describing it as part of normative culture. In the second stage of the prank, the wannabe snipe hunter is given a flashlight and a bag while the pranksters make noise or instruct the dupe to utter sounds to summon the snipe. The practical joke ends with the literalization of the phrase, "he was left holding the [empty] bag," much to the delight of the pranksters (Dundes 1989a, 105; Bronner 1988, 170–71). The conclusion, if the structure holds, is that the novice turned initiate joins the group in a good laugh.

Participants in the snipe hunt usually single out a youth to play this joke on, but it is not just fun at the youngster's expense. There is a lesson to be gained. The deception is that the snipe hunt is actually hunting; hunting has been defined, one learns, in more aggressive terms characteristic of manly endeavors or in Freudian terms of parricide, thus separating the joke of the snipe hunt from the ritual of blooding. It appears laughable that a hunter would engage in a contest of strength against a creature uttering the high-pitched tones of the peeping snipe. The dupe looks foolish because of the incongruity of making feminized whistles and bird noises in the company of men in the rugged woods. The bag and flashlight are no match for gun and scope. The hunting context is viewed as a coming-of-age experience, and authority is vested in experience, just as reverence is given to tradition. Structurally, the tripartite narrative of pranks follows what Arnold van Gennep (1961) calls "rites of passage," which have the function of ceremoniously facilitating the transition from one life stage to another. The rites compress life experience into three stages marked by the youthful, innocent past ("separation"); the daunting present, a liminal betwixt and between state in which the initiate has to prove him- or herself ("transition"); and the celebrated future in which the initiate is incorporated into society and has a heightened sense of the values, wisdom, and traditions of the community ("incorporation"). An implication of this maturational process is that a power struggle occurs between youth and experience; the elders are reminding the initiate of the authority of the community and the significance of tradition, though the youth often has strength, attractiveness, and vitality on his or her side (Dundes 1989a, 109).

At many camps I visited, there was less hunting going on than telling stories about hunting. In fact, part of the custom for many hunters is "camp hopping," that is, visiting other hunter-gatherers and engaging in storytelling. As hunter-storyteller Robert Hruska writes, "The stories that came in from the hunt [were] really part of the exciting camp life. It seemed that you could stretch the truth telling them as long as they were reasonable" (1999, 14). In light of the previous argument, the narration involved in stretching the truth and playing practical jokes also serves to create a distinct social world. It is a primitivistic world in which men reenact the experience of the hardscrabble wilderness not only by going out into the woods to provide sustenance but also by engaging in storytelling around a fireplace in a preindustrial setting. This reenactment is a play frame that uses metaphors of animal-human relations to redirect anxieties about aging and family relations as well as tradition and modernity. The background of the crackling fire provides warmth, to be sure, but it also suggests the patriarchal quest for fire in the wild; fire is heralded in classical literature as the only one of the living elements that humans can produce themselves, and it is observed in the "firearm" symbol of the camps (Biedermann 1994, 129). Its flames may suggest the mystery of yore and invite the suspension of belief in the fictive plane of storytelling. In the context of hunting, fire made with wood gathered from the outdoors harnesses explosive power in the hands of man. The setting is supposed to be rugged and manly, as indicated by Hruska's comment that when younger members asked for insulation at his camp, "Grandpa would say, 'That's for sissies.'" The experience, he emphasized, was intended to be rough, to teach "character, perseverance, and a hearty personality." As a veteran hunter, he noted the physical transformation in the smell and color of youngsters new to camp. He reminisced that after two weeks at camp, his own father had told him, "You look two shades darker and smell like the rest of us," which "was like an earned badge of honor. Like being accepted into the veteran hunters' group" (Hruska 1999, 14). Stories reenacted every year at camp reminded them of the badge, of the identity, of the manliness they had gained.

When filmmakers Kenneth Thigpen and George Hornbein filmed *Buck Season at Bear Meadows Sunset* (1984) at a Pennsylvania deer camp, their ethnographic revelation was that the men at camp apparently spent more time joking and gaming than going out and pursuing prey. When the men of Bear Meadows Sunset joked or related more sobering stories, they centered the narratives in hunting experience and drew notice to the fact that their ranks were graying. They were having trouble getting young people to replace the members who had passed away. An oft-repeated narrative at Bear Meadows Sunset and at other camps I visited tells of the young hunter who hears the gathered elders blurting out numbers to the response of great laughter. Impressed by the good cheer of the exchange, the youngster interjects a number into the conversation, but dead silence ensues. Feeling dejected, he sheepishly asks, "What did I do wrong?" An old hunting sage responds, "Well, son, some can tell 'em and some can't" (compare Dorson 1972, 19–20; Dundes 1989b, 34). On its surface, the story speaks to the high-context world of the camp and the significance of storytelling to maintain it. Embedded in the story, too, is the importance of acculturating youth to the customs of camp. New members are certainly needed, the story conveys, but they require initiation, including becoming versed in exaggeration as the stuff of conversation.

The pervasiveness of hunting as, in Hufford's words, "a conversational resource" may be even more widespread than she acknowledged. J. Russell Reaver, surveying manuscript archives of 2,378 American tall tales from thirty-two states collected from 1949 to 1951, concluded that the most popular motif was X1110, *the wonderful hunt* (Reaver 1972, 370; tale type 1890 in Uther 2004, 2:478–79; see also Baker 1986, 3–12; Burrison 1989, 169–75; Creighton 1950, 136–38; Lindahl 2004, 102–5, 479–80; Roberts 1955, 145–47; Sackett and Koch 1961, 15–17). The most prevalent story using this motif is described as a person shooting many animals with one shot. It figures prominently in folklore collector Vance Randolph's summary of hunting yarns from the Ozarks in *We Always Lie to Strangers* (1951, 95–130). Although the motif gives the impression of a single set of variant stories, the documentation suggests a structural difference between the single-shot wonder or accidental kill and the remarkable pursuit. As an example of the former, Randolph documents stories told as a third-person narrative about legendary hunter Abner Yancey, who, armed with a single-shot rifle, was trying to get two squirrels lined up so as to kill them both with one bullet. The squirrels fell when Ab fired, and just then he heard turkeys in a nearby tree. Seven hens and a gobbler were sitting on a branch, and Ab's bullet had sped on to split the limb and catch their feet in the crack. Ab climbed the tree and wrung the turkeys' necks, but on his way down he fell into a brush pile, killing two big rabbits and a covey of quail. On the story goes, following the structure of a catch tale, until a button popped off his shirt and killed a big buck that Ab never even saw (1951, 120–21).

Regarding the second form, Randolph states that "every backwoods child has heard of the hunter who chased a giant buck, which always dodged around a knoll before he could fire" (1951, 117). Many of these stories prompt listeners to think about the significance of firearms to the hunt; as the machine that empowers the hunter, the gun is the physical extension of the person that invites exaggeration. Randolph relates, for instance, the story of the man who asked the blacksmith to bend his rifle barrel so that he could shoot around the mountain. He pulled the trigger just as the big deer disappeared, and the animal ran completely around the hill four times, with the rifle ball in hot pursuit. Finally, the exhausted deer slowed down and was killed by the bullet. Closure to the narrative is provided by noting that the buck fell dead "at the hunter's feet" (1951, 117; see motif X1122.3.1 and type 1890E in Baughman 1966). Variations of this "lie" are hunters who bend a gun to conform to angles on a fence (and hit all the birds sitting on it) or to curves on a stream (shooting all the ducks on a winding waterway), and the ones who change barrels of a double-barreled gun to shoot sideways (the bullets round up all the game on both sides of the hunter) or twist them to shoot up and around a tree trunk. The incongruity in these different lies is that the gun is unnatural by virtue of being straight and mechanical but is naturalized by bending and curving to match the contours of streams, mountains, and trees. One indication of the symbolic opposition of the straightness of the machine and the circularity of nature is the motif for "hunter bends gun barrel in curve, shoots game standing in circle" (X1122.3.3 in Baughman 1966; Baker 1986,

9; Lindahl, Owens, and Harrison 1997, 219). The exaggeration works because the machine that is out of place in the wilderness becomes integrated into the landscape between human and animal. It playfully inserts the mechanistic gun in the primitivistic picture of the hunting scene. One commonly reported variant even has the bullet substituting for the man chasing down the deer: "hunter bends gun in curve, *bullet chases deer* around mountain several times before catching up with, killing deer" (X1122.3.2 in Baughman 1966; emphasis added).

The big lie in narrative is a compensatory way to show self-confidence in one's abilities as a hunter, a pursuit that is considered daunting and could reveal one's inadequacies to peers in a test of manly prowess in combat with animals (see Thompson 1975, motif H1161). The narrator as hunter, and senior, is fearless and peerless. Alone in the woods, he exerts complete dominion over nature in the tall tale—an inversion of reality. As joke, a story can relate the maturational process of gaining the identity and self-confidence of the hunter. One of the favorites at Camp Hunter, for instance, is about the youngster who is given tips about hunting at camp. Having heard stories about bears roaming the woods, he asks, "What should I do if I see a bear?" His veteran guide tells him, "Just do everything the bear does, and you'll be fine." He goes out on his own and comes across a ferocious-looking bear. The animal roars, "Rrraaah," and the youngster roars right back. The bear returns an even louder growl, and the novice answers in kind. Just then, the bear drops a huge load of feces, as bears in popular imagination are wont to do. ("Does a bear shit in the woods?" is a response implying affirmation in folk speech.) The youngster blurts out, "Damn, I did that at the first 'Rrraaah!'" Even with many repetitions, the story always draws laughter at the idea of defecation as a result of fright (as in, "that bear scared the shit out of me"). Like the stories of buck fever, it draws attention to feelings of inadequacy and, in this case, the narrated gulf between initiated hunter and youthful novice. In a variant reported by folklorist James Leary, the bear's defecation is described as "Mother Nature calls," suggesting the narrated ambiguity in the wild between human and animal dominion and the symbolism of defecation as infantile and feminine (2001, 187–88). A hunter, the joke relates, has a higher status in which natural urges are controlled; not being afraid unties the strings to mother.

Randolph deserves credit for drawing attention to these stories, but he offers little to guide their interpretation, and it appears that few other folklorists picked up the trail of hunting yarns as a narrative genre connected by the praxis of hunting. Randolph hints at the meaning given to the stories by Ozarks residents by noting that they begin with an exaggeration of the abundance of game in the old days. Another significant pattern in the stories is the hierarchy of animals from the pigeon and squirrel, usually considered deserving of slaughter, to the monarch of the woods, the buck, highly regarded as a dangerous opponent. Another factor in evaluating the yarns is that Randolph, like many collectors, was primarily looking for set fantastical pieces that might be called "fabulates," hardly taking into account the more prevalent deer camp tradition of narrating the personal experiences of hunting. In the set pieces often intended as humorous, what is laughable—that is, incongruous—is the success of the hunter. Human dominion over the land and its creatures is extraordinary, drawing attention to the ordinary routine of human struggle in the woods. The buck is arguably the monarch in these narratives told by men for other men because of its rack of horns, imagined as a weapon as well as a crown, and its manly attributes.

What about the "old days"? In many narratives of the abundance of earlier times, one finds a historical recounting of a pioneer theme of encountering an unspoiled Edenic garden. For many hunters, the location of hunting in the backwoods and the insistence on primitivizing the experience are tied not only to reenacting a primal male experience of provision but also to conquering an American wilderness. Lamar Underwood's introduction to *Classic Hunting Stories*, for instance, explains the appeal of the activity reflected in the hunting narrative: "The exhilarating details of the chase, the moments of suspense when failure loomed, the skills that prevailed through great difficulties—these classic elements of hunting talk were no doubt as much in evidence for the pioneers as they are today for the pursuers of whitetail deer, and all other game" (2003, ix). My point is that hunting as praxis is both imagined as a redemptive root of the present and normalized as routine in a region with a pioneer heritage.

The connection to hunting as local knowledge is evident in modern legends of "dumb hunters" who come, of course, from out of state. Californians are characterized thus by Utah hunters, urbane Chicagoans turn out to be not so woods smart in Wisconsin, and in Pennsylvania, the unfit hunters are from New York or New Jersey. Their crimes of naivete involve shooting horses, cows, mules, and other domesticated livestock or, worst of all, does instead of the manly bucks (Poulsen 1974). Brunvand lists "The Deer Departed" in the *Encyclopedia of Urban Legends* as a prime contemporary example of the dumb hunter type (2001, 110; see also Brunvand 1999, 341–42). In this story containing rhetoric of the marvelous single shot, with one bullet a deer hunter has dropped a huge buck sporting a magnificent rack of antlers. He decides to take a picture of himself with his prize, placing his new rifle across the deer's rack. But while the hunter is arranging his camera on a tripod, the deer—merely stunned from a flesh wound—gets up and walks into the woods, carrying the expensive rifle away. Brunvand reads the story literally as the animal's revenge against the hunter, who is often depicted as a weekend hunter or consuming tourist. Not mentioned is the symbolism of the dumb hunter replacing the potent, or phallic, gun that ejects a bullet with the camera that receives an image. Both can be said to shoot, but the aggressive, traditional firearm is replaced by the passive, modern camera. The dumb hunter does not just look stupid; he is, in essence, feminized and associated with modern cosmopolitanism. The legend's effect depends on the image of the buck's rack carrying the gun. The hunter is symbolically castrated, and a slot is created in the story for gun and horny rack as equivalent manly symbols of phallic triumph made possible in the wild.

There is an animal welfare reference in the story because of the frequent rhetoric in animal rights literature that the camera should replace the gun for those people who want to capture nature. The subtext of the rhetoric is that the camera as a modern invention has replaced, following evolutionary thinking, the old, barbaric, destructive gun. The classic example is Carl Ethan Akeley's transformation from Theodore Roosevelt's avid hunting companion to a fervid opponent of sport hunting. Akeley worked for the American Museum of Natural History and gained famed as a taxidermist, but during the 1920s he became convinced that killing animals was not necessary for museum dioramas. He advocated photography as a means of studying as well as appreciating nature and developed improvements in the technology for working in the wild. He helped make the camera less of a huge encumbrance and more of a hand-held tool, raising comparisons to the gun (Haraway 1993, 259–61). Akeley became especially polemical concerning the protection of endangered gorillas in Africa, and his comments on using cameras rather than guns by so-called sportsmen on safari have been quoted frequently in feminist and animal rights literature: "according to any true conception of sport—the use of skill, daring, and endurance in overcoming difficulties—camera hunting takes twice the man that gun hunting takes" (Akeley 1923, 155; see also Haraway 1993, 260). Feminist scholar Donna Haraway comments that this quote is a criticism of patriarchy: "the true father of the game loves nature with the camera; it takes twice the man, and the children are in his perfect image" (1993, 260). The implication is that the camera is reproductive and feminine because it moves the focus of capturing nature from the intrusive phallus of the gun to the recessive eye of the camera. In this view, Haraway argues, "The eye is infinitely more potent than the gun," given that potency is defined as feminine reproduction rather than masculine destruction (1993, 260).

Sport in a masculinist view is the enactment of combat. Critics are skeptical of hunting as sport because they think of sport as enlivening play and competition with other humans rather than animals. Smearing it as blood sport taints hunting as an unsportsmanlike praxis about death rather than about the pleasure of life. Hunters like the label of *sportsman* because they believe that hunting encapsulates the primal essence of sport: action made thrilling because of high-stakes competition—man against nature. It is the ultimate test, in this view, of triumph over adversity. Hunters ask, what is more basic, more vital, than that? No wonder *sportsman* is synonymous with *hunter*, they say. They also refer to the ethical basis of hunting as sport. Sportsmanlike conduct, expressed for hunters in the idea of the "fair chase," is defined by the Boone and Crockett Club (2008) as "the ethical, sportsmanlike, and lawful pursuit and taking of any free-ranging wild, native North American big game animal in a manner that does not give the hunter an improper advantage over such animals." It is the centerpiece of hunters' ethics and is crucial, in the words of the club, to "the hunter's experience of the relationship between predator and prey, which is one of the most fundamental relationships of humans and their environment" (Boone and Crockett 2008). Hunting, governed by a social code yet also a primal instinct for the pursuit of prey in the invigorating outdoors, is in this view simultaneously manly and gentlemanly. One source contrasts this sense of sportsman with the desire to maintain bureaucratic control in characterizing the members of his yacht club: "Some have been true sportsmen—and as I take it, the phrase true sportsmen includes everything that is manly and gentlemanly—others have been rare sticklers for red tape and etiquette" (Kenealy 1894, 400). Whether in racing or hunting, he offers sport as a release from work. The frame of sport is controlled battle, remembered fondly in war stories.

Evidence for the function of hunting as male combat is found in folklorist Robert Bethke's laudable fieldwork among hunters in the Adirondacks of northern New York State (1981). What drew my attention in the narrative performances he recorded was the repetition of a proverbial comparison: "He was as excited as a guy with a deer." This statement is even applied to a character whose masculinity is questioned because, as narrator Ham Ferry declares, "He don't like to hunt deer, but he loves to hunt ducks!" Laughter ensues from the story of a hunter who shoots pellets, rather than the single rifle shot. In the narrator's words, the pellets "didn't even penetrate at all . . . And none of them pellets went into that thing—only the ones that hit 'em in the head. And you could see the pellets hitting them all over out there on the pond. They [the geese] wasn't in the air; they were sittin' on the pond. He shot three times, and they were all hit right in the head, the two he got. And the other ones got up and flew. They were just bouncin' right off, them pellets, bouncin' right off the feathers" (Bethke 1976, 133–35). Ferry's story underscores the superiority of the single penetrating shot. The contribution that Bethke makes is to show that the hunting story in modern performance is not so much a staged piece as a artful extension of the personal-experience narrative often told conversationally. The tall tale associated with the magic and mystery of the wilderness is told as if true and with a realistic setting, but it has an absurd incongruity or exaggeration of the truth. The implication of this performative observation, though, is that the lie is enacted for the function of entertainment, but we are provided no explanation of the content that produces the incongruity.

My thesis is that hunting is a male display whose effectiveness depends on the establishment of combat with another male foe in a natural environment depicted as feminine. The result of the combat in this fictive plane is the joining of the animal to the feminine environment and the fantasy that the man represented by the phallic extension of the gun is the only male left standing. To be sure, this act is not narrated without respect for the animal. The guilt over killing an animal is compensated narratively, I propose, by exaggerating the danger posed by the animal and, frequently, the representation of a lucky or accidental shot doing the killing. The vulnerability of the hunter in this high-context situation is ritually and narratively verified in enactments with sexual overtones: buck fever, in which the hunter fails to shoot in the presence of the deer, and shirttail cutting for the hunter who misses his shot at the buck. In both cases, the hunter is punished for impotence or for being in a feminine position. At Camp Hunter, I took note of narrative compensation in the recounting of dream images. Setting up the fantasy frame of dreaming, hunters could tell of shooting themselves in the foot or being shot in the rear end, and thereby project their anxieties of inadequacy in a position where an aggressive stance is necessary in a life-and-death situation. What has been interpreted or dismissed as the prankish milieu of deer camp can be explained by the belief systems around the sparing and taking of life as a male prerogative.

A context that is often overlooked is the association of hunting with a son's coming-of-age in companionship with the father. As I have pointed out, the killing of the first buck, accompanied by rituals of drinking blood and eating entrails, suggests replacement of the father. Indeed, the son is sometimes referred to as a "young buck" who needs to take the position of the patriarchal hunter rather than being cast in animal terms. The stakes in hunting, then, underscore the achievement of manhood in several ways, and they are higher than in other non-blood sports. One can detect this symbolism in the story of the stunned deer that is similar to the "deer departed." The cue for the story is often a report of someone who has hit a deer while driving home and hauls it into his car. He attempts to claim a rifle kill by affixing a state hunting tag to it, but the deer revives and, in the struggle to get out of the car, delivers penetrating kicks. In the story, the driver typically swings at the deer and hits his hunting dog by mistake, causing the dog to attack him. Closure occurs when the man escapes into a telephone booth or some other enclosure that entraps him (see Brunvand 2001, 203). Instead of a symbolic castration, though, the key detail that has escaped interpretation is the hunter's juvenilization by being entrapped in a womblike enclosure. And the dog, placed in a motifemic slot with the son, has turned on him for being less than a man.

The argument is related to Dundes's contention, anticipated by

psychoanalyst Richard Sterba in 1947, that hunting is especially important—perhaps even the ultimate test of manhood—because it is a
repeatable experience of phallic triumph in a penetration contest. In
contrast to the phallus, which cannot sustain an erection constantly,
the gun is a constant hard extension that is reliably ejective, according
to Dundes. In the context of the woods—considered the appropriate
setting for hunting, but not necessary to it—man against a background
of fertility "confronts," in Dundes's words, "his (own) animality" (1997,
29). Dundes generalizes all blood sports in this perspective, but I have
tried to answer the question of why hunting in particular represents manhood by pointing out the coming-of-age implications of the father-son
relationship in ritual and narrative. One might reexamine a frequently
reported legend about a hunter's prank in this light. Called "Shooting the Bull" by Brunvand (2001, 382), it is about a hunter who asks a
farmer's permission to hunt his fields. The farmer gives his consent on
the condition that the hunter shoot an old bull he had been planning
to eliminate. The hunter goes back to the car, where his two buddies
are waiting, and decides to pull a gag on them. He tells them that the
farmer has refused their request and curses him as an old coot (replaced
by the more vulgar "cunt," "bitch," or "shit" in camp versions I have
collected). They take off, but he tells the driver to stop when they pass
the bull. He gets out and shoots the bull, yelling, "That'll take care
of that rotten old coot," whereupon his two companions each shoot a
cow, commenting, "That'll REALLY take care of that rotten old coot."
Brunvand views it as a celebrity joke, with a macho figure such as Iron
Mike Ditka hunting with athletes or a Texas governor hunting with
legislators.

Brunvand is at a loss to integrate the celebrity theme of "Shooting
the Bull" with the variant of the prankster who, having shot the farmer's animal, wonders what it would feel like to shoot a man. When the
prankster turns his rifle playfully toward his companions, they panic
and shoot at him. Yet seen as a structural system in which the ethics of
male combat have been violated, the prankster loses his humanness in
each case. In the first story, the function of hunting as male display is
undermined by the shooting of the domesticated cows (which, in comparison to combat with the bull, appears rapacious); in the related second narrative, it results in the projective inversion of the man as animal.
Desiring to prove his manhood by shooting the bull and thus feminiz-

ing the animal, along with feminizing the farmer as a "cunt," the hunter is the one to be feminized because he does not engage in a fair chase. Use of the tamer term "coot" may also be symbolic because of the equation of the weak-flying, lobe-footed aquatic bird with nonvirile old age.

In 2005, when folklorists produced a series of radio programs for the Vermont Folklife Center around what they called "deer stories," one could read in the introduction a crack in the normalized facade. It stated, "Hunting is as fundamental to Vermont's cultural heritage as dairy farming, and its lineage reaches back beyond the arrival of the first European settlers. But as Vermont has changed, knowledge of hunting is no longer universal and some Vermonters are entirely outside its culture" (Vermont Folklife Center 2006). Gregory Sharrow, who worked on the series, told me that the folklorists were advised to avoid interpreting the material and even dispatched this disclaimer: "The Deer Stories series does not advocate for hunting but rather explores the experience from an insider's point of view." Obviously, something had markedly changed in the perception of hunting as a cultural resource, at least from the vantage of professional authority; in fact, hunting seemed to be portrayed as an anachronistic activity rather than a tradition because it is nondomesticated. Brunvand epitomizes this view when he states in the *Encyclopedia of Urban Legends*, "Hunting is an anachronism in modern life, and those who engage in the sport seem to be pictured in the folk stories as reverting to an earlier, more primitive way of life or mentality" (2001, 204). For nonhunters, the change was prompted by modernization, resulting in the elimination of the need to hunt to provide food and dress. Others taking a modernist position comment on hunting as a symbol of violence and patriarchy that is unacceptable in a civil society. For hunters, the change was prompted by a fringe element of loony radicals, a "subspecies of human," according to hunting advocate James Swan, otherwise known as "animal rights activists" (1995, 9).

The animal rights movement threatens the tendency of hunters in a high-context environment to normalize hunting as praxis. This is evident, I find, in an emergent tradition of stories in which the foe is the anti-hunting animal rights activist, or "anti." Often the intention is to show the hypocrisy of the antis, or the story exaggerates the threat posed by the anti-hunter. Having recorded rituals and narratives at deer camp for several years, I was used to hearing the personal narratives that often became fabulates, but the closure of "Do you believe it?" increasingly became, "What would those anti-hunters think of that?" An example from Camp Hunter in Mifflin County, Pennsylvania, follows:

> I was at Cooper's Gap when I saw a buck in between the trees. I shot, kabam, and that sucker runs past me with guts hanging out. I said, oh shit, a gut shot. He motors on, got his paunch out, and I let him go an hour. I walk on and I see a pile of guts in a pile. The liver's there and other stuff and I see a hemlock with a branch out. The buck was 25 yards away. The hemlock must have ripped him and dropped his paunch. I looked at him and saw the bullet must have ricocheted off a tree and cut him across the paunch. When he ran he tried to jump over the tree and it got him. He killed himself! What would those anti-hunters think of that, huh?

"That's quite a story," one of the listeners said, and someone else repeated, "Yeah, he killed himself." The key detail conveyed is that the gore of the kill was caused by the deer, not, as animal rights activists would assert, the hunter. Noting the tendency of sportsmen's groups to tout the conservation and wildlife management function of hunting, the hunters were uncomfortable abandoning the master narrative of the appeal of the kill. Then followed a discussion of anti-hunters as a group. They were characterized as pet-owning urban women who have little awareness of animals in the wild. The portrayal of anti-hunters as fearful comes through, for example, in narratives of the famed Hegins pigeon shoot protest (covered in the next chapter), relating the way protesters ran onto the field between the shooters and their targets but scampered and screamed when confronted by dead pigeons.

One common personal experience among hunters that is channeled into a structured and elaborated story deemed worthy of repeating is the deer that would not die, in contrast to the lucky one shot of tall tales. The spark for the telling of such a story is often the anti-hunter belief that deer are gentle; the narrative serves to show the animal's toughness as an adversary who "won't go down." Related one hunter: "I thought that big buck was dead, but he was only stunned, and jumped right to his feet. I grabbed him by the antlers to try to stop him, and when he slung his head around, he throwed me right up onto his back, and away we went through the woods. We must have been going forty miles an hour, maybe forty-five, 'cause he was scared and he was a big one and had not been hurt none to speak of." The raconteur had to be asked how the deer was killed. He replied, "I just hung on with one hand and got my knife out with the other and cut his throat while I was riding him." The story accentuates the battle of males to the death in old-fashioned hand-to-hand combat. The end comes with a signal castratory slit of the throat and the spilling of blood.

The motif of the deer's showing guts, both literally and figuratively, also comes through in a story about deer drives:

> After driving the mountain over an hour, Jack sighted a deer, and drove him down the mountain toward Bill. Bill and the deer came practically face-to-face near a stream. Seeing the deer, Bill fired six shots, tearing a hole in the side of the deer. But the deer kept right on moving, reached the stream, and swam across, with his insides floating around in the water. On the other side of the stream, the deer started up the bank, faltered, and fell. When Jack and Bill reached the other side of the stream, the deer was still alive and trying to climb the bank. Jack fired another three shots before the deer finally died.

The mountain backdrop is important to the story because of the implication that it marks the wild, a zone in which grit and determination run rampant. The hunting story distinguishes this landscape from the domesticated lowlands of streets and suburbs.

The woods test one's survival skills—both human and animal—and can appear to elevate one's powers. Another personal-experience narrative I collected has the legendary qualities of giving reverence to a remarkable animal in the heat of battle:

> Here's one that animal rights idiots aren't going to like, but it goes to show what life in the woods is about that they don't understand. Two men were out hunting deer, and one of the men went up on the mountain to drive the deer down, while the other, the "watch" stayed at the foot of the mountain and waited for the deer to be driven down to him. Finally he saw a deer streaking down the mountain and headed toward him. As the deer passed the hunter, he emptied his gun at the deer. The

deer fell, and the hunter walked over to him, and believing him to be dead, gave him a boot, saying, "There you son of a bitch, let's see you run some more now!" Suddenly the deer got to his feet and started to stagger away. The hunter was so stunned that he just stood there and watched the deer, but luckily, by this time the driver had come down the mountain and arrived just in time to see the deer staggering away. He raised his gun and fired, also emptying his gun. The deer fell down—dead. They checked that sucker out, trying to figure how it could get up. They found nineteen bullets in the buck. They had fired only twelve shots between them, and even if every shot had found its mark, there were still seven [extra] bullets. The buck had been carrying these bullets around for a long time.

The storyteller's cueing device of "Here's one the animal rights idiots aren't going to like" refers to prolonging the death of the animal. The teller conveys that he wanted to take the deer out with one shot but could not. The adversary was too tough. Reminding listeners of human vulnerability in the wild, the teller narrates the buck as possessing superphysical powers. Life in the woods, he implies, is a separate world with different rules. The men to whom he talks nod, agreeing that they are not the brutish beasts animal rights activists portray.

Hunters also have stories that cast animal rights activists as the oppressors, taking away the liberty that hunting represents. Reminiscent of the dumb hunter story, hunters relate stories of anti-hunters trying to disrupt a deer drive with the use of bullhorns or grabbing a horse, mistaking it for a deer. To counter the view that animal rights have become mainstreamed, the anti-hunter is characterized as an obsessive, antisocial fanatic; in narrative, she (for the anti-hunter is regularly depicted as female) is presented as demonic. The present in this constituted world is a time when family and community values associated with rural life have become disrupted, and the good old days of the past are the times when hunting pervaded society. Frustrated at not being able to fight back as they can in the wilderness, with gun and scope, hunters gathered around the fire at camp narrate their social and moral superiority over animal rights activists. There is a symbolic transference in the narratives from animal species as endangered and therefore in need of protection to the hunter as a marginalized figure in a redemptive community. The expansive tall tale of the "wonderful hunt," of lore representing the bounty of the land and the perpetuity of human dominion in hunting, has turned into the wish-fulfillment personal narrative of the subordinated tradition. Whereas animal rights activists portray gun-toting hunters gloating in their tall tales about their despotic, destructive power, deer camp storytellers function to convey, and compensate for, human inadequacy in the face of regnant nature and the company of male peers.

The Ritualization of Deer Hunting, the Socialization of Deer Camp

Several feminist animal rights critiques explain the bloody and meat-consuming rituals of triumph over animals, and the consequent bonding among men, as a sign of the violation of women. Often they view, and condemn, the continued popularity of hunting—and meat eating, for that matter—despite hunting's loss of practical function, as a reaffirmation of patriarchy in society. For Carol Adams (2003), Brian Luke (1998, 2007), and Charles Bergman (1996), for instance, deer hunting as a process is related to reading pornography or even predatory stalking and rape. Luke's explanation is that hunting persists because it is doubly sexual: "it is a source of erotic enjoyment as well as an expression of masculine gender identity" (1998, 635). Adams comments on an advertisement appealing to deer hunters to "check out our buck naked girls": "The sexual conquest of the object, identifying and stalking the prey, the thrill of capture, degrading, ejaculating in, or killing the victim—with this narrative, one could be reading pornography, the testimony of a victim of sexual assault, a hunting story—or all three" (2003, 90). Ehrenreich makes much of bleeding as a characteristic of reproductive turning points in women's lives, suggesting that blood smearing is a rite of passage to men, but she does not follow this observation along the lines of my argument that hunting marks the defloration of a virgin or an imitation of menstruation (Ehrenreich 1997, 104–9). More commonly, bloodletting, usually reserved for males, is seen as a symbol of domination because of the perceived masculine predation and penetration in the act (Bergman 1996, 278–80; Luke 1998, 652).

The trouble with the interpretation of hunting as predation against women is that it loses sight of hunting large game as ritual combat between *males*. To be sure, an affirmation of manliness occurs ritually in hunting, and as Dundes has pointed out, men tend to feel compelled to prove their masculinity repeatedly, presumably because of insecurities caused by the temporariness of the male erection. "Women," he writes, "do not feel nearly so obliged to prove their femininity" (1987b, 166). The social environment of deer camps discourages women from participating; reinforcing the exclusion of women is the folk belief that seeing a woman on a hunt is bad luck (Hand, Casetta, and Thiederman 1981, 2:1019). The structure of ritual male combat applies to hunting bucks as a competition. To add to the manly warrior image of the buck, hunters relate stories about the dangerousness of the animals. They may point to the aggressive behavior witnessed during "rutting" or "bucking" season, a period of sexual excitement that occurs in the fall, when it is common to see "sidle displays" between bucks of nearly equal position in the hierarchy, their heads in the high threat posture (Wegner 1987, 167). "During this period the old stags are very ugly to each other," folklorist Henry Shoemaker notes, and "when two of them get into a fight it is a fight to a finish" (1992, 68). This narrative suggests that man is part of that hierarchy, "locking horns" with the buck. Shoemaker incredulously relates the belief that "deer are said to attack men during the rutting season"; even if this is not true, the belief reinforces the idea of hunting as combat against a dangerous, hypermasculine opponent (Shoemaker 1992). In this regard, Shoemaker also records beliefs through the twentieth century related to bucks' horns being made doubly phallic and dangerous by the poison of snakes: "In Pennsylvania the points of deer horns and their hoofs were supposed to be poisoned, as the deer killed with them so many venomous snakes" (Shoemaker 1992, 41). The symbolism of the buck's sexual potency is indicated by the use of its antlers as a male aphrodisiac. An advertisement for "Red Bullet," composed of deer antler velvet, claims that it "turns every man into a sexual dynamo" by raising testosterone by 500 percent, increasing penis size up to three inches, and maintaining harder, stronger erections for hours.[9]

In cartoons, the buck is phallically threatening when he mounts the hunter from behind and says, "Here's your deer meat, mother fucker" or "That's what you get for shooting all the damn does" (Dundes and Pagter 2000, 266–67). The image of homoerotic attack suggests that the buck is doing to the hunter what the hunter is metaphorically doing to the buck in real life. In another widely circulated photocopy titled "Basic Rules for Deer Hunting," one of the rules states: "If you forget your rifle and meet a Deer, hide in the bushes" (Dundes and Pagter 2000, 264). Without the phallic gun providing power, the cartoon implies, the hunter is helpless. One folk cartoon that emphasizes the possibility of the buck's triumph shows a buck in hunter's garb grabbing the penis of a man hanging by his feet from a tree limb. The usual caption reads, "This one's barely legal" (Dundes and Pagter 2000, 268–71). The reference is to the size restriction on bucks killed—generally a minimum number of points on a buck's antlers (three on each side in Pennsylvania in 2003). The implication of the folk humor is that the size and potency of the man's phallic power are diminutive compared with the buck's. The buck and the human charge at each other, in this image, with phallic power. From the hunter's viewpoint, which differs from the anti-hunter's, the man derives a sense of satisfaction from vanquishing a stronger, more dangerous foe.

A way to view blooding in buck hunting is to draw comparisons to the cockfight as ritual male combat in which the good fight to the finish is marked by vivid displays of blood by both parties. In this homoerotic phallic duel, the winner emasculates the loser through castration or feminization (Dundes 1994). In both these "sporting" events pitting symbolic cocks against each other, women are excluded or discouraged from attending, and the fighting spirit of the participants is intensified by a heightened sex drive. Indeed, the rooster may be referred to as a "stag," suggesting a correlation between the antlered stag and spurred cocks. The theme of the sport is arguably an all-male preserve in which one male demonstrates his virility, his masculinity, at the expense of a male opponent (Dundes 1994, 250; 1997).

Is there a further connection to Dundes's idea that male ritual combat begins with two *men* but ends, symbolically, with one victorious *man* and a vanquished, indeed consumed, *woman* (Dundes 1994, 250–51)? The belief in oral tradition is that the buck cries, that is, exhibits feminine behavior, only when it is killed (Cartmill 1993, 76–91). Arguably, however, the symbolic castration in the traditions of hunting camp is more emasculation than feminization. For example, hunters report the folk imperative to bleed the animal by slitting his throat, removing his tarsal ("male musk") glands and genitals, and later mounting his antlered head not as sexual transformation but as sexual (or masturbatory) defeat. In hunters' photo albums, it is not uncommon to see them assuming a comical pose with the buck's head held between their legs simulating an exaggerated phallus, as a sign of either virility gained from the kill or transference of potency from the buck. More than the cockfight, the deer hunt adds the element of pursuit and suggests that the victory is significant for demonstrating virility because the aggressive, dangerous buck may also be pursuing the hunter as a competing male. In a widely copied postcard, a buck is shown up against a drowsy hunter with the caption, "Who's Hunting Who?" In the setting of the woods, the boundaries between animals and humans become less distinct.

The metaphoric refocusing of the deer hunt as deep play relates a coming-of-age narrative marking another transformation in society for the dominant male: from a mother-raised boy to a male-bonded man (see Mechling 2005). In addition to being separated from the mother and bonded to a group of male peers as his extended family, the man realizes that he must get out of the shadow of his father. Many of the rituals, after all, surround the new or young hunter and emphasize an experience-based hierarchy with intergenerational familial overtones. If it was only a coming-of-age scenario, the rituals would not be re-peated at other times, but because of the male ego's need for reaffirma-tion, reenactments are necessary. Instead of coming-of-age, the hunter at deer camp may find himself in an asserting-of-age competition with vigorous younger members. He may feel that his potency is challenged. Around forty, the average age of hunters, he may question his mortal-ity, pursue wild, invigorating primal experiences, and seek social sup-port (Brandes 1985). The narrative of escape is toward the wild, where males' supposedly savage or primal instincts are normative, and away from the domesticated home of the hunter's wife or feminized modern society (Douglas 1977; Ames 1992).

Dundes (1997) questions the function of violence and war rooted in male folk sports and games but leaves open for debate whether the purpose of those practices is to control aggression or to encourage it. Implied is a philosophical discourse over whether male aggression, the "fighting spirit," is acquired or instinctive. Most hunters regard their activity as playing out a primal human instinct; they see it as a recre-ative release, a tradition worth maintaining for its social and ecological good. Anti-hunters, in contrast, view tradition as an obstacle, as anach-ronistic and counter to the societal goals of peace and equality (Dizard

1999, 2003). Shooting at targets, if demonstration of sporting skill was the main issue, or resorting to photography to appreciate nature would not resolve the debate, since hunters value the regenerative power of taking animal life in the wild, establishing humans as monarchs by deposing the king of the wild. And anti-hunters might still object to the phallocentric use of guns and the implied social hierarchy and dominance. What is at issue is the perceptual basis of systems (i.e., of traditions as part of larger, integrated webs of boundaries, domains, and routines) governing human behavior (Mechling 1989). In other words, hunters view the restriction of deer camp tradition as a violation of an entire cultural system involving human dominion over the land and its creatures. A struggle exists in modernity for moral control of cultural systems, and the battle over hunting, with its symbols of human-animal-environment-society relations, is a striking manifestation of a larger culture war that often pits tradition and local-centered worldviews against universalist, or cosmopolitan, calls for change (see Bronner 1998).

One way that this cultural confrontation is played out is in a debate on the entitlement to rights in a democratic society. Anti-hunters declare animal rights as a way to achieve a civil, egalitarian society, while pro-hunters see an imposition on individual liberties. Sportsmen's reaction to anti-hunters in Pennsylvania is a campaign for legislation declaring hunting a basic human right. On February 16, 2004, Bill 1512, calling for an amendment to the Pennsylvania Constitution "to provide for the right to hunt and fish," was passed by the state's house of representatives. The Fund for Animals countered with a letter-writing campaign pointing out that "any constitution typically addresses fundamental *rights* necessary to life and liberty"; therefore, "adding a recreational *privilege* is contrary to the purpose of the constitution." The bill was not enacted into law, but proponents vowed to redouble their efforts to declare hunting a constitutional right in answer to the claims of animal protection organizations. This skirmish raises the issue of whether hunting is a right based on its status as a basic human instinct or "natural law," or whether it is a recreational privilege, a matter of choice or tradition that can be altered or banned if, as animal rights groups point out, it is no longer necessary or desirable.

Other states have enacted legislation under the rubric of hunting heritage. Effective January 1, 2005, Illinois' Hunting Heritage Protection Act calls for the state to promote hunting on lands managed by its

Department of Natural Resources. The governor's message touted the hunter as an agent for environmental conservation with roots in the country's founding principles: "This new law recognizes the important role hunters and trappers play in conserving wildlife, habitats and the ecosystems on which wildlife depend, while at the same time enjoying a form of outdoor recreation that has been part of our state's heritage from its founding. Recreational hunting is perhaps the most important component of effective wildlife management, and this legislation helps remind us of the importance of our hunting heritage" (Blagojevich 2004). In Maryland, home to the anti-hunting Fund for Animals, the Hunting Heritage Protection Act became law in 2005, guaranteeing that when state land is made unavailable for hunting other properties will be substituted. The declarations of the original bill emphasized hunting as a conservation strategy and "an important and traditional activity." In 2007, Missouri added its name to the list of states passing laws using the rhetoric of "hunting heritage protection." In Governor Matt Blunt's comments upon signing Senate Bill 225 into law, he underscored a connection to America's pioneer past and the perpetuation of traditions. He stated, "As Lewis and Clark made their way up the Missouri River they encountered some of the richest land in North America. They recognized immediately that this land was perfect for hunting and offered tremendous potential for agriculture. This legislation helps protect the very lands on which they hunted, ensuring that today and for generations to come Missourians will be able to continue the traditions that have been passed from generation to generation" (Blunt 2007). The heritage being protected thus carries a double meaning of ecology and culture, with the implication that both are traditions at risk. Whether from the effects of animal rights activism, mass culture, or land development, the danger to hunting is not specified in the texts of the bills, but the state interest is clearly to protect hunters as an identity and hunting as an activity.

The "no net loss" provision of several state laws is a key feature of federal bills introduced annually since 2000. In addition to protests from animal rights groups, the Hunting Heritage Protection Act (HR 4790) introduced in 2000 drew opposition from the executive branch's Bureau of Land Management (2000) as unnecessary and costly. Animal rights groups view such legislation as attempts to institutionalize the "right to hunt" with ecological and cultural justifications that they find objectionable. The Fund for Animals' position is that "besides being a piteously unfair and cruel slaughter of innocent animals, sport hunting is also ecologically destructive" (Hennessey 2004). Animal rights groups pose the biting question, "If hunting is in decline because it is unnecessary, unpopular, and harmful, why should the state protect it?" One answer, judging from the rhetoric of hunting heritage advocates, is that hunting is symbolic of traditional values at the heart of American culture, or a communitarian version of it. In Maine, for example, a referendum to limit bear hunting drew the ire of one sportsmen's advocate, who warned that if it passed a domino effect would occur, "encouraging future anti-hunting initiatives aimed at ending the hunting heritage symbolic of this state" (Hennessey 2004).

The appeal of hunting as heritage is that it signifies continuity from generation to generation, a characteristic of family tradition that is viewed as threatened in an individualistic postmodern society. When Georgia Republican Saxby Chambliss introduced a Senate version of the Hunting Heritage Protection Act in 2007, he opened his speech by saying, "I cannot stress how important this piece of legislation is to ensure that our Nation's rich hunting heritage is passed on to future generations." His motivation in sponsoring the bill, he avowed, was that "the best times" of his life had been spent hunting with his son or with friends. He expanded on the connection between hunting and children's coming-of-age: "It is hard to put a price tag on seeing the joy and excitement in a child's eyes during their first hunting experience. I believe that recreational hunting should be an activity that everyone has the opportunity to experience." He closed with an appeal to the value of tradition as "vital," or, in other words, as being about regenerative life: "It is vitally important that we, as Members of the Senate, do all we can to protect and preserve the tradition of hunting so that future generations will be able to experience this great outdoor recreational activity." If that rhetoric did not stir his fellow legislators, he reminded them that hunting deserved their patriotic support because it was part and parcel of "our Nation's rich heritage of hunting" (Chambliss 2007). For the opposition, the tradition of hunting nurtures killing and violence as "recreation" that is not only unethical but also dangerous in modern-day life, given an expanding human population, increased firepower, and efficient technology. As animal liberation philosopher Lisa Kemmerer declared, hunting constitutes "killing that lacks almost every vestige of tradition because it is now unnecessary for survival" (2004a, 14). For animal rights groups, animals need preservation, not hunting.

Realizing that many millions of Americans are not engaged in either hunting or animal rights advocacy, the two sides mounted campaigns to provide the public with images of their work. Whereas the hunting heritage lobby portrayed hunters as wildlife managers who care deeply about the environment and animals, as well as the role of hunting in promoting "traditional" American values, anti-hunters strove to depict hunters as destroyers of the wild and abusers of life. The discourse showed that hunting was indeed a broad cognitive category or praxis for most Americans, and the two sides sought to redefine it in modern terms, with a special concern for an egalitarian ethic that curbed violence. While hunting heritage advocates proclaimed deer camps as places to engage in wholesome outdoor recreation, healthy wildlife management, and culturally sensitive intergenerational bonding, animal rights groups showed films of pigeon shoots likened to bird "holocausts" and baited bears brutalized by anything but an ethic of fair chase. Heidi Prescott, national director of the Fund for Animals, offered a frank observation of the situation in a speech at the fourth annual Governor's Symposium on North America's Hunting Heritage:

> What do people who may not have strong feelings about hunting either way think when they see a man or woman in camouflage sitting in a tree over a pile of rotten food waiting for a bear to come along? What do they think when they watch someone track an animal with dogs outfitted with radio-collar devices? What do they think of outdoor ethics when a story runs in their local newspaper about someone paying thousands of dollars to kill a tame lion or sheep on a fenced-in ranch? And what do they think when birds are released one a time from a box and shot from twenty yards away? Do you think that the average person who looks at this practice thinks that hunting is a spiritual outdoor experience, and that hunters respect the wild and are the great wildlife managers and conservationists they claim to be? I can tell you what they think, because they call the Fund for Animals' office to express their horror, their sorrow and ask what they can do to help. (Prescott 1995)

Prescott claimed that the picture of hunters shooting at animals benefits anti-hunters "much more so" than defense of the practice on the basis of conservation helps to save hunting. "Remember," she advised the gathering of hunters, "when people see a person shooting at an animal, that is hunting to them, and all hunting is lumped into the same category. If they watch a bird shot and crippled at the Hegins pigeon shoot—that is hunting. If they watch a tame lion under a tree being shot at a canned hunt—that is hunting" (Prescott 1995).

I have more to say about the symbolism of the pigeon shoot in the next chapter; here, it is important to note the basic philosophical difference between what is instinctual in humanity—the drive to hunt or to care for animals—and how those portrayals tend to be gendered, with hunters viewed as brutishly masculine and animal rights advocates as sensitively feminine. Understanding that their ethical positions could not be easily reconciled, the groups used hunting as symbol and practice to address larger issues involved in determining America's cultural future. Whereas hunting heritage bespoke the protection of so-called traditional values associated with the protection of family, land, and nation, animal rights implied the creation of a civil egalitarian society.

In light of the anti-hunting campaigns by animal rights groups, hunting heritage advocates implied that it was more than hunting grounds they sought to maintain; they urged protection from animal rights activists, sometimes pejoratively labeled "eco-terrorists" in legislation such as the Animal Enterprise Terrorism Act (2006). Under the terms of this act, what animal rights advocates viewed as lawful protest, whistle-blowing, and boycott in the spirit of a civil rights campaign in defense of animals could be criminalized as harassment or intimidation. Hunters were outraged at some of the anti-hunting field tactics—scaring game with screeching over bullhorns, admonishing orange-clad sportsmen, and videotaping animals being dragged in the woods. They claimed that it disrupted the ritual setting—the sacred, natural silence of the woods that shut out the modern world, urged commune among one's fellows, and allowed concentration on the human-animal struggle. The rhetoric of "terrorism" applied to animal rights rather than the label "activism" suggested that animal rights subvert society rather than work to improve it, particularly in a post-9/11 age, when terrorism is associated with dastardly attacks on

America. Whereas animal rights groups bemoan hunting as a killing tradition, hunting heritage proponents denigrate activists for seeking to kill American tradition.

Back at camp, outside the court of public opinion, why are traditions and rituals significant in explaining why men hunt? My answer is because they embody relations among men, with the environment, and through time that set their place in a cultural system. The traditional experience of hunting dramatizes dominion, hierarchy, and patriarchy for men working in community. The fact is, though, that hunting is changing, and traditions of deer camp are changing along with it. More women are encouraged to participate, and the lands available for hunting are dwindling (Hiss 2007; Hurst 2007). It is more expensive, and for many hunters, it is not the primitive experience in the wild that it once was.[10] It is certainly under more scrutiny by citizens' organizations as well as governmental agencies. Challenging the family apprenticeship model of generational learning, the training for and conduct of hunting are more regulated, legislated, and scientific. It is more difficult, men say, to get away from their jobs for stretches of time. The continuities between generations— "the heart of the matter," to quote the men at Camp Hunter—appear to be disrupted. Why, then, are rituals and traditions *more* important now? Perhaps because the cultural system is threatened, and the rituals reaffirm the generational link. It may also be that the modern cultural critique of masculinity as overly patriarchal and aggressive has led to an uncertainty that has fostered the desire to reserve certain domains for the playful dramatization of manliness (Mechling 2001; Sommers 2000; Pollack 1998; Raphael 1988).

Rather than scoffing at, or repressing, affirmations of manhood, there is a renewed compulsion to express it. Whether hunting is the best way to do so is a contentious issue. Arguably, hunting is the main symbol of manliness and tradition in America, and for many proponents, it provides a needed outlet from what they perceive to be the enervating, feminizing effect of modern mass culture. Country music star Brad Paisley tapped into this sentiment with his chart-topping hit of 2008, "I'm Still a Guy." The song opens with the line, "When you see a deer you see Bambi, and I see antlers up on the wall." On the surface, "you" refers to women, but it also symbolizes feminized urban mass culture, evident in the closing verses:

These days there's dudes getting facials
Manicured, waxed and botoxed
With deep spray-on tans and creamy lotiony hands
You can't grip a tackle box

With all of these men lining up to get neutered
And headin' out to be feminized
I don't highlight my hair
I've still got a pair
Yeah honey, I'm still a guy.

Oh my eyebrows ain't plucked
There's a gun in my truck
Oh thank God, I'm still a guy.

This message of resistance echoed in narrative and song forms a division between country and city and can be equated with other binaries of male and female, tough and soft, hunting and anti-hunting. It longs for the pioneer, preindustrial spirit of America when the countryside reigned, and it asks whether there is still a place for old-time values. Many animal rights activists answer negatively when these values depend on hunting as ritual and praxis.

For the men of Camp Hunter, hunting's representation of heritage or tradition and its ritualization of the social make it worthy. Sitting around the dinner table for a traditional Thanksgiving meal with the family, staring at a symbol of wild game associated with bountiful Americanness, the men may realize that the traditions and the continuities between the generations need reconfiguration when the question comes up, "Are you going to deer camp?"

CHAPTER 2

The Pigeon Shoot Controversy

At the end of the twentieth century, pigeon shoots, often described in media coverage as "folk tradition," made front-page news. Every Labor Day from 1987 to 1997, animal rights activists protested the community-sponsored shooting contest in the rural Pennsylvania German hamlet of Hegins.[1] Stories about the protests were carried on national wire services, in mass-market magazines, on radio talk shows and television news programs, and even in the tabloid press. The campaign against Hegins was intended to protest live animal shoots nationally, but organizations targeted the Hegins event because it was a large public festival, and the pigeon shoot symbolized the excesses of animal abuse in traditional activities. Pennsylvania drew special attention because the state is recognized as the national center of the tradition, with shoots at private "rod and gun clubs" nearly every spring and fall weekend. Also of concern to animal rights organizations, Pennsylvania is a major hunting state, often leading the nation in the number of hunting licenses issued. Heads of the major national animal rights organizations—People for the Ethical Treatment of Animals (PETA), the Fund for Animals, and Trans-Species Unlimited—believed that media attention to this horrific event would lead to public pressure to ban the shoots and turn public opinion against hunting. Implicit in their strategy as a social movement calling for fundamental change was to erode what they viewed as America's irrational attachment to "tradition."

Yet targeting central Pennsylvania was a risky move, for it repre-

A shooter waits for the official to pull the strings, releasing the pigeons from the traps, at the Hegins pigeon shoot, Labor Day, 1990. (Photo courtesy of Historical Society of Dauphin County, Harrisburg, Pennsylvania)

sented one of the animal rights movement's first forays against folk practices of the rural American heartland. Chronicles of the animal rights movement frequently trace its roots to a 1980 conference in New York that brought together activists for vegetarianism and animal rights. Out of this event emerged an annual Action for Life conference that focused on protests of animal experimentation, animal entertainment, and factory farming.[2] Subsequently, the movement enjoyed success exposing animal abuse in medical and commercial research, appealing to the anti-corporate and anti-institutional sentiments of many Americans (Finsen and Finsen 1994, 108–52; Guither 1998, 73–112). The common pigeon at the Hegins shoot was hardly a cuddly, pet-like animal such as those depicted in campaigns against the wearing of fur and medical experimentation. The movement's leaders realized they would have to transform the bird's image from dirty urban pest to tender dove of peace. Once they were committed to a mass protest and civil disobedience in 1989, they expected a short, successful media blitz to exert pressure to end the tradition (Dillard 1997, 2002). Although they anticipated initial resistance by local residents, they did

Protest march on Hegins led by Trans-Species Unlimited, Labor Day, 1989. State-
ments on the signs include "Stop the Slaughter," "Murder Most Foul," "Shame on
Hegins," "Teach Your Children the Value of Life, Stop the Pigeon Shoot," "Pennsylvania, the Blood State," and "Real Men Shoot Clay Pigeons, Not Real Ones!" (Photo
courtesy of Historical Society of Dauphin County, Harrisburg, Pennsylvania)

not predict the staunch national defense of Hegins's cause, resulting in
a protracted struggle to shut the shoot down.

My purpose in this chapter is to explain the high stakes in the contested tradition by analyzing how the protest rhetorically served to
present tradition as a "problem" in the ethical modernization of society.
The battle in Hegins became a staged moral drama based on a clash of
rural and cosmopolitan values in modern America that derives from
fundamentally different views of human dominion over the land and
its creatures. In the historical context of a post–civil rights concern for
protecting victims and achieving a nonviolent society, the symbolism
of shooting birds as play and sport became especially important in the
reformation of the American concept of human-animal relations in an
urbanized modern society (see Swan 1995; Scully 2002; Phelps 2002;
Kheel 2003). The campaign against Hegins is significant in terms of
cultural interpretation because it underscores broad ethical questions

about the character of tradition, the use of the past and the rhetoric of heritage and identity, and the social conflicts in American culture. From an interpretive viewpoint, it forces reflection on how symbols such as pigeons, guns, and shooters are portrayed and perceived. Compromise became impossible in the controversies over pigeon shoots, I find, because the sides perceived symbols so differently.

Tradition, Contest, and Play

The pigeon shoot draws attention to itself because it is a spectator *contest*, offering prizes and bestowing honor for skills that are considered valuable in the cultural setting of Hegins but are considered reprehensible in cosmopolitan contexts, where animals become a metaphor for innocent victims in need of protection. As a contest, it is a central text in this community, a "deep play" or "paradigmatic human event," to use anthropologist Clifford Geertz's terminology. As "deep play," it is more than a ritualized game; it is a "metaphorical refocusing" that clarifies the meaning of assorted experiences of everyday life (Geertz 1973, 450). Geertz's study is important as background for my study because animal rights activists frequently put pigeon shoots in the same category as the outlawed, "brutal" traditions of cockfights and dogfights. It is not coincidental that in Geertz's study of the cockfight, one of the most cited methodological guides to the interpretation of culture, the significant metaphors are about animals and violence. After all, the processes that represent everyday life and social structure involve men ritualizing their dominion over nature, and these metaphors of gender and landscape evince control of the social and physical environment. The assumption is that a symbolic projection occurs by which the attitudes of humans toward animals translate into people's relations with one another; for some animal rights activists, a further step is the notion of animals as "fellow creatures," obliterating the distinction between human beings and animals (see Cavalieri 2003; Diamond 2004; Mechling 1989; Rachels 1990; Singer 1990; Wolgemuth 2000). If that step is taken, animals have rights and are capable of feeling pain, desire, and understanding. In this thinking, humans as a dominating species need to avoid "speciesism," which carries the injurious ring of "racism" and "sexism"; it holds that the respectful treatment of animals will result in a civil, egalitarian society

(Adams and Donovan 1995; Dunayer 2004; Epstein 2004; Jasper and Nelkin 1992; Midgley 1983; Rollin 1981; Ryder 1989; Singer 1990; Regan 2001; Wolfe 2003).

The animal rights movement literature consistently adds the connotation that animals are childlike or feminized victims in need of protection and advocacy (see Adams 2000; Arluke and Sanders 1996; Brady 1994, 140–41; Donovan 2003; Fudge 2002, 70–78; Wise 2000). The Fund for Animal's motto, for example, is "We Speak for Those Who Can't." PETA's Web site declares, "Animals deserve basic rights—consideration of their best interests regardless of whether they are useful to humans. Like you, they are capable of suffering and have interests in leading their own lives; therefore they are not ours to use" (PETA 2005). Philosopher Tom Regan's "The Case for Animal Rights" greatly influenced this view by describing animals as "moral patients" and giving the examples of human infants, young children, and enfeebled humans as "paradigm cases of human moral patients" (2004, 17). Moral patients are not accountable for what they do, whereas moral agents, such as adult humans, are accountable because they bring moral principles to bear on their actions. Animals deserve respect and protection not just because they are alive but also because they are the "subject-of-a life," that is, they have beliefs and desires, perception, memory, and interests. They feel pleasure and pain, and they possess an "individual welfare" in the sense that their experiential life bodes well or ill for them (Regan 2004, 20). This state separates animals from blades of grass, potatoes, or cancer cells, which can also be said to be alive. This state also gives them an "inherent value" shared by moral agents and moral patients because they are unique and irreplaceable. Regan thus argues that humans and animals, having inherent value, possess the fundamental right to be treated with respect and receive justice, but he realizes that many traditional moral systems are obstacles to these goals, especially the "conditional" view that humans are morally justified in controlling and killing animals if they are harmful, dangerous, or diseased or if doing so provides some benefit to humans, such as food or subjects for experimentation. Regan observes that moral agents can do what is right or wrong in ways that affect or involve moral patients, and animal rights activists take that as a pronouncement to work to change unjust moral systems (2004, 18).

Change is not possible, activists often explain, until "tradition" as a positive social value is altered; as Mary Midgley states in *Animals and Why They Matter* (1983, 144), the animal rights goal is "removing barriers which our tradition has erected against concern for animals." From this vantage, tradition is a static instrument of human dominion that people mindlessly follow without regard to the harmful consequences to animals. Although most folklorists would argue for a more dynamic definition of tradition, animal rights philosophers and folklorists share at least one perspective: traditions that are often dismissed as play are crucial to challenge, because they are avenues for change in belief and moral systems (see Ben-Amos 1984; Bronner 1998). Other philosophers argue that inherent value derives from the capacity to make moral judgments and have a consciousness of duty (Cohen 2003; Rickaby 1976; Ritchie 1976). In that sense, humans have rights that animals do not; humans can be stewards for animals, and in most cases humans imagine themselves in a higher order over the lower order of animals. Presenting a symbolic contrast between the respected human and the disrespected rat, for example, Carl Cohen states, "Although both may have value as lives, only humans have inherent value in the sense from which rights may be inferred" (2003, 28).

A more positive view of tradition is implied by the assignment of inherent value solely to humans. Since value is inherited, some cultural transmission from one generation to another is assumed to distinguish the experience of being human. Tradition expressing the development of community bonds and continuity across generations rhetorically refers to a higher cultural order. It gains prestige by giving identity not just to humanity but also to the differentiation of group or community based on place. Tradition—and therefore folklore—has an intrinsic value by representing the social basis or cultural root of identity. Folklorist Jay Mechling tests the boundaries implied in an anthropocentric view of tradition in a study of play traditions that humans form with their pets (Mechling 1989). One view of the common tradition of "fetch" with dogs is that pet owners anthropomorphize their animal companions; they attribute intentional consciousness—that is, human qualities—to the animals (Mechling 1989, 315; see also Grier 2006, 58–181). Characteristic of folklore as a human tradition, humans intentionally create a repetitive communal, informal, and aesthetic connection with animals as if they were human. When considered as an interactive routine forming a cultural system between human and nonhuman animals rather than an extension of the autonomous human self onto animals, however, tradition can be about relationships that are not necessarily human.[3] Although Mechling's study challenges scholarly convention, it also underscores the entrenchment of the popular view that tradition and folklore rhetorically emphasize human dominion and priority, as well as the importance of historical and cultural precedent in establishing an identity for a human community.

In Geertz's analysis, play and tradition are human creations that reveal social structure and therefore human needs and desires. Leaders of animal rights organizations would extend Geertz's conclusion that deep play with animals, such as the cockfight, uncovers a situated social structure by exposing patriarchal dominance and exploitation and the encouragement of or desire for the physical abuse and victimization of people. Their detractors often argue that play with animals is more benign—a fantasy that distorts, indeed inverts, reality for the purpose of emotional or spiritual release.

A critical, if rarely asked, question after reading Geertz's study is why the cockfight, and not some other folk expression, represents the social structure. One can hypothesize that such human-organized contests affirm the core values of a society through ritual combat with animals and therefore provide centrally significant symbols. I test this idea of significance by uncovering the reasons some symbols in an event such as the pigeon shoot were pressed into service in a highly publicized cultural clash—reasons that were often outside the awareness of participants. This query forces a revision of the interpretation of deep play from a close reading of a cultural text for its reflection of social structure to an explanation of the process of symbolization. Guiding this revision is Alan Dundes's folkloristic call to understand the unconscious symbolic dimensions of human behavior (1994, 275). Dundes cogently criticizes Geertz's idea of deep play as "shallow play" because it reduces traditional events to reflections of social structure rather than explaining why these events need to be symbolized in the first place. Dundes's perspective views the feminization of opponents in male ritual combat as a folk root, he argues elsewhere, of the social predilection for war (1997).

I elaborate his symbolist approach by suggesting a semiotic layering and a representational significance placed on historical precedent, especially in contested traditions in which conflict arises over the symbolic meanings perceived in, and communicated through, intensified folk events (see Ardener 1980; Foster 1980; Cohen 1980). The idea of layering suggests that a cluster of meanings, such as the pigeon as pest and the pigeon as reference to pioneer life, can exist together, and indeed work together, to offer significance to the shoot as ritual play representing community values. To interpret this layering ethnographically is to consider for whom symbols carry meaning in an event, as well as to consider their historical sources.

If the frame of the *contest* provides a source for the intensified attention the tradition draws to itself for a community, it follows that *contesting* the pigeon shoot in the form of disruptive protests draws attention to the relation of such events to the values and morals of a dominant mass or alternative society. The focus often shifts in the staging of the event from the action in the separate ring, field, or pit to the open confrontation between sides, often referred to by participants in the rhetoric of combat as the "tussle." When the tradition becomes contested, the resulting drama off the main stage forces tradition-bearers to justify their behavior; the clash often results in intense arguments about the function of a tradition for a community and a society. The national director of the Fund for Animals explained to me, for example, her reason for suspending protests of the shoot in 1997: "the focus was on our battle with Hegins rather than on the plight of the birds." In an appeal to pragmatism, arguments against the tradition entail the practice's instrumental function in the current day and the consequences it engenders. The burden is to rationalize the tradition, because animal rights protesters sound the progressive chord that since shooting events and hunting are no longer necessary for food provision or environmental control, their only purpose is to support killing as fun. For the protesters, the point is that the overwhelming message is one of promoting violence and brutality; for supporters of the shoot, it is that it fosters a necessary sense of cultural identity and community by building on the legacy of the past.

Contestation adds pressure to resolve conflicts between groups by changing traditions. Why would Hegins *not* substitute clay targets for live pigeons, for instance, if that allowed the event to keep going? In the contest, we may learn what the tradition is; in its contestation, we learn what it is not. Contestation frequently results in an illumination, and indeed a polarization, of symbols—pigeons as sacred doves of peace versus pigeons as profane rats of evil—even if the targets previously had some symbolic ambiguity. Protesting events such as cockfights and pigeon shoots is a challenge not just to the activities of the tradition but also to the very idea of tradition as a social force and moral system.

An examination of the process of contesting addresses the question of why cockfighting would be singled out for protest when other supposedly brutal sports such as foxhunting remain legal (Howe 1981; Newall 1983; Hufford 1992; Dundes 1994, 245–46; Fukuda 1997). Dundes suggests that the cockfight is objectionable to moralists because it provides the offensive image of "grown men playing with their cocks in public" and its symbolism of masturbation. This behavior is deemed inappropriate in feminized, "polite" society and implies, in fact, that the moralists acting on behalf of animals feel threatened by the actions of masculine domination in the ring. The violence of ritualized combat, in Dundes's view, is a demonstration of masculinity by feminizing a male opponent; it is not necessarily an affirmation of status hierarchy, as Geertz maintained.

The pigeon shoot provides another comparative perspective on what is objectionable and cruel to some yet emotionally and culturally fulfilling to others. The contradictory perceptions of the pigeon's symbolism and the process of the contest contributed to protests of pigeon shoots from their inception. In the discourse of this contestation we learn, in folk parlance, what "the whole shooting match was about." This folk phrase suggests that the intensity of a shooting match, and particularly one involving animals, signifies the whole of an idea. In representing pursuit in the wild, the shoot mythologizes the process of the event and the identification of a winner as central to the formation of values, even sacredness, or what Mircea Eliade calls the "symbolism of the centre." The center is outlined and made sacred by establishing and ritually eliminating what is unclean or profane (Eliade 1991, 41–47; 1987). As I will show, the Hegins pigeon shoot ritually constructed a narrative of the values of the community, even if its members did not participate in the shooting, and it mythologized how the community came into being. The protests served to disrupt the practice and malign the community as a way to highlight the need for a new universal morality granting animals justice.

The Shoot as Process and Precedent

The process of the pigeon shoot is a metaphor for the pursuit of prey, without the reality of movement in the wild. At the Hegins pigeon shoot, approximately 250 contestants, predominantly men, step up with shotguns on six fields laid out on the grass in the town's only community park.[4] In the fields are rows of small wooden boxes, called traps. Strings attached to the traps lead to an apparatus controlled by an official sitting in an open wooden structure. The official pulls the strings to release pigeons from the boxes, and the contestant shoots at the birds taking flight. The shooter's challenge is to anticipate the box chosen by the puller and predict the released birds' flight path (Blechman 2006, 73–99). Contestants score points for downing birds within the field. Typically, 70 percent of the birds are killed. After all the pigeons are released, "trapper boys," usually between the ages of ten and fourteen, run out on the field and gather the birds on the ground in sacks. They bring the birds back to an area behind the puller's station and deposit them in a metal barrel. The boys kill any injured birds on the ground by wringing their necks. For many years, the destroyed birds would be used for fertilizer, but some old-timers recount occasions during the Depression years when birds were collected by residents to make a variation of a Pennsylvania German "potpie" (see Weaver 1993, 34–35; 1983, 55–57; Glassie 1968, 67–74).

The fields surround an interior layout of dining pavilions, children's playgrounds, and concession stands. Beer is openly consumed, supplied by the Yuengling Brewery of Pottsville, Pennsylvania. This family-run operation in Schuylkill County claims to be America's oldest brewery (established in 1829)—yet another reminder of the importance of tradition as a reference to cultural continuity with the past. But to protesters, the visibility of beer signals a dangerous combination of guns and alcohol, especially in a social environment where children are present. Chickens are barbecued in open pits and hamburgers are grilled for attendees, with women volunteers doing most of the serving. Spectators can watch the shooting from the bleachers, but most people gather in the interior to socialize while the all-day event drags on. By the end of the day, around 7,000 birds have been shot and killed, and as many as 2,000 have escaped back into the wild.

The competition in Hegins is a "straight shooting" contest, a nineteenth-century development that emphasized the act of shooting over the training of birds, probably in imitation of shooting at massive flocks in the wild. In straight shooting, large quantities of common or barn birds are brought in for the shoot and arbitrarily placed in traps. The likelihood is that participants will be successful, that is, chalk up a large number of hits. Winners are declared in different categories, but the straight or public shoots are celebrations of shooters' efficiency. The privatized form of the shoot, still practiced at numerous rod and gun clubs, is "trap and handle" shooting or "match shoots," which are structurally similar to male ritual combat because an opponent is defeated (see Krider 1966, 272–77; Canfield 1992, 14–19; Song 2000a, 176–85). The trap is located twenty-one yards from the shooter, and the field's bounds are forty yards from the center of the trap. If a hit bird lands beyond the forty-yard boundary, it is considered a miss (Canfield 1992, 14). The birds in match shoots are "brushed," that is, trained to fly in particular patterns unknown to the shooter. The trapper's training device is typically a wire five inches long with a small bell attached to the end. The "rig," as it is called, is tied with string to the middle feathers of the bird's tail and extends to either side of the head or above the head (Canfield 1992, 15). Crepe paper may be inserted into the bell. The jingling of the bell and the fluttering of the paper, trappers say, scare the pigeon and prod it to fly more quickly out of the trap.

Example of a spring-action wooden trap used in the Hegins pigeon shoot—before the string is pulled. (Photo by Simon Bronner)

Example of a spring-action wooden trap after the string is pulled. (Photo by Simon Bronner)

Shooter Patrick Canfield explains the trappers' techniques: "If the trappers want the bird to fly to the right, the rig is placed on the left side of the bird's head, and vice versa. If the bird is to fly low and straight, the rig is placed directly above its head. However, the birds do not always adhere to the predicted flight pattern, and some matches are won and lost because the pigeon does not perform as programmed" (1992, 15). Most trappers, who are experts in the craft of breeding and training pigeons, have as many as 300 or 400 birds in their home pens, and for each match they select 20 or 30 pigeons to be brushed (Canfield 1992, 15). As boys, they learned the skills of training pigeons and building pigeon houses from their fathers or other older relatives, and the techniques passed down to the present generation have been consistent since the nineteenth century (see *American Boy's Book* 2000, 332–51; Allen 1975). Trappers and shooters team up, and each shooter has to shoot the bird trapped by the opponent's trapper. Gamblers bet on the overall outcome of the shoot and on particular traps.

Pigeon matches are typically between two teams. Each team member contributes money to bet against the opposing team. The match is a winner-take-all contest. The object is to eliminate the opponent as well as the birds. There may be additional bets placed for each shot; bettors yell out "Ten for a hit!" or "Twenty for a miss" as the shooter squares to shoot. Tension rises, because the shooter might intentionally miss to make money on side bets. In fact, one resident reminded me, "One must be very careful at a pigeon match because people will take advantage of you any way they can" (Wiscount 1989). The bettor wants to be sure he does not become, in the local lingo, a "pigeon mark." There is an association between the duped loser—humiliated and therefore feminized—and the targeted bird. Ritualized male combat is evident in the match between the trapper and the shooter as well as between the two shooters. Straight shooting tests the skill of the marksman rather than that of the trapper and trainer. Every contestant is out for him- or herself rather than playing for a team and seeking to reduce the opposing side to nothing. In direct shooting, the score is valued, whereas in the match shoot, the objective is elimination.

Both match shoots and straight shoots attracted protests during the 1980s and 1990s, but the straight shoot on Labor Day became the main focus because it was a public event attended by families and children. In addition, protesters emphasized the scale of the slaughter at the

Hegins shoot; the large numbers of birds killed drew comparisons to a massacre and a "bird Holocaust" (see Patterson 2002). The Labor Day straight shoot in Hegins is usually preceded by match shoots through the weekend at a private rod and gun club in Valley View.[5] Besides decrying the spectacle of killing the pigeons, protesters objected to the extended "pain and suffering" of injured birds, using the legal rhetoric of human victimization (see Sontag 2003, 40–58). Yet for many shooters who were also hunters, the pigeon shoot fit into the sportsman's ethic of the "quick kill" as well as the "fair chase" because the traps had springed wooden "launchers" with bells that encouraged the birds to take flight (Posewitz 1994; Dizard 2003; Dugan 1993). Other shooters shifted the ethical argument to one of human supremacy, maintaining that pigeon shooting provided enjoyment, and the birds were dispensable natural targets there for the sportsman's taking. In libertarian rhetoric, such a motive of basic freedom should not be subject to interference from governmental regulation or outsider moralizing. Still another rhetorical response was that participating in tradition provided value because it benefited the community and invoked a foundational American heritage.

Notable twentieth-century writers have reflected on the masculine attraction to shooting pigeons. The theme of birds as dispensable natural targets is baldly stated by Ernest Hemingway in "Remembering Shooting-Flying: A Key West Letter." In the essay, written in 1935, he recalled shooting pigeons in childhood and commented on birds generally, "I think they were made to shoot because if they were not why did they give them that whirr of wings that moves you suddenly more than any love of country? . . . I think they were made to shoot and some of us were made to shoot them and if that is not so well, never say we did not tell you that we liked it" (Hemingway 2001, 185). Novelist John Updike, who grew up in Berks County, Pennsylvania—the next county over from Hegins and the site of many pigeon shoots—creatively described the "joy" of killing pigeons for a boy coming of age in *Pigeon Feathers and Other Stories* (1962). He even suggested a regenerative function and having "the sensation of a creator" after killing barn pigeons:

> Standing in the center of the floor, fully master now, disdaining to steady the barrel with anything but his arm, he killed

two more that way. He felt like a beautiful avenger. Out of the shadowy ragged infinity of the vast barn roof these impudent things dared to thrust their heads, presumed to dirty its starred silence with their filthy timorous life, and he cut them off, tucked them back neatly into the silence. He had the sensation of a creator; these little smudges and flickers that he was clever to see and even cleverer to hit in the dim recesses of the rafters—out of each of them he was making a full bird. A tiny peek, probe, dab of life, when he hit it, blossomed into a dead enemy, falling with good, final weight. (Updike 1962, 146–47)

Updike's explanation of their status as enemy is found later when the narrator proclaims, "these birds bred in the millions and were exterminated as pests" (1962, 149).

The first public Hegins shoot was held on Labor Day 1934, as part of the community's homecoming celebration. Into the twentieth century, Labor Day in this rural central Pennsylvania region was traditionally a time for family reunions, and the shoot was a festive event that drew many returning residents to the community. The shoot honored Fred Coleman, a world-champion shooter and local hero who was born in 1874 on a farm near Hegins. Beginning in 1890, the Pennsylvania State Sportsmen's Association organized state championships with cash purses for live bird shooting. Such events had previously taken place in private clubs, hunting lodges, and informal social settings. Coleman won his first of several state championships in 1900, including six successive titles from 1902 to 1908. On the basis of this notoriety, he made a tour of England, which was considered the main source of the pigeon shooting tradition that had spread through America during the colonial period. Coleman moved to Maine, but his legend as a great sportsman continued in central Pennsylvania.

The heyday of the region, based on a coal and agricultural economy, had already passed, and the rise of homecoming celebrations was an indication that many young people were leaving the area for better opportunities in the cities. Many factories that were offering employment produced textiles and clothing and hired primarily women, forcing some to question the "male provider" model for the area's families (Song 2000b; Marsh 1987). Adding a pigeon shooting contest that honored a local hero drew on memories of a better day for the region

Fred Coleman and two of the trophies he earned for competitive pigeon shoots, c. 1900. (Photo courtesy of Jennifer Miller)

and emphasized traditional gender roles. It encapsulated the pioneer cultural heritage of the region symbolized by hunting and shooting, as well as the associated values of male-led families and community bonding. Preparing for the shoot became a year-round community volunteer effort organized by the Labor Day Committee. It was the major public festival for the entire valley, surpassing other events such as the firemen's carnival and the agricultural fair.

By using Coleman's name, Hegins organizers hoped to put the small town on the shooting map, taking advantage of Pennsylvania's large population of hunters interested in gun skills. Lodged between imposing mountains, Hegins was not easily accessible, but it had a reputation for prime hunting lands, and it vied with Chicago and Kansas City for champion-level contestants. Hegins strategically added entertainment, such as dancing girls and musical bands; it brought in celebrities to host the event and lured contestants from the state championships held around the same time. The first few shoots featured both clay and live bird contests, but as the town sought to distinguish the event by linking it with a pioneer heritage and differentiating it from the official trapshooting world, which had exclusively adopted clay targets, it promoted live bird games as a festive tradition.

Illustration of a pigeon shoot on Long Island in the 1890s.

Whereas the renowned Grand American Trapshooting Tourna-
ment had dropped its pigeon shooting competition in 1903 to modernize its image, Hegins intentionally retained its live bird shoot because it
was associated with the past (Trapshooting Hall of Fame 2004). Starting with 73 entries in 1934, the Hegins shoot allocated profits from the
event to the maintenance and expansion of the community park. The
shoot attracted a high of 380 entries in 1946. The number of contestants leveled off to around 100 during the 1960s but grew again during
the 1980s, including 335 entries in 1983. Some of the growth during
the 1980s could be attributed to more contestants from outside the
state, especially since live bird shooting had been outlawed by most
state legislatures. In 1984 an animal-loving couple in the county seat
of Pottsville alerted Trans-Species Unlimited, an animal rights organization based in Williamsport, Pennsylvania, of their objection to the
event. In ensuing years, a handful of protesters from the area demonstrated at the Hegins shoot but attracted minimal media attention. The
organization stepped up its efforts by inviting national animal rights organizations with abolitionist zeal, such as PETA and the Fund for Animals, to intervene. What was at first a loose series of protests became
highly organized in 1989, and many busloads of protesters descended
on Hegins. At the same time, attendance at the shoot increased dra-

matically into the thousands. The height of the protest was in 1991 and 1992, when hundreds of protesters were arrested after running onto the fields to rescue birds from their traps.

The busloads of urban protesters created an immediate contrast with the rural attendees of the shoot. Another contrast frequently mentioned on both sides was the predominance of women among the protesters and the predominance of men among the supporters. In 1991, I estimated that 75 percent of the protesters were women, whereas more than 60 percent of supporters inside the park were men. Major animal rights organizations represented at the shoot were led by women, whereas the main spokesman for the Labor Day Committee was a man. Although the supporters were not overwhelmingly male, men were especially conspicuous and dominant as shooters, trapper boys, officials, cooks, and vendors. The percentage of women participating in the protests was consistent with composite profiles of animal rights activists, which placed female participation between 68.4 and 78.3 percent in the early 1990s (Guither 1998, 71). In addition, according to surveys conducted by Harold D. Guither (1998, 71), most activists were urban (73.4 to 85 percent), professional or executive (44 to 46 percent), college educated (40.2 to 48.4 percent), white (92.9 to 96.9 percent), and, on average, between 30 and 49 years old (48 to 56.6 percent). I observed a younger cohort at the Hegins protest, and some women brought children with them, although there were more children inside the park among the supporters. Activists have also been characterized as unaffiliated with official religions and predominantly vegetarian and feminist (Guither 1998, 67–72). Seeking to determine activists' attitudes toward occupational groups, an Oregon State University study scored animal rights advocates' views of farmers, businesspeople, and scientists as extremely negative (Guither 1998, 69). Inside the park, supporters described themselves to me positively as the descendants of farmers, even if they were not presently engaged in farming. They made frequent reference to being family oriented, hunters or sportsmen, and religiously affiliated. Supporters and protesters shared a belief that their lives were devoted to sustaining the environment, as well as a distrust of government and politicians.

When protesters suggested that live birds be replaced with clay targets, they were rebuffed with the declaration that the unpredictable flight of live birds made the event more sporting. Live bird shooting

Pigeon shoot supporter carrying a sign stating, "Pigeons Are Rats with Wings! Shoot 'Em!!" and holding an artificial rat fitted with bird feathers. His T-shirt and hat are emblazoned with "THE AMERICAN CAUSE," an organization launched in 1993 whose stated mission is to "advance and promote traditional American values." Hegins pigeon shoot, Labor Day, 1994. (Photo by Simon Bronner)

also appealed to the Labor Day Committee because it represented an unofficial, community-oriented tradition. The Fund for Animals offered to pay the Labor Day Committee to cancel the shoot, matching the amount of money that would have been raised for the park, but the committee insisted that the tradition should continue as an affirmation of Hegins's distinctive sense of family and community. In addition to having the taint of a "sellout" with the implication of submission to a moral or corporate authority, the offer negated the reference to hunting and human dominion in staged live bird events.

The protests at Hegins have precedents in campaigns against largely urban pigeon shoots in the nineteenth century, following successful efforts by animal welfare organizations to ban cockfights and dogfights associated with the seedy parts of cities. These fights to the death were not quick kills; participants expected the animals to suffer injuries and create a bloody mess in doing so. The *New York Times* in 1873 joined the Humane Society in calling dogfights a "national disgrace," citing their audiences of "thieves," "brawlers," and "ruffians." The "hideous details" of the "savage cruelties" inflicted by the dogs on each other was

Trapper boys collecting shot birds from around traps. They are wearing T-shirts stating, "SHOOT PIGEONS, NOT DRUGS." Hegins pigeon shoot, Labor Day, 1990. (Photo courtesy of Historical Society of Dauphin County, Harrisburg, Pennsylvania)

matched by fighting and profanity in the crowd, leading the journalist to call the scene "the worst display of human brutality in its most degraded form." Realizing that the participants ascribed manliness to involvement in the event, the *Times* closed with an appeal: "It is time that the ruffians who do these things should be told that they are not to be done, and that the fair fame of the nation is not to be sullied by men so infamous or deeds so unmanly" ("National Disgrace" 1873). The *Times* and the Humane Society found legislative resistance to the link between dogfights and pigeon shoots, at least in part because of differences in class, with pigeon shoots being associated with the club set. Arguments could even be heard that pigeon shoots were "wholesome" endeavors. For example, in a debate in the New York State legislature between Samuel Slater of New York City, sponsor of an anti–pigeon shooting bill, and Horace White of Syracuse, the latter argued, "I don't believe Senator Slater has ever been at a pigeon shoot. He may have been at a dogfight, but not at a well-regulated pigeon shoot. I have attended them. The birds are fed and strengthened to give them greater flying power. Shoots are well conducted and wounded birds retrieved at once. Men stand at the extreme limit of the killing power of their guns. I believe it is a good sport. I believe in all such American sports, football especially. It is wholesome for the American youth" ("To Prohibit" 1901).

The rise of pigeon shoots as a sport was noted in the mid-nineteenth century by Philadelphia gun maker John Krider. In his widely circulated chronicle of field sports of 1853, he discusses the use of the now extinct passenger pigeons for trapshooting, and that may be a clue to the emergence of competitive target shoots. They probably grew out of pioneer hunts of passenger pigeons, once so abundant in the wild that oral tradition referred to the way they "darkened the sky" (French 1919, 17–22, 229; Leffingwell 1967, 129–46; Schorger 1973, 129–98). The pigeon shoots of the nineteenth century demonstrated in a more regulated way the hunters' shooting skills and provided an occasion for gambling, since passenger pigeons were considered easy marks in the wild. The center of the tradition in the middle Atlantic states may be explained by the fact that pigeons were especially abundant in the "hardwood belt" spreading westward from the middle Atlantic into the Midwest and upland South (French 1919, 11–14).

In America, the pigeon shoot refers to a form of regulated target contest, but in Europe, and particularly in the British Isles, pigeon shooting—a subset of sport, field, or "rough" shooting—is what Americans would call hunting in the wild (see Lynn-Allen 1942; Arnold 1956; Gray 1988; Coats 1970; Hall 1995; Batley 1996). In Britain, shooting is differentiated from hunting; the latter refers to the pursuit of prey with hounds, as in foxhunting, and competitive live pigeon shooting has been outlawed since 1921 (Swan 2003; Hall 1995, 13). Accounts of English events typically refer to betting and drinking. At an English shoot that Peter Hall recalls:

> Several men took it in turns to shoot the pigeons, which were released quite haphazardly as far as I can remember by a man pulling a piece of string outside the circle. Any one of the five cages would open, and a pigeon would immediately fly out and try to gain height before the poor thing was shot. There were plenty of rows as I recall—not so much as to whether each pigeon was getting killed because that was pretty self-evident, but about where the thing fell or where it had been shot in the air. That side of things seemed to be very important indeed, and to score maximum points the gun had to shoot the bird within a prescribed time or distance. (1995, 13)

Today, pigeon shooting on British estate fields is common to control "agricultural pests" (Swan 2003; Gray 1988). Because the pigeon is identified as a pest, there is no season for the bird, and they may be shot year-round. In Britain, too, protests have been mounted against field sports, but defenders claim, "A pigeon shooter is not a rural vandal gratuitously slaughtering wildlife, nor is he solely a crop protector. Rather he is a lover of the countryside and its creatures, appreciating the ever-changing moods of weather and sky and the quiet places, where he may be alone with his thoughts whilst exercising the perfectly natural hunting urge which still exists in modern, largely urbanised man" (Gray 1988, 14). In both Britain and America, catapulted clay targets called "pigeons" have largely replaced live birds, but much of the terminology from live bird competitions remains. In clay target shoots, the command "pull" is still used to signal the "trapper" to release the "bird" or "pigeon"; a hit is registered as a "kill," whereas a miss is termed a "lost bird" (Weston 2002).

Another key feature of European shoots is the use of dogs to retrieve the birds, suggesting a symbolic equivalence between Hegins's trapper boys and dog companions. The darting of dogs, like that of young boys, seemed to raise the betting fervor among the crowd. For example, in 1883 Lord Randolph Churchill described for the House of Commons his experience with pigeon shooting: "One of the pigeons was struck and fell to the ground; but when the dog went to pick it up, the wretched bird fluttered again in the air, and for an appreciable time it remained so fluttering, just a little higher than the dog could jump. While the bird's fate was thus trembling in the balance, the betting was fast and furious, and when at last the pigeon tumbled into the dog's jaws, he would never forget the shout of triumph and yell of execration that rose from the ring-men and gentlemen" (Stratton 1915, 166–67).

The American colonial heritage of shooting passenger pigeons was among the first protested hunting activities. In James Fenimore Cooper's *The Pioneers* (1823), the elderly Leatherstocking expresses his disgruntlement with the mass slaughter of pigeons, which he calls "harmless as a garter snake," in upstate New York. An "uneasy spectator," Leatherstocking protests, "This comes of settling a country! Here have I known the pigeons to fly for forty long years, and, till you made your clearings, there was nobody to skear or to hurt them" (Cooper 1964, 235). "Sportsman" Billy Kirby humiliates Leatherstocking by feminizing him as weak, impotent, and sentimental, calling him an "old cornstalk," "old fool," and "sapless stub." In language echoing some of the Hegins supporters' resentment of outsiders who are unaware of the pigeon's adverse effect on crops, Cooper describes Kirby's response to Leatherstocking's sympathy for the pigeons: "What! Old Leatherstocking," he cried, "grumbling at the loss of a few pigeons! If you had to sow your wheat twice, and three times, as I have done, you wouldn't be so mass-fully feeling towards the divils. Hurrah, boys! Scatter the feathers!" (Cooper 1964, 235–36).

The piles of birds that resulted from the shooting asserted the power of the settler to reap benefits from the lush environment. Leatherstocking leaves, saddened by the "destruction," being careful to be respectful of life by not stepping on the birds. The sheriff has a different take on the event, seeing play and pragmatic consequences for what has transpired, exclaiming, "Sport! . . . it is princely sport! There are some thousands of the blue-coated boys on the ground, so that every old woman in the village may have a potpie for the asking" (Cooper 1964, 239). In his plaint, the *old* Leatherstocking remembers the days before civilization dominated the wild and defiled the virgin land, whereas the sportsmen and sheriff optimistically see the promise of a new land of plenty, intended for human exploitation. To the sportsmen, the "clearing" of the pigeons is a metaphor for the opening of the western frontier and the rising national optimism growing out of a pioneer heritage and the violent eradication of natives (see Smith 1970, 59–70; Slotkin 2000, 466–516). According to Richard Slotkin, Cooper's scenes underscore how settlers considered violence to natives and nature necessary to mythologically do away with the old and regenerate a sacred sense of a new people and place. A bit of historical evidence that supports this view is the tradition emerging in the nineteenth century equating the celebration of America's founding and American abundance at Independence Day and Thanksgiving with the staging of pigeon shoots ("Puritans" 1882; "Plans" 1893).

During the 1870s, the youthful optimism enacted in pigeon shoots became publicly debated in New York City. Unlike the cockfights and dogfights associated with the lower class, pigeon shooting was being taken up, according to the *Times*, by elite young gentlemen "who court the reputation of 'sporting' characters" ("Pigeon" 1872). It was indeed common for bachelors of the upper class to engage in sports perceived as "manly" to compensate for the enervating and emasculating effects of cosmopolitan life (see Chudacoff 1999, 217–50). Pigeon shooting gained some legitimacy among this class because it was not as bloody as cockfights and dogfights and was staged at private clubs. It could be rationalized as being about keeping individual scores rather than metaphorically murdering an opponent. But John Emory, in a letter to the *Times* published on April 2, 1901, questioned the differentiation:

As a matter of public policy and for the promotion of sound morals, would it not be desirable to treat pigeon-shooting contests as we have treated cock fights, dog fights, and other brutal sports? It will be no answer for the offenders to say that the birds would be killed anyway. Killing for the sheer sport of the thing is out of joint with the best ideals of the day. Even from the point of view of the sportsman, who fights fair, so to speak, and seeks his quarry in its native haunts, the "pigeon shoot," as described in your paper to-day, would appear to be as mean as it is cold-blooded.

Whereas cockfights and dogfights were outlawed because they encouraged crime in the slums as well as animal cruelty, pigeon shoots persisted, much to the chagrin of animal welfare organizations and urban reformers. Calling the pigeon an "emblem of peace," the *New York Times* in 1872 editorialized, "In a country like ours, where recreation bears so small a proportion to hard work it would ill become us to do anything to abridge youthful tendencies to healthy exercise; but this pigeon shooting not only includes the eminent disadvantage of useless cruelty, but also offers no proper and adequate field for manly endeavor" ("Pigeon" 1872). Sounding the progressive cant of cosmopolitan modernism and cultural evolutionary doctrine, the *Times* blasted pigeon shoots on February 28, 1881: "It seems as though our stage of civilization was sufficiently far advanced to enable us to do away with the barbarous so-called sport known as pigeon shooting. . . . Pigeon shooting is mere slaughter, and it is not true sport." Such editorials resulted in letters defending the practice, including this one on June 29, 1881: "The sentimentalists pretend that it is an act of cruelty to shoot pigeons from a trap merely as a sport. They allege that no good purpose whatever is served by the wholesale butchery of twenty thousand birds, and that it is demoralizing not only to the butchers but to the community which tolerates them. Of course, this is a narrow-minded and superficial view of the subject, and it needs very little argument to convince any fair-minded man that pigeon-shooting is, perhaps, the noblest occupation in which a man can engage."

Other arguments in favor of pigeon shoots cited their virtue in eradicating pests, honing shooting skills that could be used in defense of the country, and improving the economic condition of the community. A petition carrying 20,000 signatures calling for the preservation of the tradition was presented to the New York legislature as it considered an anti–pigeon shooting bill in 1901. After long debate, the bill prohibiting pigeon shooting in New York became law in 1902, and the pen used by the governor to sign the legislation was handed over to the president of the New York Society for the Prevention of Cruelty to Animals.

In my survey of the 238 articles in the *New York Times* regarding pigeon shoots from the mid-nineteenth century to 2004, a clear pattern emerges: as a matter of public debate, media attention to the shoots was concentrated in the late nineteenth and late twentieth centuries. During the late nineteenth century, controversy revolved around New York City shoots, whereas during the late twentieth century, the focus was on the campaign against Hegins. As a result of the publicity surrounding Hegins, wire services during the 1990s reported other contested pigeon shooting traditions in California, Nevada, Arizona, Texas, Florida, North Carolina, and Wyoming. Both fin de siècle eras were notable for rapid transformations of society resulting from industrialization and urbanization in the nineteenth century and computerization and suburbanization in the twentieth. Both eras also engendered reflection and heated public debate on society's future directions and the status of traditions threatened by what was widely perceived as an accelerating rate of change, especially as the new millennium approached (Bronner 2002). During the 1990s, publicity was given to "culture wars" as skirmishes over the preservation of traditional values and maintenance of the traditional family structure in a sexually permissive and increasingly individualistic society (see Ravitch 2002; Bronner 2000a; Goodheart 1997; Foley 1995; Hunter 1991). In both eras, there was a crisis of masculinity in which men questioned their feminized domestication in a modernizing society (see Douglas 1977; Rotundo 1993; Kimmel 1996; Bronner 2005b, 31–41). In the nineteenth century, the culprit was the first wave of the women's movement and the emasculating character of industrial work, whereas in the twentieth century, accusative fingers were pointed at the feminist movement and modernization.

At the end of both the nineteenth and twentieth centuries, reform movements aroused sympathy for social victims to advocate for new public policy. The animal rights movement emerged in the late twentieth century following the campaigns for civil rights and women's rights. According to Lawrence and Susan Finsen's chronicle of the animal rights movement, human rights issues in the forefront during the 1960s created an intellectual climate conducive to the challenge of "morality as usual" (1994, 55). Especially provocative for animal rights activists was the comparison between the persecution of animals and blacks in America. For many activists, the most influential text was Peter Singer's *Animal Liberation* (1975), which opens with the declaration that the struggle against the tyranny of human over nonhuman animals is "causing an amount of pain and suffering that can only be compared with that which resulted from the centuries of tyranny by white humans over black humans" (1990, i). He goes on to proclaim that the animal rights campaign is as important as "any of the moral and social issues that have been fought over in recent years" (Singer 1990, i).

The title of Singer's book, *Animal Liberation*, raises comparisons with the radical rhetoric of women's liberation and black liberation made popular during the 1960s. Another rhetorical connection between the civil rights and animal rights movements was the March for the Animals on June 10, 1990, which was intended to do for animal rights what the 1963 March on Washington had achieved for civil rights. The national park police estimated that 25,000 animal rights activists attended the 1990 march in Washington, D.C. A humanistic link between animal rights and civil rights was the popular impact of Harper Lee's Pulitzer Prize–winning novel *To Kill a Mockingbird* (1960), made into a critically acclaimed film in 1962 (it won four Academy Awards, including best screenplay and best actor). The title refers to lawyer Atticus Finch's advice to his children about firing their rifles at birds: "Shoot all the blue jays you want, if you can hit 'em, but remember it's a sin to kill a mockingbird." He explains that the blue jay is a common bird, often perceived as a bully and a pest, whereas mockingbirds do nothing but "sing their hearts out for us." Tom Robinson, the innocent black victim of racism in the small southern town, is a metaphoric mockingbird who is attacked despite doing nothing but good. Arguably, his character is also feminized like the bird because he could not have committed the rape of which he is accused. Both the bird and Robinson are sinless and considered less than human, and when they are killed, innocence is metaphorically destroyed. The book and movie had a powerful anti-prejudice theme as racial unrest over segregation mounted during the 1960s, and they used sympathy for an innocent bird to drive home the message.

In keeping with the struggle against human tyranny as a form of slavery and discrimination, many animal rights activists distinguished their movement from that of animal welfare with the rhetoric of "abolition" (Spiegel 1996). Other animal rights activists referred to genocide, holocaust, and male exploitation, implying that the cruel treatment of animals predisposed humans to create destructive social inequalities (Patterson 2002; Adams 2000). Although some observers viewed animal rights as tangential to the struggle for human rights and social reform, animal rights advocates insisted that their movement reached the root cause of injustice. For example, Josephine Donovan, writing on animal rights and feminist theory, pronounced that "the domination of nature, rooted in postmedieval, Western, male psychology, is the *underlying cause* of the mistreatment of animals as well as of the exploitation of women and the environment" (2003, 47; emphasis added).

Calling for the abolition of human exploitation of animals, the animal rights movement supplanted the protectionist animal welfare organizations of the nineteenth century, and its leaders came largely from domestic abuse and feminist ideological backgrounds (Mackinnon 2004; Guither 1998, 35–72; Adams 1995). According to the national director of the Fund for Animals, her outrage over violence in the form of animal abuse came directly from her experiences fighting spousal battery, child abuse, and rape. During the Hegins protests, the rhetoric for and against pigeon shoots focused on the moral significance of tradition in maintaining community and the exposure of children to violence. Fueling the heated exchange between opposing sides in Hegins was the frightening and shocking news of Jeffrey Dahmer's serial killing and butchery of young boys, with the animal rights movement playing up reports that he and other publicized predators had reportedly abused animals as children (Clifton 1994; Morella 1998; De Angelis 1998). When the national director of the Fund for Animals wrote to a high school that was considering excusing students from class so they could work as trapper boys at a pigeon shoot, her argument was as follows:

This is not only an issue of legality. It is also a question of ethics, compassion and core values we want to teach our children. There is ample scientific evidence that allowing young people to treat animals inhumanely can desensitize them to violence and can eventually lead to violent acts toward people. Recent studies show that seven out of ten people who are cruel to animals eventually commit crimes against other people, about half of which are violent crimes. We are not suggesting that every child who abuses an animal grows up to be Ted Bundy or the Son of Sam, but we are raising the question of whether we want to promote violence or compassion as a core value in our young people. In light of the recent shooting tragedy in an

Arkansas middle school last week, we should be especially cautious of any activity that potentially could give young people the impression that violence is not only acceptable, but also a good excuse to skip school. (Prescott 1998)

For Hegins supporters, though, the news of the serial killings, alien to the region, was affirmation of the depravity of cities and of family values gone wrong (often associated, they said, to the acceptance of homosexuality, abortion, and radical feminism). Hegins was, supporters repeatedly told journalists, a peaceful, sociable place rooted in the land; it was a place where everyone knew one another—a rarity in urbanizing, modernizing America. Animal rights organizations decried the pigeon shoot as extreme violence because of the extent of the killing. In a post-Holocaust concern for social genocide and urban decay, manifested by rampant random violence perpetrated by roaming youth gangs, the animal rights organizations repeatedly hammered away at the Hegins bird "holocaust," "massacre," "slaughter," and "murder."

Despite the growth of American folklore studies on threatened traditions and cultures through both fin de siècle periods, pigeon shoots and shooting and hunting practices in general rarely attracted folkloristic notice before the Hegins protests, despite being widely recognized in the media as one of America's most enduring, if privatized, folk traditions (see Bronner 1998, 417–34).[6] What made the Hegins pigeon shoot newsworthy was animal rights activists' protest against a public practice they called "barbaric" and "cruel." It was also picture-worthy, and the media often sought shocking images of the bizarre, anachronistic ritual for public consumption. As it turned out, it was not the bloodbath that animal rights protesters predicted, but they pointed their cameras at boys wringing the necks of injured birds and the massive accumulation of dead birds in barrels.

Inevitably, the question of the tradition's meaning for communities as well as shooters in the modern age came to the fore. Was it sport? Was it slaughter? Was it festival? Was it sickness? Was it heritage? Journalists could easily solicit positive answers to all these questions from the various sides, and they often attributed differences of opinion to culture wars between the traditional values of heartland America and the moral imperatives of cosmopolitan culture. Yet also evident in the reporting was skepticism that all the fuss over pigeons was really merited. I stood with shocked wire-service reporters as protesters risked their lives by running onto the field of fire to rescue pigeons, and hundreds of individuals were arrested over the course of the protest.

Structurally, the protests featured the type of civil disobedience characteristic of human struggles for racial and gender equality. The "rescues" represented the seriousness of the issue and signified the idea that animals have individual lives worth saving. But the rural residents of Hegins aroused sympathy in the court of public opinion because they appeared to be unfairly victimized by the animal rights protesters. They also appeared to be the underdogs in the fight owing to their marginalization by modernizing society, and they claimed that their values and community, not the birds, were in need of protection. The residents repeatedly moved the focus from cruelty to the birds in a "backward" slice of Americana to the threat posed by animal rights to mainstream cultural features such as leather and meat consumption. In the mid-1990s, after animal rights organizations failed to convince the legislature to pass anti–pigeon shooting bills, Hegins supporters felt confident that they would be able to continue the public shoot without interference.

Ironically, what gave the animal rights organizations their ultimate triumph was an alliance with the moderate animal welfare organization the American Society for the Prevention of Cruelty to Animals (ASPCA) that resulted in court rulings to enforce animal cruelty statutes. It was not the media or public opinion that ended the Hegins shoot in 1999 but rather the courts. The fact that the Pennsylvania Supreme Court decided against the community's preference only fueled broader suspicions, with residents blaming distant legal authorities for undermining the coal industry through environmental regulation and subverting the freedom to hunt in the wild. For Hegins supporters, it was a signal event in the decline of tradition and liberty in America. They anticipated a domino effect that would doom other venerated customs in the area such as hunting, trapping, and fishing. When the Hegins shoot was canceled in 1999 as a result of the court's ruling, the headline in the local newspaper blared, "Court's Decision Doomed Tradition," and it offered the representative statement, "It's part of our Schuylkill County heritage to shoot pigeons" (Edmondson and Hessinger 1999). "Many people consider the shoot a Hegins Valley tradition," journalist Vicki Terwilliger (1999b) wrote, noting that "many boys in the area grew up

T-shirt worn by supporters of the Hegins pigeon shoot, 1993. (Photo by Simon Bronner)

with the event and later took their own children and grandchildren to see the marksmen perform."

Taking the rhetorical stance of victim, shooter Carl Specht told a reporter, "I don't think we (hunters/gun owners) have any rights anymore," and others referred to a betrayal of the American sense of freedom (Terwilliger 1999a). Larger questions related to the shoot came to mind: "I don't believe it's just about pigeons. It's going to come down to the confiscation of guns"; others predicted an assault on hunting and meat consumption (Terwilliger 1999a). The unclean status of the birds was frequently mentioned in the aftermath: "Pigeons are such dirty birds. I think they should catch all the pigeons and put them in the living rooms or in the cars of those people who are opposed to this"; "They poison the pigeons in the city, yet complain when we shoot them here. We didn't turn out to be murderers" (Terwilliger 1999b). Meanwhile, the Fund for Animals issued a statement focusing on the event rather than the people of Hegins and recognizing the importance of the shoot's cancellation for the animal rights movement: "The Hegins pigeon shoot has often been called the world's cruelest event. It is a hallmark for the humane movement to put an end to this annual atroc-

♀ WOMEN ♀

JOIN IN SOLIDARITY TO EXPOSE
PATRIARCHAL VIOLENCE

❝ *Pigeon shoots are one of the most bizarre forms of the violent male bonding ritual called sport hunting. Trapped urban birds or those bred for hunting are shot as they attempt to fly when a string opens a box that imprisons them. The lucky ones die quickly, others, wounded but still conscious stagger and flap in the dirt...* **❞**   Dana Forbes, MS Magazine, Jan/Feb 1992

Please join us —
Labor Day,
September 7, 1992,
in Hegins, Pa.

More than 50 women were arrested last year in Hegins, Pa., to protest the violent killing of innocent pigeons. We are expecting hundreds this year. Help stop the violence against women and animals.

For more information, contact Beth Beck at PETA 301/770-7444, Ext. 430.

Officers arresting a women trying to rescue a wounded pigeon.

PEOPLE FOR THE ETHICAL TREATMENT OF ANIMALS
P.O. BOX 42516
WASHINGTON, DC 20015
(301) 770-PETA

The typical pigeon shoot supporter watching the days' "activities."

Flyer distributed by PETA against the pigeon shoot, 1992.

ity and save thousands of animals from suffering" (Edmondson and Hessinger 1999).

The Hegins decision was invoked in campaigns against pigeon shoots elsewhere as the new millennium approached. The Fund for Animals teamed with Sacramento-based United Animal Nations (UAN) to lobby for cancellation of the Champion Flyers Pigeon Shoot in Sierra County, California, in 1998. The director of UAN issued a statement echoing the arguments against Hegins: "We are appalled that pigeon shoots could be considered sport by anyone; as Californians, we don't want this type of barbaric massacre—particularly one which involves children in the killing of innocent animals—taking place in our state" (Fund 1998). Failing to shut down the shoot by pressuring the promoters, the animal rights organizations succeeded in acquiring an opinion from the California attorney general in 2000 that the pigeon shoot violated the state's animal cruelty laws because "disoriented and defenseless" pigeons were "released from their cages for purposes of being shot" (Fund 2000). Around the same time, animal rights groups applied similar tactics in protests of shoots in Dallas, Texas, Sarasota, Florida, and Phoenix, Arizona (Bensman 1998; Johnson 1997; Plank 1995). Meanwhile, back in Pennsylvania, the Fund for Animals continued its litigation to ban pigeon shoots at rod and gun clubs in a major test of the government's power to regulate private activities. In 2004, the Fund suffered a setback when the Pennsylvania Supreme Court upheld a lower court decision that the shoots did not violate the state's cruelty statute as long as "reasonable efforts" were made to minimize the number of animals treated cruelly. The Fund's national director responded, "We were able to stop this barbaric and inhumane practice in Hegins and it should be stopped throughout Pennsylvania" (Animal News 2004).

Tradition on Trial

For many residents of Hegins, hunting and shooting contests, particularly within the confines of private sportsmen's clubs, are subject to folk law rather than state law. According to Alison Dundes Renteln and Alan Dundes, editors of the landmark *Folk Law: Essays in the Theory and Practice of Lex Non Scripta* (1994), folk law is a socially defined group's orally transmitted body of traditional obligations and prohibitions, sanctioned or required by that group and binding on individuals or subsets of individuals (e.g., families, clans) under pain of punishment or forfeiture. Animal rights groups wanted to give the impression that the customs governing events such as pigeon shoots had to be condemned because they belonged to a barbaric place and time that modern, progressive society needed to repress. It is more common to think of folk law existing in non-Western societies than in America, because of the legal view that modern societies have rationalized knowledge that is translated into rule of law, whereas primitive, non-Western societies have irrational bases of judicial order based on superstition, rigid custom, and even mysticism. Renteln and Dundes point out, however, that the idea of a common, unwritten, living, or customary law is an integral part of the American legal system, although legal practitioners and scholars in common-law nations "sometimes seem not to have the slightest inkling of what folk law is" (1994, xv). Of particular interest in a transnational context are cases in which a "cultural defense" is used, that is, when an argument is made that a person should not be punished in the United States for engaging in activities that are customary in his or her country of origin. The cultural defense raises a central issue in *Folk Law:* conflicts between the state and a folk group with nonnormative practices. A presupposition is that groups that adhere to folk law or tradition are not in power in the larger society. Renteln and Dundes state, "Often the dispute involves conflicting state or 'official' law and folk law, and at stake may be legal practices that are crucial for the maintenance of group identity" (1994, xv).

In *The Cultural Defense*, Renteln (2004, 94) offers animals as a special category of cultural conflict in the courtroom. She comments that the treatment of animals "represents a classic example of the manner in which enculturation affects moral intuitions." Of legal interest is the way court cases involving animal cruelty determine whether animals have rights, particularly if they are personified to have duties. Of cultural interest is the way ritual activities with animals are necessary to the maintenance of group identity and moral code, especially in a society that promises tolerance of different belief or religious systems and allows peaceable assembly. Devoted to providing legal protection to "any person," the U.S. Constitution does not specify the protection given to animals; much of the jurisprudence on animal-human relations is based on cultural norms. Animal cruelty laws that protect animals and punish humans are justified by the traditional human tendency to personify animals; as declared in the constitutional challenge of *New York v. Blunt* (1983), cruelty to animals is defined as "unjustified, needless and wanton inhumanity." It is left to interpretation what is "unjustified" or "inhumane," especially when it comes to legal activities involving animal destruction, such as hunting and food processing. A paradox that Renteln points out is that whereas a minority defends the proposition that animals have rights, "there seems to be a common presumption that the protection of animals trumps the right to culture" (2004, 95).

A special contemporary problem of invoking animal rights in the cultural defense is that it disrupts the balance of state interests against a minority or powerless group. In many cases of animal advocacy groups versus organizations accused of animal abuse, both sides have cultural claims. Often at issue are conflicting claims between the need or right of a community to treat animals in a manner prescribed by tradition and the need or right of animals to act as a community with interests in a society. Since animals do not have a voice, animal rights advocates act as moral agents for them, much as children might be protected from abusive parents. This situation is different from animal welfare cases in which the main concern is upholding a public interest.

Folk Law, for instance, includes a report on the nineteenth-century decision in *People v. Harriet* (1819) that denied citizens the right to keep pigs in the street (Hartog 1994). The defense asserted that keeping pigs was a custom among members of an artisan community and that labeling pigs a nuisance was an attack on the life of the poor. The court decided, however, that the practice was unsafe, immoral, and therefore illegal. The case did not consider whether animals had rights but rather whether the city had the authority to exercise control over public culture. A cultural assumption made by the prosecution was that swine were more objectionable than other animals and that the community of pig keepers constituted a criminal subculture. In his commentary on the case, Hendrik Hartog mentions that the law did not, in fact, eliminate the practice; however, it transferred power from the artisan community to establish guidelines of conduct according to tradition and vested legal authority in those who opposed pigs in the streets. The case drew attention to a particular difficulty of American law that implicitly recognizes pluralism—an acceptance of customs founded on multiple sources of legal authority—while also establishing consistent, universal guidelines on rights and rules of conduct.

Of cultural significance, in animal rights cases the courts inevitably consider the relation of a group's practices to the greater society. Whereas the legal question is often about conflicting claims of animal and human rights and the moral responsibilities of human owners of animals, the cultural issue that looms large in shaping a modern philosophy of action is the role of tradition in the maintenance of a society. This issue has historical, social, and psychological dimensions. In cases in which the continuation of a tradition is at issue, the historical question is why a traditional practice (such as pigeon shoots) that was condoned for years should now be criminalized. Socially, the relativistic question is why a group's practices that benefit the group and do not adversely affect society should be prohibited. The psychological aspect is often the most difficult to grasp, whether in folkloristics or jurisprudence: should groups be held accountable for the unconscious effects or latent symbolism of their practices?

In the pigeon shoot cases, defendants claimed that tradition had an intrinsic psychological and social value to the community and that its effects were positive. Ultimately, the court established a principle criminalizing long-held shooting events because they were linked to unresolvable problems of social violence. The cultural significance is that in the absence of empirical evidence of cruelty or inhumanely inflicted pain, the court was swayed by the symbolic implications of tradition. Although Chief Justice Flaherty recognized the cultural conflict between opponents of the shoot, who "view it as a cruel and moronic exercise in marksmanship," and proponents, who "view it as entertainment, exemplifying the state of sportsmanship in this Commonwealth," the court avoided the cultural defense, instead focusing on the right of an agent of the ASPCA to request injunctive relief. As with the "pigs in the street" case, the pigeon shoot practice continued, but it became part of a larger public discourse on animal-human relations and rights claims.

In court, the direct examination and cross-examination centered on the question of whether pigeon shoots were cruel to the animals—not whether killing pigeons was cruel, but whether any abuse took place. Once it was determined that pigeons indeed qualified as animals subject to protection, the question was whether the following guideline applied, and if so, who was authorized to monitor its enforcement: "A person commits a summary offense if he wantonly or cruelly ill treats, overloads, beats, otherwise abuses any animal, or neglects any animal as to which he has a duty of care, whether belonging to himself or otherwise, or abandons any animal, or deprives any animal of necessary sustenance, drink, shelter, or veterinary care, or access to clean and sanitary shelter which will protect the animal against inclement weather and preserve the animal's body heat and keep it dry" (18 Pa.C.S. 5511[c]). The question of tradition entered the trial because of the defense's assertion that experience gained from traditional knowledge was sufficient for the "duty of care." The defense also maintained that the context of the ritual was for the participants, not for the spectators, since that would put it in the category of illegal activities such as dogfights and cockfights. Pigeon shoots, the defense argued, were in the category of hunting because the animals were not captive but were from the wild.

Consider the following exchange when Ray Buffington, a member of the organization sponsoring the shoot, was called to the stand:

Q: Do you know what kind of training the trapper boys are given in the handling of the birds?

A: We get all the trapper boys together in the morning before the shoot starts.

Q: Who's we?

A: Usually myself and the referees basically explain to the trapper boys what's expected of them, how they're supposed to handle the bird, how they're supposed to place it in the trap, what they're supposed to do when they retrieve it. They get a good explanation of what's expected from them in the morning before the shoot starts, and that's done at every shoot we have.

Q: Fine. Tell us what you tell them.

A: That they're supposed to take the pigeons from the crate, put them in the carrier, carry them to the trap, place them in the trap faced a certain way, close the door on the trap. We show them how to do that. Tell them that when they retrieve the birds after a shooter's finished, they're supposed to put them in the bag, bring them back and hand them to the person in the—we usually have an adult back supervising the trapper boys, because they are younger, younger. I wouldn't say children. They're twelve to sixteen years old. Some are older than sixteen, but we always have an adult there, twenty-one or over, that is responsible for decapitating any of the wounded birds.

Q: What training have you and the referees had in the proper handling of pigeons?

MR. PERLSTEIN [defense attorney]: I object to the form, Your Honor, training or experience.

THE COURT: If he had any. Is there any required? I don't know. Go ahead. From who, from a vet? I'm not sure.

MR. BROOKS [prosecuting attorney]: I'm just asking generally.

THE COURT: I don't understand the training.

MR. BROOKS: In the proper handling of pigeons.

THE COURT: What is the proper handling of a pigeon for a shoot? What am I supposed to assume there is?

MR. BROOKS: Well, if he hasn't, he hasn't.

THE COURT: From where? Who gives this training or what's out there, from a vet? Can you be a little more specific?

MR. BROOKS: That's why I'm asking him.

THE COURT: You said have you ever received any proper training. From who, from where?

MR. BROOKS: Any training in the proper handling of pigeons.

THE COURT: What is that? I don't understand that.

MR. BROOKS: Well, I think as distinguished from pulling the wings off live pigeons would be improper handling. I think we can agree on that, Your Honor.

THE COURT: I would agree with that, but that still doesn't solve the problem with your question.

MR. BROOKS: How about anything that would violate the cruelty statute?

THE COURT: I honestly don't understand that at all.

MR. BROOKS: The cruelty statute's fairly clear.

THE COURT: You have to be more specific with your question. I think the answer is, no, I don't. I think that's the answer.

MR. BROOKS: That's all I want to hear him say.

THE COURT: But proper training. Have you had any training at all in how to handle a pigeon, if there is such a thing?

THE WITNESS: Not more than when I was little, I was a trapper boy and the referee told—

Q: Okay. Have you ever had any training in the proper technique for decapitation?

MR. PERLSTEIN: Objection.

THE COURT: What's the objection?

MR. PERLSTEIN: The word *proper*.

THE COURT: I understand. Have you had any training at all in decapitation of pigeons?

THE WITNESS: Not more than—

THE COURT: What you did on the farm or what you did somewhere?

THE WITNESS: Yeah.

THE COURT: All right. Prior experience at it?

THE WITNESS: You know, *tradition*.

Q: So you never received training by a vet?

A: No.

Q: Who are the twenty-one-year-olds who are selected to do the
decapitation?

MR. PERLSTEIN: Objection, Your Honor, relevance.

MR. BROOKS: I don't need names.

THE COURT: How are they selected?

MR. BROOKS: Sure.

A: They're members of the club that volunteer.

Q: Okay. Is it fair to say they've never received training in appropriate methods of decapitation also?

MR. PERLSTEIN: The same objection, Your Honor.

THE COURT: All right. If you know.

A: Other than basically the same way I got the training I got.

Q: On the farm?

A: Yeah, or from the referee when I was younger.

In this exchange, the prosecution tried to use the idea of professional authority as necessary for the normative or, in the rhetoric of the examination,
proper, treatment. The answer by the witness is that cultural experience, or
tradition, constituted training. In legal terms, the question was whether
a veterinarian needed to be present to administer euthanasia. Or could
community or folk standards gained from years of practice suffice?

Another issue was how the "perceived value of the animal" per-
tained to its treatment. If the pigeon was a pest rather than a pet, did
that make a difference in its treatment? The prosecution tried to show
that universal moral standards for the protection of life applied, but the
defense countered that cultural categories were pertinent and that the
elimination of pigeons was perceived as a service to the community. On
the stand to address the point was Dr. Gordon Stull, a veterinarian:

Q: Doctor, on the zoological chart, we go from humans at the top to single-cell animals at the bottom, am I correct?

A: Yes, fungi, viruses.

Q: Doctor, every animal, even single cell, will respond to negative stimuli, am I correct?

A: Yes, in one form or another.

Q: And there is a limit, is there not, as to what point, where on the zoological chart, we are going to provide veterinary care to an animal?

A: There certainly is. We wouldn't take antibiotics if we wouldn't feel we should kill bacteria. There certainly is a limit, and that limit is determined by people based on their perceived value of the animal.

Q: Have you ever had someone bring in their cockroach collection for you to take care of?

A: I've cared for cockroaches at the Pittsburgh Zoo actually, yes.

Q: How about—is that because they had value to the Pittsburgh Zoo?

A: They most certainly did. They're expensive. They cost more than a pigeon apiece.

Q: So the decision was made, am I correct, that the cost of the care and the effect of the care were worth it based upon the value of the animal to the Pittsburgh Zoo?

A: Yes, and that value again was determined by the owner of the Pittsburgh Zoo.

The defense used the term "negative stimuli," because it insisted that pain and suffering were human terms, and one could not determine whether a pigeon suffered or felt pain, anxiety, or fear. In addition to the comparison to cockroaches—with the implication that living creatures are subject to a hierarchy of value—the defense later pointed out the categorization of pigeons, along with rats and rabbits, as small pest animals (see Mechling 1991; Mechling and Wilson 1988). During cross-examination, attorney Brooks countered by asking Dr. Stull whether a kitten or puppy shoot would be cruel, if a pigeon shoot is not. The court sustained the defense attorney's objection, and Brooks followed by asking, "Where do you draw the line . . . as to cruelty or not cruelty?" But another objection was sustained.

One cultural definition of cruelty from the American Veterinary Medical Association (AVMA) that was introduced into the proceedings referred to spectator events with the intention of causing injury or death to animals. Criminalized activities such as cockfighting and dogfighting fall under this category. Dr. Stull answered that a pigeon shoot was a sportsmen's event. "It's not set up for the spectator; it's set up for the sportsmen," he testified. Brooks pressed with a line of questioning that suggested a negative cognitive category for pigeon shoots:

Q: So by your analogy, a rodeo is not a spectator event, but it's for the people who want to ride the bulls?

A: No, I believe a rodeo is a spectator event.

Q: So if we have spectators observing the pigeons being killed, you're disagreeing with the proposition that that's a spectator event?

A: No. The design of a rodeo is set up as entertainment for a group of people. As far as I'm aware of, a pigeon shoot isn't to set up entertainment for the people watching it, but rather as a method of—it's designed as a resource for the people in the sportsmen's club.

Q: Resource?

A: Well, as a method to perfect their skills, and it's a method of recreation.

Q: Not unlike a bull rider perfecting his skills in riding a bull or roper perfecting his skills in roping a horse or a dog and cattle, any of those particular sports that are scored and prizes are awarded just like this, correct?

A: Prizes are awarded at a rodeo, yes.

Q: And they're awarded at a pigeon shoot.

It appeared that Brooks was mounting what could be called a "mass cultural offense" by suggesting that the subcultural context of the pigeon shoot was misrepresented by Hegins advocates. His line of questioning was leading the witness to say that a deeper meaning of the shoot was about promoting violence and the wanton destruction of animals for entertainment rather than wholesome recreation and the development of skills. But the court intervened:

Let me just stop you right here. Does it make any difference, Mr. Brooks, in terms of what veterinary care should or should not be given, whether it's a spectator, whether it's a sporting event? I'm going to be the fact finder in the case. Whether it's a spectator, whether it's a bull fight, it's still going to be the reasonableness of the treatment, the care provided. It really doesn't matter to me what label you put on it, or ultimately whether the AVMA says it's a spectator event or not, or a sporting event. To me, that doesn't change the underlying responsibility of the animal's treatment as appropriately as you're able.

The trouble with using medical authority to criminalize animal abuse was that veterinary standards did not define abuse; the courts did. And as the questioning of the witness showed, the community and the animal rights organization held different views of abuse.

Perlstein for the defense then explicitly introduced cultural standards, if medical standards did not apply:

> Q: Let me ask you this, sir. You're familiar that there is something that goes on in our culture today called hunting of animals, am I correct?
> MR. BROOKS: Objection.
> THE COURT: Sustained.
> THE WITNESS: There is something that goes on—
> THE COURT: Sustained. You don't have to answer the question.
> Q: Now, are you aware that in hunting, animals may be wounded?
> MR. BROOKS: Objection, Your Honor.
> THE COURT: Sustained. He's here as a witness on the treatment and care provided at the shoot.
> MR. PERLSTEIN: I know, Your Honor.
> THE COURT: I'm not going to let you get into any hunting questions.
> MR. PERLSTEIN: May I make an offer of proof, Your Honor?
> THE COURT: Sure.
> MR. PERLSTEIN: The only reason I'm asking these questions, Your Honor, is I'm not getting into the philosophy of hunting. It's not my point.

THE COURT: Okay.

MR. PERLSTEIN: My point is to show the bias and prejudice of this witness in that there are other situations—and I want to question this witness. There are other acceptable and legal situations that exist, and I want to question this witness as to his own opinions regarding them. For instance, we know that in hunting, I want to ask questions regarding the retrieval of animals, how they're handled in the field, also what he believes is the duty owed—the reason this is important, Your Honor, and I will do this at sidebar, but I won't do it in front of the witness. . . .

Q: Now, are you aware that in hunting oftentimes an animal is wounded and not killed immediately?

A: Yes, sir.

Q: And animals that are for hunting are rabbits or birds or deer, for instance, am I correct on that?

A: Yes, sir.

Q: Am I also correct that when an animal is hunted, there may be some amount of time before the animal is retrieved?

A: Yes, sir.

Q: That when the animal is hunted, when it's retrieved, it may not be dead?

A: Yes, sir.

Q: Now, Doctor, my question is, in your opinion, if an animal in all other respects lawfully hunted is retrieved and it is not dead, must it be given veterinary care?

MR. BROOKS: Your honor, now we've gone beyond the scope. This is about a pigeon shoot, which is not a hunt. It doesn't fall under the definition of hunting. The characteristics are not the same. We've deviated way—

THE COURT: Overruled. Go ahead.

A: From my understanding, pigeons are not a hunted animal.

Q: We've just heard Mr. Brooks testify. Could you please answer the question?

A: That the—as I understand, the laws regarding hunting allow a hunter to dispatch the animal any way he pleases. The humane considerations are not taken into account for hunters.

The judge again intervened to ascertain the line of questioning:

THE COURT: Are you trying to say to the court, well, he somehow has some bias because he feels that in hunting, animals are killed and they're not given veterinary care, that that somehow demonstrates a bias on his part, is that the point of this?

MR. PERLSTEIN: There's also another very important legal issue here, Your Honor, but Your Honor just absolutely made the witness understand, and that's the question, what status or category do the pigeons fall into.

THE COURT: But that's going to be my decision.

MR. PERLSTEIN: Exactly.

THE COURT: He's an expert in the care and treatment.

MR. PERLSTEIN: That's why it becomes relevant. If the pigeons are within the purview of hunting, if this witness says the humane considerations do not apply.

THE COURT: All right. I think I understand. Go ahead.

It might be concluded that the defense was undermined by this argument because it got away from the principle that the pigeon was property.

Q: Now, animals you realize, do you not, whether it be a dog, a cat, a thoroughbred racehorse, a pigeon, has a value, it's property which is bought and sold, and there's an amount that one pays for it; is that correct?

A: Yes, sir.

Q: There are those who believe that no value can be put on the life of any animal, is that correct? . . . And am I not correct, Dr. Stull, that the owner of an animal has the right, as far as you know and understand, to make a decision to put down or kill an animal, even if it's healthy?

A: I'm not comfortable with the law on that, sir. I don't know the law on that. When someone brings the animal to me, I always try to find a way to save the animal.

Q: But there's no legal proscription if someone wants to have a healthy animal killed?

MR. BROOKS: Objection.

THE COURT: Sustained. That you're aware of. Are you aware of any?

THE WITNESS: Legal proscription?
THE COURT: Yes.
THE WITNESS: That someone can't destroy their own animal?
THE COURT: Right.
THE WITNESS: No, I don't believe there is any legal proscription.

In the end, the court underscored the priority of scientific authority but did not go so far as to prohibit pigeon shooting. The court also sidestepped the conflicting rights claims of the community as owner of the animals and the animal rights organizations as their agents. Although both sides tried to introduce cultural arguments, the court instead focused on the definition of cruelty. The judge ruled that pigeon shoots as a traditional practice were not illegal, but tradition as a basis of knowledge to care for animals was not legitimate. Although the defense argued that serving as trapper boys was a civic service and maturing experience, Chief Justice Flaherty seemed to be convinced that the boys were adversely affected psychologically. He commented, "The trapper boys retrieve the wounded pigeons from the circle area and kill them by a variety of methods. These include tearing the birds' heads from their bodies, throwing or smashing them against objects on the ground, crushing the birds by falling on them, and suffocating the birds by tossing them into a barrel filled with other dead and dying pigeons. All of these methods are contrary to accepted veterinary methods of euthanasia and cause the birds additional pain and suffering. Wounded pigeons also fly into the crowd of spectators, who further injure and kill them. Spectators ostensibly derive great enjoyment from this chance to participate in the slaughter." His choice of "slaughter" rather than "resource" to describe the event denied its cultural significance as a signal of the hunting season to come and a metaphor for control of the land. For Justice Flaherty, "The pigeon shoot is conducted primarily for entertainment and fund-raising purposes. The pigeons that are killed are not used for food." Although the decision was based on a legalistic issue, it was clearly influenced by the worldview of the dominant culture that the event was a sign of a backward rural culture. It points out the conclusion of Renteln that judges often "discount arguments about the importance of the animals to minority groups" (1994, 112).

It appears that the court was even less sympathetic to rural enclaves than to ethnic groups as minorities. It might have been a detriment that the pigeon shoot was associated with a Pennsylvania German ethnicity because of its historical link to a lack of education and irrational beliefs. Although credited with successful farming practices, the community's ability to understand the ecology of wildlife was summarily dismissed. Its customary or folk laws of animal hierarchy, based on a biblical idea of dominion, and its experience in animal husbandry were viewed as contrary to scientific authority. Especially detrimental to the Labor Day Committee's case, in my view, was that in asking for tolerance of the tradition, the committee could not show that the shoot was desirable or necessary. Of folkloristic significance, the committee conveyed the view that animals were property, part of the cultivable land, and not social beings, whereas the Fund for Animals personified animals as experiencing pain and suffering. For the former, animals were externalized tools or objects; for the latter, animals were persons or subjects of life.

A general conclusion is that as a result of the cognitive association between animals and children in a postmodern society and the concern, whether defensible or not, that hunting and the use of guns foster social violence, the traditional sporting practices of folk societies are likely to be banned from public life. To be sure, pigeon shoots are still held in the Hegins Valley, but they are hidden from public view within the confines of private clubs. In a case that many observers view as critical to the "right to culture," the Fund for Animals has called for extension of the Hegins ruling to private clubs. "We should stress," lawyers wrote in an internal memorandum, "that annually conducting an event where, as part of the event, you know that hundreds will be wounded, is itself unlawful conduct." In other words, in stressing its objection to an *annual* praxis, animal rights advocates declare tradition at fault. In this case, at least, the cultural defense has been shot full of holes.

The Shoot as Symbol and Metaphor

Although animal rights organizations frequently make comparisons between pigeon shoots and cockfights or dogfights, labeling them all barbaric "blood sports," some notable differences exist. As "fantasy play," Dundes observes, the cockfight and dogfight are ritualized combat between male animals that extends symbolically to the fighting of men to the death. He places them in a pattern of male combat games by which men have a need to repeatedly demonstrate their virility or manliness (Dundes 1987a, 1997). The trainers are usually men, and the fight's mostly male spectators engage in the sport by gambling, which Dundes also argues is symbolically related to the masturbatory acts of handling excited cocks in the pit or ring. Dundes finds it ironic that in demonstrating virility, male combatants engage in a form of homosexual attack that feminizes the opponent. Supporters of the pigeon shoot do not categorize it as a fight but rather as a trapshooting or target sport. The shooter is human, usually male, armed with a potent shotgun.

Then what does the act of shooting represent? A common Freudian interpretation of the male attraction to shooting is the phallic extension of the gun; thus the feminist outcry against gun ownership is at least in part a symbolic castration of male power (Freud 1995, 339; Luke 1998; Stange 1999). That being the case, shooting the gun is ejaculation, and folk speech for sexual climax such as "shooting a wad" or "shooting white" supports this interpretation. In this perspective, virility is gained from shooting a gun at a live target because of the penetration achieved and the demonstration of potency; in fact, a "shooter" is sometimes cited as derisive street slang for a would-be tough, and "shooting the agate" means pursuing a woman for sexual intercourse (Partridge 1961, 621; Wentworth and Flexner 1967, 470). In relation to hunting, shooting is about the pursuit of prey, and many songs and jokes refer to hunting for sexual conquest (see Randolph 1992, 42–43; "Hunting" 2004). In his analytical survey of traditional Anglo-American erotica, Frank Hoffmann lists several under narratives of seduction, particularly symbolizing female animals as targets: hunter seduces girl by telling her he is hunting bonny black hare and asking if she knows where it is; man seduces girl by showing her how a gun is shot; and man seduces girl by showing her how to play a game called "shoot the cat" (Hoffmann 1973, 260–61; see also Randolph 1992, 42–43). Conversely, an "unloaded gun" in folk narrative is code for impotence (Hoffmann 1973, 275 [X735.9.1]; see also Randolph 1976, 58; Lindahl 2004, 485–86). In American popular culture, Hank Williams Jr. had a major hit on the country charts in 1983 with the song "Gonna Go Huntin' Tonight," with lyrics about pursuing women as "wild game": "Don't fire on the first one, Don't waste your bullets on a little bitty baby, Get yourself a grown woman." Since the gun provides lethal power and connotes male power, the implication is that the pursuit is predatory. The action shows complete dominance, often resulting in the elimination of an opponent, as indicated by the folk speech of feeling "shot down." In cards, "shooting the moon" leaves all the other players with nothing; "shooting the works" means betting everything.

It is important to point out, as an example of semiotic layering, that shooting guns at animals carries significance in terms of the provision of sustenance and independent self-sufficiency. In its imagery of the settler obtaining food and clothing from adventure in the wild, shooting guns invokes the sense of hunting as human dominion over the land. The land, especially in pioneer American mythology, is bountiful and capable of meeting all the settlers' needs; the city, in contrast, is considered contrary to the hunting ethos of being in touch with the natural cycle of life. Russell Nye calls this American belief the myth of superabundance, related to Dundes's reference to the American folk idea of unlimited good (Nye 1966, 277–79; Dundes 1972). The historical gun is therefore a referent to tradition; it is the tool for control of the land, the sign of providing for one's family through independent self-sufficiency. The process of clearing the land with other settlers leads to the formation of social bonds characteristic of community. Dundes adds a crucial point: the belief in abundance breeds optimism for the future as well as social self-confidence; however, in this worldview, change can undermine the perception of the bounty's source (Dundes 1972, 98). This background helps explain why the stakes were so high for Hegins supporters: it was not just the past they were upholding but also the outlook for the future. At Hegins, there was a perception, for example, that governmental regulation and cosmopolitan interference threatened the cultural insulation as well as the natural bounty and socioeconomic independence of the residents. Particularly in the historical context of the region's economic decline, the annual pigeon shoot provided a ritual reaffirmation of a regional worldview based on a pioneer hunting legacy. That connotation of the pigeon shoot is often expressed by hunters, and it is why they do not relate the pigeon shoot to the savage combat of cockfights and dogfights.

The phallic symbolism of the gun is important to consider because another difference between cockfights and pigeon shoots is that in the latter, the animal is symbolically feminine. In folk speech, a *pigeon* refers to a girl or young woman, and *dove* is frequently a term of endearment for a child or an attractive woman (Wentworth and Flexner 1967, 389).

However, *pigeon* also carries the pejorative connotation of a woman being available for sex or being an object of sexual conquest. For example, the rap band Sporty Thievz hit the pop charts in 1999 with the song "No Pigeons," which opened with these lines: "A Pigeon is a girl who be walkin' by, My rimmed up blue brand new sparklin' five, Her feet hurt, so you know she want a ride."[7]

The dove arguably has a more genteel image. In the Song of Solomon from the Hebrew Bible, the romantic male singer seductively croons, "O my dove . . . Let me hear your voice; For your voice is sweet, And your face is comely" (2:14). The symbolic contrast is then made between the dove and the predatory male fox (see Hufford 1987). In the "Ages of Man and Woman," one of the most popular broadsides of the eighteenth and nineteenth centuries in Europe and America, the gendered symbolic contrast between the feminine youth of doves and the predatory fox is extended (see Bringéus 1988; Kammen 1987):

> The ape, the lion, the fox and the ass,
> Resemble the age of a man in the glass.
> Foolish as apes till twenty and one,
> Bolder than lions till forty is gone,
> Cunning as foxes till three score and ten,
> Then, stupid as asses, they're called no more men.
>
> The dove, the hen, the magpie and the crow,
> Resemble the age of a woman also.
> Harmless as doves till twenty and one,
> Hatching like hens till forty is come,
> Chatting like magpies till three score and ten,
> Like crows in the autumn farewell to all men.
> (Stein n.d., 45; Smith 1935, 14)

The characteristic "cooing," gentle disposition, domestication, and smooth facial features of the pigeon are often cited as feminine traits. Like the folk term *chick* to describe a young woman, the pigeon is associated with pronounced breast and tail portions, suggesting sexually desirable parts of the body. The word *pigeon* comes from the Latin *pipire*, meaning "to peep," and refers to the soft cooing of the birds (Martin 1993, 143). Whereas *peep* is often associated with the short, high-pitched sounds of a baby bird (hence the infantilizing admonition, "I don't want to hear a peep out of you!"), cooing, defined by dictionaries as a vocal characteristic of pigeons, is perceived to be an amorous or gentle murmur.

The pigeon's physical and vocal features probably contribute to the frequent representation of the white dove as a sacred symbol. The dove repeatedly appears in the Hebrew Bible as an emblem of peace, purity, tenderness, and affection (Levi 1957, 4). Doves and pigeons also are held sacred in Islam, probably based on the legend that God spoke to Mohammed through a dove he had domesticated (Ingersoll 1923, 135). Recounting the folklore of pigeons, Ernest Ingersoll quotes an Algerian source for doves being called *imams* (leaders of prayer in the mosque) because they "prostrate themselves by inclining their necks in devotions to the Creator" (1923, 136). Many sources claim that Muslims in Asia indeed hold doves and pigeons in much greater esteem than do European Christians. The most frequently cited example of this difference is a 1921 riot in Bombay that erupted after two European boys killed pigeons in the street. According to Ingersoll, "the stock exchange and other general markets were closed, and a wide-spread strike of workmen in India was threatened, as an evidence of the deep feeling aroused by the boys' sacrilegious act" (1923, 136–37).

One explanation for pigeons being targeted for killing, despite their symbolic spiritual connections, is their historical role as a prime sacrificial animal in purification rites. The Hebrew Bible provides details:

> If his offering to the LORD is a burnt offering of birds, he shall choose his offering from turtledoves or pigeons. The priest shall bring it to the altar, pinch off its head, and turn it into smoke on the altar; and its blood shall be drained out against the side of the altar. He shall remove its crop with its feathers, and cast it into the place of the ashes, at the east side of the altar. The priest shall tear it open by its wings, without severing it, and turn it into smoke on the altar, upon the wood that is on the fire. It is a burnt offering, an offering by fire, of pleasing odor to the LORD. (Leviticus 1:14–17)

The sacrifice of a pigeon for purity is especially imperative when a woman gives birth, and it is distinguished from the sacrificial lamb because the killing of the pigeon is redemption for sin (Leviticus 12:6). This association suggests a spiritual cleansing and regeneration after destroying the unclean bird. Wendell Levi connects this sacrifice to veneration of the mother-goddess Astarte, the Sumerian goddess of war who is symbolized by the dove (1957, 3). Killing the dove allowed for a transformation from war to peace and from unclean to clean, and this imagery of the dove as a sign of resurrection or regeneration is still evident in contemporary Easter celebrations.

Ingersoll reports the belief in several cultures that touching a dove would render a person "unclean" for the rest of the day (1923, 129). The pigeon as an omen of death and the sacrifice of pigeons to cure life-threatening fevers are widely reported in British-American tradition (see Opie and Tatem 1989, 308–9). The idea of sacrificing pigeons to cure human ills attracted religious commentary when Anglican bishop Jeremy Taylor in *Rule of Conscience* (1660) pronounced, in favor of the idea of human dominion, "Cruelty to beasts is innocent when it is charity to men; and therefore though we do not eat them, yet we cut living pigeons in halfs and apply them to the feet of men in fevers" (Opie and Tatem 1989, 308). In this belief, men live, and come back from near death, because pigeons die.

This ancient folk root for the symbolism of the pigeon may seem a long way from contemporary pigeon shoots, but it is relevant because of the conflict over modern categorizations of the bird as a symbol of both sacredness and profanity. Indeed, the Bible was a source for both sides in the pigeon shoot controversy at Hegins: the protesters cited the need to protect the sacred dove of peace, whereas the supporters cited the opening passages of Genesis dictating that humans rule, master, or have dominion over—depending on the translation—the "birds of the sky, and all the living things that creep on earth" (Genesis 1:28). The dominion idea was also invoked in the first major court case on whether pigeon shoots violated animal cruelty statutes, *Commonwealth v. A. N. Lewis*, in 1891. In maintaining the legality of pigeon shoots, Chief Justice Paxson of the Pennsylvania Supreme Court declared, "Is the bird in the cage any better, or has it any higher rights, than the bird in the woods? *Both were placed here by the Almighty, for the use of man*" (140 Pa. 261, 21 A. 396, February 23, 1891; emphasis added). Animal rights activists often argued that animals, defined biblically as "living souls," deserved protection and kindness from humans; dominion could be reinterpreted as a call to love animals and show them mercy or even to promote vegetarianism (Fuchs 2003; Linzey 2003; Phelps 2002; Scully 2002). Countering this view is the frequent anthropocentric reference to Genesis 9:1–3: "God blessed Noah and his sons, and said to them, 'Be fertile and increase, and fill the earth. The fear and the dread of you shall be upon all the beasts of the earth, and *upon every bird of the air*, upon everything that creeps on the ground and all the fish of the sea; into your hand they are delivered. Every moving thing [creature] that lives shall be food for you; and as I gave you the green plants, I give you everything'" (emphasis added).[8] With this rhetorical conflict in mind, some animal rights activists went to church services in Hegins to challenge residents' religious views about dominion. Indeed, an influential animal rights tract written by Norm Phelps called *The Dominion of Love: Animal Rights According to the Bible* (2002) has emblazoned on the dedication page, "For the pigeons who died at Hegins."

Referring to the biblical idea of the provision of animals for food, John Updike describes a mealtime discussion in a coming-of-age story set in central Pennsylvania. After "Granmom" brings a "forkful of food to her mouth," the boy's father comments, "Only human indi-vidu-als have souls . . . Because the Bible tells us so," in answer to the boy's mother's notion that "the land has a *soul*" (Updike 1962, 122). The biblical connection comes up again as the boy piles dead pigeons in the intriguing concluding line of the story: "As he fitted the last two, still pliant, on the top, and stood up, crusty coverings were lifted from him, and with a feminine, slipping sensation along his nerves that seemed to give the air hands, he was robed in this certainty: the God who had lavished such craft upon these worthless birds would not destroy His whole Creation by refusing to let David live forever" (Updike 1962, 149–50).

An alternative view—one more sympathetic to animal rights—of pigeon shoots as a male coming-of-age ritual is also a strong theme of Jerry Spinelli's *Wringer* (1997), which was named a Newbery Honor Book and won other awards in 1998. Based on the Hegins pigeon shoot (called Waymer in the book), the "wringer" in the title refers to the trapper boys who wring the necks of injured pigeons. In the story, one boy develops an emotional attachment to a pigeon that he personalizes by calling him "Nipper." He saves the bird from being shot, "cradling his pigeon in both hands," and the narrator recounts that the boy "felt a peace, a lightness that he had never known before, as if restraining straps had snapped, setting him free to float upward" (Spinelli 1997, 228). In contrast is the unsympathetic character of Beans, who "hoisted the bird above his head and gave a long, ripping screech of triumph." Then he "shook the bird in the shooter's face" and yelled, "'It's yours! It came back! Kill! Kill.'" The narrator develops the reader's sympathy for the helpless bird, and pity for the boy, with the line, "He slammed the bird to the ground and ran for cover" (Spinelli 1997, 226–27).

The symbolic behavior of creeping or crawling in Genesis is significant because of the idea that "lowly" creatures connected to the ground are unclean. The characteristic "prostration" of the pigeon on the ground, which is a source of sacredness in Islam, is a source of profanity in Christianity. The common description of the pigeon as a "rat with wings" is symbolically important, in fact, because of the profane connection of pigs and mice (Isaiah 66:17). Animal rights activist Ingrid Newkirk understood this cognitive category when she made her oft-quoted statement, "a rat is a pig is a dog is a boy," and the comparison came up repeatedly in response to pigeon shoot supporters' assertions that a pigeon is a "flying rat" (McCabe 1986, 115). In fact, the addition of the dog is important because of the symbolic replacement of hunting dogs in the pigeon shoot with trapper boys; besides suggesting an equality of species, the analogy can also signify that violence to rats is a violation of children. With her provocative analogy, Newkirk tried to subvert the traditional moral distinction between "lowly" or dirty animals and clean humans by pointing out their emotional equation. After she made the statement to a reporter, she explained, "They are all mammals. They all feel pain" (McCabe 1986, 115). Alan Dundes, in his study of Sabbath taboos, interprets the predominant association of pigs and mice in the profane sphere as a shared proclivity for eating feces (2002b, 117). The taboo is therefore based on the idea that eating feces "is considered the ultimate despicable, disgusting act, which is why God reserves it as a punishment for those who disrespect him" (Dundes 2002b, 117).

Dundes also could have cited legends of the hoopoe bird, which, like the pigeon, is associated with stupidity in European tradition and is distinguished by nesting in a hole. Such legends bear out God's disfavor of eating feces and its equivalence with female avarice. Folklorist Moses Gaster recorded one legend explaining why the bird feeds on droppings: Representing divine dominion, God gave all creatures the food he thought best for them. When the hoopoe's turn came, God offered millet seed, but the bird was not satisfied. "She," as the bird is referred to, did not think it was good enough for her. God offered alternatives, but still the hoopoe was not satisfied. According to Gaster's version, "So God got angry, and said, 'Thou impudent and greedy thing, I have given thee the best food that is in this world, and in which even man rejoices and is satisfied, but as this is not good enough for thee, thou shalt find thy food henceforth in the droppings of other animals.'" Making the leap from food to domicile, Gaster relates that "the same happened when God arranged the dwelling-places of birds, where they should build their nests. He had at first given the hoopoe sweet-smelling bushes and flowering trees to build her nest in. But she wanted something better, and she was punished in the same way as with the food. She now makes her nest in places which are anything but clean and sweet-smelling" (Gaster 1915, 160).

Animal rights activists believe that humans are at fault for despoiling the pigeons' environment. At Hegins they complained vociferously that the pigeons were kept in cages filled with their own feces. Shoot supporters pointed out that pigeons are pests that need to be eliminated because they pollute barns and people with their droppings. Killing the pigeons as one would kill mice or rats offers sacred human redemption, since the birds are associated with an unclean state. Killing them ritually establishes the "symbolism of the centre" by emphasizing sacrificial elimination of all that is impure, thus offering spiritual purity. In the Bible, pigeons are associated with sin, and their blood provides atonement (Leviticus 5:7), especially for the "unclean" state of menstruation (Leviticus 12:1–7).

Several contemporary examples of folklore can be cited to show pigeons' association with feces and vermin, especially among male groups. Many jokes comment on the abundance of feces produced by pigeons. Here is one I collected in 2004:

> It seems there were these two statues and they were a couple hundred years old. One day, a fairy flew over them and tapped their heads with her wand. "You have 24 hours to do *whatever you want*," she said to the statues. Fast-forward 23 hours, 57 minutes later. . . . The male statue says to the female statue,

"Why don't we do it again?" The female statue says, "We don't
have enough time!" The male statue says, "Sure we do! Just *one
more time*, please?" Whereupon the female statue says, "Oh, all
right! But this time *you* hold the pigeon and *I'll* crap on it!"

On this same theme, also connecting pigeons with urban filth and a defiling of status and wealth, is this joke: What's the difference between a
bankrupt lawyer [or stockbroker] and a pigeon? A pigeon can still leave
a deposit on a Mercedes [or BMW].

Besides being resented for their droppings on public places and
monuments, pigeons are considered unclean because they scavenge for
food in garbage and on the ground. One legend has pigeons and spar-
rows eating crumbs off the street as a punishment from Christ. According to some versions of the story, at the time of crucifixion the birds
flew around the cross, mocking Christ. He cursed them and said, "May
you live only on the crumbs which you will pick up on the roadside, and
henceforth, becoming smaller, you will be snared by little boys and tor-
mented by them, and the passersby shall hit at you with whips, and kill
you" (Gaster 1915, 195). In addition, the folk idea circulates that the
birds are expendable because they carry diseases, look ordinary (dull
gray feathers), are stupid (e.g., being "birdbrained," or Aesop's fable
of the thirsty pigeon who flies into a picture of a goblet of water), are
found in abundant numbers because of their reproductive prowess, and
are indiscernible from one another, thus preventing sympathy for their
individuality (see Lawrence 1997, 97–98, Johnston and Janiga 1995,
257–80; Schwartz 1989, 34; Hodge 1985).

Like the cocks that Dundes connects to the shady (or masturbatory) practice of gambling, so too are pigeons. Significant is the idea
of gambling as a kind of ruse or wile, casting an image of falseness or
incredulity on the participants' objects, thus making them expendable.
Contemporary pigeon shoots held at rod and gun clubs are gambling
activities, often between two sides. The association with gambling is
ancient in origin, as indicated by the prohibition of "those who race
pigeons" from being witnesses or judges (Babylonian Talmud Tractate
Sanhedrin 3:3). They are disqualified because they are gamblers and
are therefore implicated as liars or thieves (Levi 1957, 4). This tradition
may be the source of modern folk speech equating a "pigeoner" with
a gambler or a swindler (Wentworth and Flexner 1967, 389; Partridge

1961, 511–12). "Pigeon numbers" are false numbers used by managers of illegal lottery games called "policy" (Partridge 1961, 512). Gambling continues in contemporary urban folklife in the form of pigeon flying fights, which are structurally more consistent with ritual male combat than pigeon shoots are; the fights are referred to in many Brooklyn neighborhoods as *la guerra*, or "the war" (Kligerman 1978; Schwartz 1989). Flyers use a special breed of domesticated pigeon and pejoratively refer to common street pigeons as "rats," thus marking them as socially undesirable and unclean (Schwartz 1989, 34). Police informers are also called "pigeons" (or "stool pigeons") and "rats," at least by criminals (Partridge 1961, 692).

One additional piece of evidence for the unclean or masturbatory nature of gambling at pigeon shoots is the campaign by some supporters of the shoots to eliminate gambling from rod and gun clubs in the late nineteenth century. Ed Sandys, for example, wrote a long editorial in *Outing* magazine complaining that the "stimulus" of the heavy wager was "unsportsmanlike" and had "no place in the amusement of gentlemen," even though he was in favor of live bird shooting (1894, 80). He complained that gambling promotes the kind of man who goes to the club "for the money he can rake out of their pockets." Believing that gambling was threatening to other "manly" members of the club, he advocated the protection of members from "fleecing," raising the image of sheep being stripped naked of their wool covering. He called on sportsmen to shoot for the "love of shooting" rather than selfish gain and ignoble enjoyment (Sandys 1894, 80).

Probably because of their symbolically unclean status, pigeons are also associated with victims and dupes. In American folk speech, a pigeon is an unsuspecting target of criminal violence or fleecing (Partridge 1961, 511; Wentworth and Flexner 1967, 389). From the shooters' viewpoint, this association with weakness further reduced the possibility of sympathy for the birds, but the animal rights protesters used this image as evidence of the birds' need for protection, just as social movements in the post–civil rights era argued for legal assistance and social sympathy for "victimized" groups. Connecting child and spousal abuse with the plight of the pigeons, animal rights protesters declared the birds' "innocence" in contrast to the socially predatory men and set up first-aid stations to care for injured birds that managed to escape the killing fields. These stations also reinforced the view of the birds as moral patients. Protesters made the symbolic equivalence of birds and children visible by parading youths holding large, bloody targets in front of their bodies.

Animal rights advocates vocally complained that the purpose and consequence of the pigeon shoot were violence, for it lacked any pragmatic rationale such as the provision of food. The protesters represented themselves as modern and progressive and therefore not bound to constraining and irrational, if not immoral, tradition. They advocated an end to culturally ingrained violence and suggested that an end to animal abuse would result in an end to war; to support this view, animal rights organizations distributed black armbands with an image of a white dove holding an olive branch in its beak below a message of "GIVE PEACE A CHANCE."

Proponents of the shoot labeled the protesters spoiled or wacky urbanites and feminists, or even homosexuals, who should be advocating for more important issues such as curbing abortion and drugs or at least paying attention to their own problems in the cities. In short, supporters wanted to be left alone to decide their own cultural character, and they retaliated against what they perceived to be the cosmopolitan attack by outsiders intent on subverting the basis of their heritage. Resenting the hoots of "country bumpkins," "barbarians," and "murderers," many supporters in the showdowns of the early 1990s countered by calling the protesters "faggots," "bunny huggers," and "druggies"—thereby emphasizing the depravity, rather than the progressivism, of the protesters. Whereas protesters carried placards pointing out the brutality and horror of the shoot and the "shame" and backwardness of Hegins, supporters expressed the themes of freedom and dominion with sayings on T-shirts such as "LET FEATHERS FLY AND FREEDOM RING," "SHOOT PIGEONS, NOT DRUGS," "IF IT FLIES, IT DIES," and "KILL AT WILL." Humor at the expense of the protesters emerged, too, in phrases such as "SAVE A PIGEON, SHOOT A PROTESTER" and "WE RECYCLE" (with an image of dead pigeons). For many supporters, coming to the shoot was like coming to battle, for it was common to see men wearing military camouflage clothing. The prevailing motto for supporters, emblazoned on shirts and hats every year of the protest, was "THE TRADITION CONTINUES."

What about the role and symbol of the shooters? The fact is that most shooters were not from the community or even from the state. But that did not matter to the residents of Hegins, who conceived of the shoot as a community event. For the supporters, the shooter embodied the pioneer hunter, because pigeon shooting was considered an antiquated kind of pursuit. The shooter eliminated the unclean from the land and thereby consecrated it. The result was socially regenerative. Several editorials set up the defense of the pigeon shoot as a last stand for hunting, interpreted as the primal impulse of humans in touch with nature, which would fall at the hands of the animal rights protesters (Slinsky 1999; Angst 1999). I concluded from my conversations and observations at the shoot that supporters were not so much defending the shoot as they were defending their agrarian tradition based on the idea of human dominion over animals and land (Berry 2003; Telleen 2003). Residents near the park resented the mess of dead birds in their yards every Labor Day, but the shoot gained importance as a symbol of the community's longing for ascendancy, an annual ritual of regenerating its past glory in the face of modernization. There were times in the shoot's history when its effectiveness as a community ritual came into question. I heard many people remark that by the 1980s, the pigeon shoot was not so appealing as a homecoming celebration, but when protesters from the cities came, they felt obliged to defend the shoot as a metaphor for "traditional" communities' self-determination not to share in cosmopolitan culture.

Hunting and gun ownership were popular in the area, and residents were aware that both were threatened by these urban moralists who were ignorant of agrarianism. The irony is that the original protests of the event were instigated by a resident of the region, but the supporters of the shoot viewed "outside" organizations such as PETA and the Fund for Animals as the enemy. To be sure, shooting pigeons and hunting are substantially different activities; on the surface, pigeon shoots do not involve the pursuit of animals in the wild, and some detractors claim that the hunter's ethic of the "fair fight" is lacking (Eveland 1992). Nevertheless, the shoot simulates the pursuit of prey and refers to a mythology of the virgin land when birds were abundant and untamed. The shoot hones the skills of the hunter because it involves taking aim at an unpredictable target, and the shoot is a prelude to the major fowl and deer hunting seasons in the fall. The choice of pigeons allows the illusion of abundant wildlife and the imminent success of the hunter in the upcoming seasons. Arguably, it is not a fair or a difficult fight, but as the warm-up for the fall hunting seasons, it is not supposed to be. In folk speech, there is a symbolic equivalence of the "pigeon mark" and the "easy mark."

Especially significant in the rhetoric describing the shoot and hunting is a reference to family tradition. In a mass society where popular novelty is privileged and family values are crumbling, many residents told me, hunting is a heritage associated with family activities and local knowledge passed from one generation to another. The shoot built on this association by promoting itself as a "family event" and a "homecoming," with children frolicking in the playground in the park where the shoot was held. Labor Day weekend, in fact, was a common time to hold family reunions in the region. Another family relationship involved the local trapper boys. Metaphorically, they took the role of retriever dogs, subordinate companions to the shooters who would evolve from energetic animals to steady, mature men. The relationship was hierarchical, with men commanding the boys (dogs), who in turn had dominion over the birds as a metaphor for nature. As an intermediary between the animal and human worlds, the boys (dogs) could touch the unclean animal in the metaphorical field of nature and deliver it back to the human world for consumption.

The incorporation of children at the shoot infuriated animal rights activists all the more because it symbolized the linkage of animal destruction with cultural celebration and violence with the upbringing of children. Supporters of the shoot answered by extolling the virtues of the shoot as part of American tradition and therefore a contribution to the threatened sense of American heritage and family based on its agrarian founding. It was not just that the shoot had been celebrated annually for sixty years; the shoot represented a legendary golden age when the valley's activities were more central to American mainstream culture. Ironically, the stability of tradition also implied the freedom to practice a community rite that ran counter to mass cultural values. Hence, it was common for shoot supporters' rhetoric of tradition to accompany expressions of reverence for freedom and flag. In retaliation, using a similar discourse of heritage, animal rights protesters compared the event to the violent blood sports of cockfights and dogfights, which were widely illegal despite their hold on tradition. Protesters complained of the exposure to guns and the "desensitization" to abuse, whereas supporters worried about the challenge to their "right to bear arms" (Fund 1997). Tradition needed to be broken, the protesters exclaimed, to prevent children from inheriting the values engendered by the event and assuming that they were normative. "Tradition" in this usage encapsulated a web of associations, including small-town agrarianism, pioneer mythology, and patriarchy. Answering the claim that the children of Hegins were more likely to be violent as a result of exposure to the shoot, the Labor Day Committee produced statistics showing a low rate of violent crime. Supporters linked the tradition to America's pioneer heritage of rural life and hunting, the culturally appropriate building of community across generations, support for charitable causes, and the wholesome ethic of competition resulting in excellence.

For all to see, the gun is an extension of the shooter, and protest-

A supporter wearing a "SAVE A PIGEON, SHOOT A PROTESTER" T-shirt confronts a protester wearing a "SAVE THE WHALES" T-shirt. Hegins pigeon shoot, 1990. (Photo by Simon Bronner)

This woman's sign draws attention to shooters' guns as compensation for phallic insecurity. Hegins pigeon shoot, Labor Day, 1991. (Photo by Simon Bronner)

ers drew out the phallic symbolism of vulturine, heat-packing men in their placards. The large-barreled shotgun was especially imposing in the image of the pigeon shooter. Many signs evident at the 1991 shoot ridiculed the phallic display of men with guns: "HUNTERS HAVE SMALL ONES," "ALL YOU TOMS, HARRYS, AND DICKS, DOESN'T IT PRICK YOUR CON-

Pigeon shoot veteran demonstrates how to kill an injured bird by severing its neck. (Photo by Simon Bronner)

SCIENCE TO USE YOUR GUN IN SUCH AN UNMANLY WAY?" and "BIG MACHO BIRD KILLER." In 1992, PETA ran an advertisement blaring, "Women: Join in Solidarity to Expose Patriarchal Violence." It included a photo of a hulky "typical pigeon shoot supporter" wearing an Adolf Hitler shirt, sporting a rough beard, and adorned with a hunting cap and military-style glasses. Another photo showed armed policemen leading away an arrested woman. It also featured a quotation from *Ms.* magazine calling pigeon shoots "one of the most bizarre forms of the violent male bonding ritual called sport hunting." Its ultimate appeal was to "help stop the violence against women and animals." The implication was that the shoot was a metaphor for a rapacious patriarchal society responsible for violence and social injustice.

Without directly saying so—probably because it was too disturbing to the female protesters—the violence and injustice implied by the shooter attacking the feminine pigeon constituted rape. In this view, the pellets from the phallic gun penetrated the unsuspecting and unwilling bird, causing the loss of feathers and blood. Several protesters told me about horrifying incidents involving male supporters taunting them with dead birds, as if they would meet a similar fate at the hands of the men. Young men declared the bird to be a pernicious, profane "rat" with wings, a comparison aimed at women, who are cast as being afraid of vermin. Some even made jokes about "flipping the bird" at the protesters, indicating the aggressive phallic gesture of extending the middle finger and the masculinization of the pigeons. The discarding of the birds by means of wringing their necks—symbolic strangulation—after the shoots thus became especially disturbing as a violation against women (Radner and Lanser 1987, 412–13). The role of the trapper boys in unfeelingly "bagging" the feminine birds and following the model of the potent, predatory shooter aroused heated emotions in the protesters, many of whom had experience in domestic abuse counseling.

Whereas shoot supporters found the idea of a first-aid station for birds absurd, tearful protesters brought injured birds that had escaped the male onslaught to the station for emergency treatment. Many brought feathers into the station as if they were torn clothing. One can discern the metaphor of the abused woman in the following reminiscence from a protester of the 1996 pigeon shoot at Hegins:

> Looking into the eyes of a bird I rescued after some men had played hacky-sack with her under a tree, and knowing, although the vets (hoping to save me some agony) told me otherwise, that *she* would die. Not of any wing damage or shock, but from internal bleeding after receiving one kick too many. And hoping that, if only for a brief moment, *she* felt the utter love and respect I had for *her* when I held *her* in my hands as *she* was dying. I hope *she* felt those feelings emanating from the vets, the technicians, the rescuers, and all the activists surrounding *her*. (Morris 1996; emphasis added)

As patient, the bird became anthropomorphized and individualized. Many women empathized with the two-legged lives frantically taking flight to escape rapacious men shooting phallic guns. The analogy of pigeons to sexual objects was apparent on full-page advertisements placed in newspapers by the Humane Society of the United States (2007), which bannered the statement, "Shooting pigeons and calling yourself a sportsman is like hiring an escort service and calling yourself a ladies' man." Complaining that birds "suffer slow, anguished deaths," the text stated that the shoots are a "shameful," "cruel," "seedy spectacle."

There is a mythological basis for the relation of hunting to rape in the figure of Orion, a giant hunter in Greek mythology. In many narratives, he rapes Merope, and the angry king exacts revenge by symbolically castrating Orion by blinding him. In some myths, he also tries to rape the Hyperborean maiden Opis. In stories of Orion's death, his end comes after he tries to rape Artemis, and she sends a lethal scorpion to sting him. In another version of feminine revenge against the predatory hunter, the scorpion is sent by the goddess Gaia (earth) because Orion has the hubris to declare that he can shoot all animals (March 2001, 570–72).

For the shooter, easy sexual conquest is implicit in the shooting of the unsuspecting or passive birds. It is a prelude to other hunting seasons requiring virility because of the risk and danger involved. In particular, the killing of pigeons, meant to be efficient, increases manly self-confidence and validates male aggression for the later contest against a tougher, stronger, more elusive opponent—the male buck. Buck season after Thanksgiving is usually considered *the* hunting season; deer are certainly the most popular hunting prey in Pennsylvania. At a deer camp I attended, one member responded to sarcastic comments about his lack of success in "bagging a buck" with the declaration, "I don't have to prove my manhood by getting a buck every year." It was a reminder of the virility gained by triumphing in ritual male combat with the large, horny buck. Although members of the camp hunt various animals, the heads mounted as trophies on the wall are of horned bucks. The connection to symbolic castration is evident in photographs of hunters with their fallen prey, where they are often shown holding the cut heads in their groin areas (Bronner 2004, 38).

Some hunters find it offensive to shoot the feminine does, much as some sportsmen consider the rapacious attack on pigeons to be somehow unsportsmanlike or unmanly. The "fair game" that provides the challenge of combat is in metaphorically masculine animals, including bears and bucks. The folk saying "shooting at a pigeon and killing a crow" to indicate a deliberate miss or bringing someone lofty down to size through a strategic assault on an underling can be explained as using the easy feminine "mark" to attack a masculine predator (Partridge 1970, 628). The phrase sets up a symbolic shift from the light, gentle pigeon to the evil, dark crow, from the passive to the aggressive, from the woman to the man. In contrast to the humble cooing of the pigeon, crowing is associated with the boastful cock. One can thus understand both the cognitive categorization of pigeon shoots with cockfights as sexual conquest and the distancing of pigeon shoots from cockfights because of their lack of a male "fight."

The structure of the match shoot suggests more of a combat metaphor between male opponents than does the straight shoot, and the typical accompaniment of gambling adds to the "action" of the match shoot, connoting emotional or sexual excitement from risk taking. From a social structural perspective, the combat may suggest fatalism about one's status and the future, since the goal of making money, and producing thrills, implies that advancement needs the intervention of luck or chance for a context in which wealth or "good" is limited (see Dundes 1972; Lears 2003). In the system of the match shoot, if one team advances, the other must retreat. One does not get the impression given by Cooper in *The Pioneers* that the supply of value as well as nature is endless. The importation of pigeons simulates a world in which the products of nature are unlimited, but the wealth at risk on them is limited, especially in the agrarian and mining environment of the Hegins Valley. Arguably, the fantasy of the match shoot compensates for a loss of confidence in the future engendered by economic decline and the attendant loss of sociocultural status. One difficulty with this social structural interpretation is that it does not account for the historical role of gambling in the valley's prosperous heyday, unless one contends that the agrarian-mining worldview was still one of a "limited good" even when the outlook for the future was optimistic.

Spectators are more involved, more engaged at match shoots, and that involvement is more aggressive and risky than at straight shoots. One indication of the ritual combat in match shoots is the special breeding trappers engaged in to produce "tougher" birds. John Bergalis said, "We crossbred the birds until we came up with a breed that was fast and scary, had big wings and small bodies and was built for speed and stamina. Let me tell ya, they were the greatest pigeons that ever took flight!" (Canfield 1992, 27). Reexamining the structure of the Labor Day weekend at Hegins in light of this evidence, one may observe that the private club "warm-up," meant as a manly activity and perhaps masturbatory in its symbolism, prepares shooters to present themselves to their families, when their sense of conquest may be more muted. In structuring the ethos of "every man for himself" in the event, organizers suggest a survivalist image that invokes a pioneer heritage of making a "clearing." The regenerative quality of eradicating unclean pests in the public shoot is heightened because it is done in front of, and on behalf of, the community. The justification of using the proceeds to expand the park—a clean, cleared, green, wholesome environment for children—is the regenerative result. Other versions of regeneration are possible; a common one at private shoots is the awarding of geese and turkeys to the winners of pigeon shoots, thus replacing the despised shot bird with a delectable symbol of human triumph and bounty. The regenerative shoot can be conceived as a purificatory transformation, using the pigeon as an offering for turning war to peace, profane to sacred, unclean to clean, and old to new.

At the 1991 Hegins pigeon shoot, animal rights activists run into the park with a sign reading "Only Perverts Enjoy Killing." In planned "direct actions," other groups of protesters ran out onto the field to rescue birds from traps as contestants prepared to shoot. More than 100 protesters were arrested. (Photo by Simon Bronner)

This girl's protest sign—a target with streaks representing dripping blood—draws attention to the connection between shooting pigeons and abusing feminized children. The woman next to her is wearing a black armband with dove of peace design and the words "GIVE PEACE A CHANCE" above it. Hegins pigeon shoot, Labor Day, 1991. (Photo by Simon Bronner)

Because pigeons in the Hegins region were treated respectfully by trappers in match shoots as local agents for a "side," ethnographers were puzzled by the virulent rhetoric of unclean profanity in references to vermin, feces, and disease at straight shoots. Elizabeth Atwood Lawrence observed that, "like any disempowered group, the pigeons have to be segregated and perceived as perpetrators of evil to justify their victimization" (1997, 98). Paradoxically, their evil was simultaneously rural and urban. As rural referent to tradition, they invoked the pioneer past, when the skies darkened with the natural bounty of passenger pigeons. As urban representative, they showed the pathetic result of being out of touch with the land, their existence marked by scavenging in garbage and producing feces. They were a nuisance to rural farmers, defiling the fertile land, and they were urban filth associated with the depravity of cities and modernism. Yet as protests mounted during the 1990s, the contestation influenced a symbolic emphasis on the birds as the urban and modern "other." Anthropologist S. Hoon Song rationally asked how the flying pests could be eliminated if the shoot resulted in a significant number of common pigeons being released back into the region. His answer: the area needed pests because its identity was marginalized in modern society. It therefore imported the pigeons for a ritual ceremony to declare an urban outsider, so that the homogeneous insider could be maintained under threats of social change. Song argued that to maintain the community's self-sufficiency, "the expulsion of the pigeons must be repeated again and again in order to establish the boundary of the interior"(Song 2000b, 225). He missed the symbolic shift, however, from the bird as a passive, feminized target to a phallic, masculinized pest; supporters of the shoot in fact identified with the pigeons as an extension of themselves in a way that was shocking to the protesters. At one confrontation I witnessed, a group of supporters spread a pigeon's wings in front of protesters to scare them. Joking comments were made that the female protesters' fright owed to the resemblance of the spread wings and the bird's beak to male genitalia; phallic metaphors uttered included "pecker," "big bird," "chicken neck," and "piece of meat."

Once the shoot became a hotly contested tradition, supporters began projecting the violence toward the animals at human targets—the protesters. This view is supported by the phrase "SAVE A PIGEON, SHOOT A PROTESTER" emblazoned on T-shirts worn by many supporters. Yet this view assumes that the shooting had only one symbolic displacement from the human target. It does not fully account for the layering of symbols for hunting, masculinity, virgin land, and family in the purificatory process of the shoot. The set of historical conditions as well as ethnographic circumstances particular to the Hegins shoot helps explain why shooting clay targets just would not do. The symbolic mythologizing of the bird as a narrative of clearing and provision offers insight into how the shoot embodied both sacred and profane functions. Even if the residents did not shoot pigeons, they symbolized the shoot as their experience; the shoot took on attributes of Eliade's "centre."

Tradition in the Crossfire

In light of the shoot's identity as a deep cultural text and its "symbolism of the centre" for the community, one may justifiably ask whether the end of the shoot changed anything in Hegins. Private match shoots continue, although the Fund for Animals is pursuing litigation to extend the ruling against the Hegins shoot to private shoots as well. For now, the sound of shotguns is still very much in the air on Labor Day weekends. But as Robert Tobash, chair of the Labor Day Committee, told me, the work of maintaining and distinguishing the community has been undermined. He believes that the hamlet needs a community festival to give it a sense of itself as well as to continue the redemptive function of expanding the park for children. The committee replaced the shoot with a crafts fair, hailing a family theme, but it was not as well attended or as profitable. The substituted symbolism of preindustrial crafts is consistent with the perspective that the public festival builds on a legacy of the pioneer past enriching the present. Yet it was not sufficiently regenerative, perhaps because it was too peaceful; no sin offering or aggressive male display was apparent. Nor was it clear how the event offered a prologue to the opening of autumn activity and the associated harvest and hunt. If anything, it reinforced the image of domestication imposed by cosmopolitan modernism on rural places and their people. Tobash regularly receives requests to revive the shoot in defiance of the courts, but he reluctantly submits to the legal agreement. Meanwhile, the firemen's carnival has difficulty mustering volunteer help, and he complains that young people are not as involved as they once were with the life of the community. To underscore the point, he mentions that church suppers—distinguished by Pennsylvania German delicacies such as stuffed pig's stomach (colloquially called "Dutch goose") and dandelion salad, drawing on the bounty of the land—have been canceled despite their popularity because of a lack of sufficient volunteer help from the aging community. In 2003, the Coleman family erected a monument in the park honoring the memory of the shoot, and the unveiling ceremony took place at a Coleman family reunion held there. The shoot was mourned as if it were a heroic person; inspired by a kind of origin legend, the monument embodied a communal myth.

The end of the shoot also signaled the beginning of a revitalized movement to preserve hunting throughout the state. In the wake of the shoot's cancellation, efforts redoubled to protect hunting and redefine it as a heritage and a right. In response to the push for "animal rights," central Pennsylvania legislators introduced bill 1512 to ensure "hunters' rights." The bill would amend the state constitution to guarantee the "right of the people to hunt and fish." In these efforts, the animal rights movement is depicted as the barbarian at the gate threatening the very core of society. Many residents fear that its goals are not just to end the killing of animals but also to erode a life of tradition and force compliance with some imagined cosmopolitan authority. In serving as the "other" from the distant "outside," animal rights organizations inspire communities such as Hegins to define their values by their attitudes toward animals and to promote hunting as a tradition passed down through families—in particular, a manly tradition emphasizing protection and dominion passed from father to son. They are also more self-conscious about the time-tested customs they promote as significant to their "tradition," and they emphasize heritage as the bedrock of survival in a new age of cultural uncertainty.

Yet the tradition is changing in response to the erosion of hunting lands and hunter numbers. Groups such as Becoming an Outdoors-Woman (BOW) actively encourage women to participate in hunting and shooting, and other organizations have lobbied to lower the minimum age for hunting to attract more young people to the sport (Eshelman 2007; Schneck 2007). To counter these moves, animal rights groups are creating educational programs for children, because the young are held responsible for transmitting society's values in the form of cultural practices. One can understand, then, the attention since the late twentieth century by both protesters and supporters to the role of children at shoots; because they are the most impressionable, they are also the most culturally potent. In Pennsylvania, sportsmen's groups have been successful in introducing several special "youth hunts" and hunting education programs for youths and women. No longer can the continuation of shooting and hunting as a family tradition between fathers and sons be taken for granted; transmission of "hunting heritage" has become organized and broadened. The public rationalization for hunting is also changing, highlighting environmental awareness and the maintenance of heritage while downplaying the primal instinct of killing in the wild (see Swan 1995). Nevertheless, social surveys of hunters frequently reveal a feeling for tradition and a desire to be close to nature—two antimodern sentiments—as primary motivations to continue hunting (Duda 1997; Dizard 2003; National Wild Turkey Federation 2003). As my argument here indicates, I also believe that a historical crisis of masculinity is attracting many to the virile meanings of hunting and shooting out of fear of domestication and modernization (Bronner 2004, 2005b).

The animal rights movement has also changed as a result of the Hegins campaign. It is less reliant on national direct action and frequently looks to litigation and legislation rather than civil disobedience (Dillard 2002; Wicklund 1998). The Hegins campaign, animal rights leaders claim, attracted many more adherents to the cause, and many of these new followers are men. This has influenced a broader social agenda, although advocacy for animals as a way to curb human violence is still prevalent. The Fund for Animals has reached out to hunters' groups to improve their image by calling for hunting ethics that would eliminate live pigeon shoots, prairie dog shoots, coyote killing contests, foxhunting, and pheasant tower shoots (Prescott 1995). Especially intense is the campaign against manly blood sports such as dogfights and cockfights. Animal rights groups were involved in a ban on cockfighting passed by Oklahoma voters in 2002, leaving only two states where cockfighting was still legal. In 2005, however, Oklahoma legislators proposed revising the ban to allow cockfighting without knives or gaffs (the cocks could be fitted with muffs).[9] Sensitive to being portrayed as antitradition and anti–American heritage, the Fund for Animals has been particularly careful to work with grassroots organizations that propose new traditions, including festivals and even shooting contests that eschew features of animal cruelty (Markarian 1997, 34).

Geertz claims that events such as the cockfight suggest that status relationships are matters of life and death; for the world of the shoot, more than social structure is at stake. In each relationship is a tension, or even a paradox, that calls for ritualized resolution between sacred and profane, redemption and sin, nature and humanity, and peace and war. In the layered metaphorical tradition of shoots and related customs of dominion, there are relationships between the traditionalized inside, conceptualized as community, and the modern, changing outside or other, often conceived as mass culture or cosmopolitan society.

In fact, much of the contestation was about the source of cultural production—from "inside" families and communities, or from "outside"
urban centers and governmental policies. The protesters sought to
subvert the "symbolism of the centre" and show it as marginal, whereas
supporters argued that animal rights was the radical "fringe" and had to
articulate symbolic meanings of the center to counter animal rights advocates' phallocentric readings of rapacious violence. Both arguments
for centeredness claimed to represent the heart and soul of America in
Hegins.

The contestation over pigeon shoots, widely used in the media to
evoke testimony in the court of public opinion, led to the examination
of other dramas that had been taken for granted—the dichotomies of
past and present, masculine and feminine, adult and child. Basic to the
tension of the tradition of the shoot in a modern age of sensitivity was
the use of violence and the elimination of the unclean to regenerate, or
redeem, the past. Killing the dirty bird appeared to consecrate the land
and bless human dominion over its wildlife, reminding one of abundance to be gained or abundance once enjoyed. Ritualizing a sacrificial
tradition promised a better day, and it purified the path for the fall
harvest of crops and animals. Challenging the regenerative property of
killing unclean pigeons with reminders of their sacred feminine symbolism associated with peace, animal rights protesters created a contest
frame of their own for the dominance of locally generated values. Much
of the battle was over how to interpret the meaning of the bird and the
process of the shoot, for that was key to the translation of human dominion in the construction of cultural tradition.

Also apparent in the battle over the Hegins shoot was the attempt
to redirect an American ethic, based on a perception of the present
state of cultural degradation. From the viewpoint of animal rights advocates, Hegins represented a tradition of cruelty or barbarism pervasive in America that was holding back progress toward the creation
of a civil society; from the perspective of sportsmen, the animal rights
movement was central to the depravity of modernizing, cosmopolitan
America that had taken over the country's soul. Even if the Hegins pigeon shoot is no longer front-page news, the major cultural conflicts it
represented, and the potent symbols it articulated, continue in various
forms, especially in the debate over the morality of hunting in modern
environments. A cluster of issues regarding the cultural inheritance of

children, patriarchal or predatory roles enacted in blood sports, tolerance for community-based values, and the place of guns and violence in culture bubbles to the surface in heartland skirmishes over animal rights.

CHAPTER 3

The Hare-Coursing Controversy

The Hunting Act 2004, known colloquially as "the ban," signaled a monumental legal change and social divide in Great Britain. The contentious effect of the act was to outlaw hunting with dogs in England and Wales after February 18, 2005. Parliament spent over 700 hours debating the ban in 2004, and one index of its political as well as social significance is that the debate consumed more time than military, environmental, social welfare, and economic legislation—although reporters noted that the rhetoric swirling about the Hunting Act involved all these matters (Prescott 2006).

Especially conspicuous in the battle over the ban were divisive cultural issues raised by animal rights activists' moral and modernist claims and hunting supporters' appeals to preserve national heritage and rural folklife. Either venerable traditions or acts of depravity, depending on the side taken in the acrimonious debate, foxhunting and hare-coursing events drew large crowds in the days before the law went into effect. The organizers of the famed Waterloo Cup in Lancashire, a three-day hare-coursing competition held annually since 1836, rescheduled its event to precede the enactment of the ban and drew major media attention as the final stand for Hunting Act opponents (Bocquet 2003).

Although it claimed fewer adherents than foxhunting, hare coursing held a central symbolic significance in the discourse, with supporters frequently referring to its revered ancient lineage; this aroused protesters to underscore its grossly anachronistic status. There are abundant references in British literature, especially from the nineteenth century,

Part of the estimated crowd of 400,000 participants holding banners and signs as they parade through central London during the Countryside Alliance "Liberty and Livelihood" march, September 22, 2002. The protesters were demanding the right to continue hare coursing and foxhunting, as well as pressing for action to help the rural economy. (Photo by Scott Barbour/Getty Images)

Marchers protest the Waterloo Cup hare-coursing event, February 14, 2005. Signs proclaim, "THE END IS NEAR," "FIGHT CRUELTY," and "HARE TODAY, SAFE TOMORROW." (Photo courtesy of League against Cruel Sports)

to coursing as the "great national sport" (Sirius 1876, 210). Whereas supporters presented hare coursing as a noble countryside tradition with wholesome images of outdoor life, protesters likened the event to shameful, vile blood sports such as cock- and dogfighting.[1] According to media analysts, coursing received the greatest negative publicity during lobbying for the Hunting Act; it was characterized as being the least necessary of all the field sports and having the smallest number of participants. However, it also raised a countercampaign warning of a domino effect extending to the human amenities of meat consumption and leather use (Thomas 1983, 198).

    Public focus on the Waterloo Cup revolved around the drama of ending a recognizable ritual of British heritage that signaled continuity with nineteenth-century imperial self-confidence. The Waterloo Cup held just before the ban went into effect attracted its largest crowd in years, but not all attendees were there to celebrate the sport. The chase

The Waterloo Cup from a "Sporting Events and Starts" card (no. 48), Senior Service Cigarettes, 1935.

on the field garnered less public attention than did the clash of protesters and supporters of hunting. Supporters characterized themselves as environmentally conscious country folk under attack from self-righteous urban "antis" who were trying to impose their views on others; antis condemned what they called the "barbaric cruelty" of the "pros" intent on tormenting or "hounding" innocent hares in a civilized country. The supporters' rhetoric of "antis" suggested that protesters were outsiders taking a stance *against* supporters rather than *for* animals. The protesters' use of "barbaric" located their ethical basis in modern, civil society, and it suggested that the supporters, in their staunch defense of tradition, had been bypassed by progress and ethical development. Police struggled to separate the antagonistic sides and appeared flummoxed by the intensity of the emotion and even the violence engendered by the issue. In late September 2004, angry pros burst into the House of Commons while a crowd estimated at 10,000 gathered outside. Other rallies drew hundreds of thousands of demonstrators. The high-water mark was a "Liberty and Livelihood" march through central London on September 22, 2002, where 400,000 participants protested the ban as governmental interference with the rights of communities to engage in traditional practices ("Timeline" 2005). At the Waterloo Cup, signs

"A Pitman's Holiday—Rabbit Coursing with Greyhounds." *Graphic*, November 15, 1890.

and shirts brandished pithy messages from both sides, often using the structure of proverbs to imply persuasive wisdom. On the pro side was "BORN TO HUNT, READY TO FIGHT" in sight of antis holding up signs emblazoned with "HARE TODAY, SAFE TOMORROW." While pros gave the government a razzing in "BOLLOCKS TO BLAIR," antis brandished pronouncements such as "MURDER IS NOT A SPORT" and "COURSERS LOVE HARES TO DEATH." Pros bemoaned the death of tradition, while antis gleefully chanted, "Last time, last time."

After the din had died down, I asked whether this rancorous debate was characteristic of postmodern animal rights confrontations in Europe and America or whether there was something peculiarly British about it. It is historically significant, I found, that heated debate over the sport has raged since the eighteenth century. Essential to this perspective is a consideration of tradition as a positive or negative process within a modernizing, urban-dominated society. Whereas each side argued over the details of hare coursing (Are hares really pests? Are brown hares endangered? Are hares always killed? Are hares terrified by hounds?), the larger, apparently irreconcilable issue was the value of rural traditions, once the basis of British identity, to a modern industrialized nation (Thomas 1983, 232–47).[2] Hare coursing as a distinctly national practice reverberated through discussions of what it meant to be British and modern and, in a more universalistic mode, how human praxis with animals reflected the postmodern possibility of a civil, egalitarian society. It was this conceptual, ethical conflict, I contend, that made the issue so politically explosive, often to the bewilderment or bemusement of the foreign press. Press coverage and publicity from advocacy organizations within Britain stressed the rural-urban split and the argument over the beastliness of the sport, but I argue that at a base psychological level, unstated social structural and gendered meanings were at work that help explain the emotional investment in the issue. Implicated in the practice is the source of cultural Britishness (use of hounds), especially in symbolic relation to the fox, hare, and cat.[3]

The Practice of Hare Coursing

As the name suggests, hare coursing requires a course in the sense of a designated or enclosed area of land in which a chase occurs. The layout of the course controls the conditions of the chase and facilitates its observation by spectators. Sight is the key feature of the coursing hounds, since they keep their eyes on the swift, evasive hare rather than using their sense of smell to track unseen prey over long stretches of terrain. Coursing differs from a hare hunt (sometimes called "beagling") primarily because it is a competition between two hounds rather than a pack event in which hounds—usually beagles, bassets, and harriers—use scent to capture the hare. Hunting hounds are bred for stamina rather than speed; they wear out their prey, which uses quickness and stratagems such as doubling back and going through fields of cattle to confuse the scent.

In coursing, people stand and watch a chase in a single field rather than joining in the pursuit of the hare through several fields. In terms of customs (use of voice and horns, hunting from horseback, riding uniforms) and even terminology (master, huntsman, whipper-in), beagling is closer to foxhunting than to hare coursing (Windeatt 1982, 38–39). In hare coursing, the hounds, usually greyhounds (whippets, salukis, wolfhounds, and deerhounds are also used), apply their speed while the hare dodges, jumps, and turns at sharp angles to evade the hounds (Co-

"Coursing, Slipping the Greyhounds."
Cover page of *Illustrated London News*,
February 12, 1887.

pold 1996, 36–39). The crowd encourages the hounds to overtake and "turn" the hare (force it in a different direction) rather than being spun by the hare, and spectators provide aesthetic commentary on the precision, timing, and coordination of the hounds in pursuit of their mark.

Whereas coursers find sport in the turns and dodges the hare is

Unmuzzled hounds chasing a hare. (Photo courtesy of Animals Voice)

"Excitement." Illustration by R. H. Moore from *Coursing* by Harding Cox (1892).

forced to make, antis label these induced maneuvers as torture and decry the sick pleasure of striking panic in the pursued "puss." As early as
1915, Lady Florence Dixie protested, "What more aggravated form of
torture is to be found than coursing with greyhounds—the awful terror
of the hare depicting itself in the laid-back ears, convulsive doubles, and
wild starting eyes which seem almost to burst from their sockets in the
agony of tension which that piteous struggle for life entails?" (quoted
in Salt 1915, 170). The betting that accompanied coursing also drew
the ire of antis. John Gulland reporting for London's *Morning Leader*
observed that he had never seen "so many bookmakers and bookmakers' clerks per head of the population" as at the Waterloo Cup. "It was
the merriest gambling I have seen for many a long day," he wrote,
"for coursing 'lends itself particularly well to betting'" (quoted in Salt
1915, 173). The gambling appeared to be a men's pursuit, with the
greyhounds acting as their surrogates in chasing down the feminized
hares ("pussies"). In one description, "just as the dog is about to hurl
himself on pussy's unoffending body, the little creature makes a deft
turn aside, his pursuer flying harmlessly past. Then follow a series of
turns, feints, dodges, and bounds. Puss may, indeed, lead his enemies

a sorry dance for a little while, but it is an unequal contest" (Salt 1915, 173). For famed writer George Bernard Shaw, it was the mob of gambling spectators that made the event cruel. He expressed revulsion and called coursing one of the "dehumanizing sports in which the killing can be seen." The gamblers egging on the dogs appeared to "revert to the excitements of beasts of prey." Shaw recalled living near a course where terriers pursued hares every Sunday morning (see Salmon 1977, 93–94). The coursing perked up his ears, and he wrote, "I noticed that it was quite impossible to distinguish the cries of the terriers from the cries of the sportsmen; although ordinarily the voice of a man is no more like the voice of a dog than like the voice of a nightingale. Sport reduced them all, men and terriers alike, to a common denominator of bestiality" (Shaw 1915, xxi). The implication is that spectators are accessories to murder, but not before terrorizing, with shouts of glee and execration, the outnumbered little creature in anything but a fair fight. Claiming that the scene of greyhounds chasing hares "utterly lacked the elements of real sport," Henry Salt proclaimed, "What an object-lesson in cruelty these meetings afford may be judged from the fact that at some of them, such as the competition for the Waterloo Cup, there is an attendance of several thousand spectators" (1915, 172).

Underscoring the greyhound's power of sight is the theory that its name originated from "gazehound." Speculation on its name followed the observation that the breed does not show much of a gray coat color, although some authorities think the "grey" in its name refers to its eye color. Others find symbolic significance in its connection to antiquity and imperiousness as a "Greek-hound." Another clue to the high status attributed to the hound is the inclusion of *gre* or *gree* in its name, which, according to the *Oxford English Dictionary*, circulates in Scotland and has roots in medieval English, indicating superiority, victory, or high rank (Genders 1975, 3–4; *Oxford English Dictionary* 1971, 393). This association between *gre* and the hound's competitive position is borne out by *The Concise Scots Dictionary*, which gives meanings such as "pre eminence," "supremacy," "first place," and "victory in a contest," while *The Concise Ulster Dictionary* defines it as "the highest honours, the prize" (Robinson 1985, 246; Macafee 1996, 154).

The hare hunt is over when the pack overtakes the hare, but in the British form of coursing, points are awarded to individual hounds. The average course lasts less than a minute, the time it takes the greyhound to cover a third of a mile. The structure of the competition is one of elimination: the winner of one course runs against the winner of the next course. The winner of a typical eight-dog stake, therefore, runs three times to become champion; the Waterloo Cup was exceptional in boasting a sixty-four-dog stake run over three days. The human followers in a hunt ride on horseback, but in coursing they focus their visual attention on action in a designated area. Coursing hounds compete in "slips"—a double-collared leash that has a mechanism for releasing the collars simultaneously. The "slipper" releases ("slips," in the folk speech of coursing) the two hounds onto the selected hare.

Coursers produce hares for the competition in two methods: walked-up and static. In the walked-up method, walkers moving in a line across the open ground arouse the hare. The slipper makes a judgment whether the prey is a good, strong running hare. If satisfied, the slipper is supposed to give the hare at least eighty yards "law" (i.e., lead on the greyhounds) before releasing the dogs, although animal welfare groups have complained that the hares are not given that long a lead before the hounds are set on them.

In the static method, "beaters" form three sides of a box and drive the hare toward the coursing field past the slipper. To antis, the role of the beaters suggests a merciless military campaign, as indicated by the following account of the Waterloo Cup, filled with the rhetoric of all-out war for control of territory:

> Stretching away into the far country (if you use your eyes) may be seen two long, thin black lines, representing quite a little *army* of beaters. In a short while dozens of hares may be seen gaily sporting between these lines, in delightful ignorance of the terrible *enemy* which is lying in wait for them in front. It is the business of the beater to divert a good hare from his playful companions; and if you keep your eye well directed on the black lines, you will soon detect the white flutter of a handkerchief passing along the *lines*, and a brown shape leaping swiftly along the ground, nervously anxious to turn to one side or the other, but kept to an inexorable straight course by the living wall of beaters. A shout from the crowd, growing every moment more excited as the short drama is about to begin, proclaims the fact that the hare is in the *battle-ground*, and is about

to *meet his Waterloo*. And, higher still, and louder than all, the raucous cry of the bookmaker, "Take 7 to 2," "Take 2 to 1," rises shrill in the air. All this time a couple of greyhounds are held tight by a slipper in a box, open on two sides, in the middle of the field. As soon as the hare is beaten past the slipper's box the greyhounds tug and strain at the leash, almost dragging the slipper with them. When the hare has had about fifty yards' start the hounds are released, and off they dash together, look- ing at first like one. This is the most thrilling part of the game, and is watched in a few seconds of almost breathless silence. Pussy hasn't, however, much chance against a greyhound, and is soon *overtaken*. (Salt 1915, 172–73; emphasis added)

Coursers insist that the chase that ensues once the dogs are slipped should not be construed simply as a race, for it involves more than a contest of speed. The chase is, as courser Steven Copold observes, a competition of skill and endurance in addition to one of speed (1996, 29). Indeed, one hound may take the lead not to reach the finish line but "to perform work" in forcing the hare to turn. Copold points out, "The turn itself, the recovery, and the runup to the next turn are the ultimate tests of a hound's abilities" (1996, 29). The dog's ability to turn a hare is rewarded because the hare can turn within its own length, while a grey- hound weighing six or seven times as much will invariably overshoot. A judge mounted on horseback follows the course and awards points. For example, one point is given for a dog that turns the hare more than ninety degrees; half a point is awarded to a dog that turns the hare less than ninety degrees. The judge signals with colored cloths which dog is the winner—red or white, to match the color of the winning dog's collar. A yellow cloth means a tie, resulting in another run later. A blue cloth comes out for a "bye" or a dog that has been withdrawn. A flag steward relays the signals to the spectators.

Kills occur in the course, although pros and antis argue over the ac- tual number of hares that die. The British Field Sports Society (BFSS) claims that fewer than 300 hares are killed in a season that lasts from the middle of September to March 10, or about one in every ten that runs. The National Society for the Abolition of Cruel Sports (NSACS) reports a count between 600 and 1,000 and estimates that as many as 50 percent of hares are killed (Clough and Kew 1993, 18–19; National Society 1968). The other contentious matter is the suffering of the over-taken hare. The BFSS insists that "in nearly every case," the hare dies instantaneously, and coursing rules call for "dispatchers" positioned in the field to finish off the animal if necessary. Animal welfare organiza-tions decry what they call the protracted suffering of the animals, which can be heard "screaming very loudly," and often give visual evidence of hounds tearing the hare apart with their teeth in what is described as "tugs of war" (National Society 1968). It is possible for the hare to outrun the greyhounds and make its way to natural escapes through a hedge or into cover (sometimes called "bolt holes"), at which point the course is over.

Another distinction in coursing is the practice of betting that of-ten accompanies the competition. These "public" or "formal" coursing events, with rules and spectators, are differentiated from an older form of "private" coursing practiced by country squires on their own lands with greyhounds they bred and kept (Richardson 1903). Advocates of formal coursing claim that its main objective is to "test greyhounds, not to kill hares"; therefore, it is "a spectator sport in which the hare is almost incidental" (BFSS n.d.; Thomas 1983, 48–49). A contempo-rary variation of the squires' private coursing is known as "informal"

"Coursing the Hare." Illustration by Francis Barlow (1626–1702) from Richard Blome's *The Gentleman's Recreation* (1686). (Courtesy of Leeds Museums and Galleries [City Art Gallery] U.K./The Bridgeman Art Library)

"Coursing." Engraving by Samuel Howitt (published 1798–1800) reproduced on "Old Sporting Prints" card (no. 2), Player's Navy Cut Cigarettes, 1924.

The Britishness of coursing is emphasized by placing the event at Stonehenge. *Illustrated London News*, November 11, 1865.

Coursers showing their dogs, Isle of Wight, c. 1920.

coursing, referring to two dogs (often crossbred dogs called lurchers) released after a hare with the intention of killing it (for food, pest control, or sport), although this is often associated with illegal poaching by a nonlandowner class.

Regional differences in coursing are apparent within Britain. The form found in England is run on open land (called "open coursing"). In Northern Ireland, coursing is governed by the Irish Coursing Club, and events take place in a secure enclosure over a set distance with muzzled dogs. Unlike the English form, the Irish form is not organized around points; the winning hound in the Irish competition is the first dog to turn the hare. According to the League against Cruel Sports (LACS), even though the dogs are muzzled, the hare can be beaten into the ground by them before a steward can reach it to wring its neck. Another objection is that the enclosed courses do not allow the hare to escape. The LACS has complained that the hares are rounded up after the event and suffer illnesses resulting from the stress of being captured and coursed ("Hare Coursing" 2006). Coursing in Northern Ireland continued to be legal after bans were imposed in Scotland (2002) and in England and Wales (2004). The LACS in Northern Ireland tried to get coursing banned on conservation grounds, claiming that the Irish hare is endangered and "one of Ireland's best-loved native species" (Keenan 2005).[4] In 2005, it circulated a flyer urging people to write letters to the minister for the environment with the message, "Stop the cruelty of hare coursing. Make sure . . . you demand an end to barbaric bloodsports." The heading of the flyer stated, "Scotland 2002 hunting and coursing banned; England and Wales 2004 hunting and coursing banned; Northern Ireland? Cruelty Continues." In the background was a photo showing two hounds with a hare on the ground.

Coursing events in Tyrone and Antrim were canceled in 2005 after the Department of the Environment in the North withheld the licenses required to trap the hares used in the coursing events, citing the animals' scarcity. The Irish Countryside Alliance denied that hare numbers were in decline and shot back that "ministers were imposing their own views on people here" (Keenan 2005). Rather than connecting Irishness to the hare, the Irish Wolfhound Foundation, based in the United States, celebrated the aggressive wolfhound as worthy of Irish national pride. In 2006 it created a bronze statue showing an Irish wolfhound coursing a hare, with the commentary that the hounds accompanied "Irish nobles to war."

Hare Coursing Venerated and Vilified

Amid the brouhaha over coursing, one question is occasionally asked: why not use mechanical lures to replace the live hares, if the purpose is to test the greyhounds? Proponents of coursing acknowledge that the advent of greyhound racing in 1927 (which uses mechanical lures) triggered a decline in the popularity of coursing, but they often mention the thrill of the unpredictable hare and the outdoor setting (Copold 1996, 18). They also give an ecological argument, claiming that the sport rids the countryside of undesirable pests that wreak havoc on gardens and fields. The brochure on coursing produced by the BFSS alludes to the appeal of the sport's natural setting, intimating that coursing is more thrilling and authentic than racing with mechanical lures. It suggests that real sportsmen stayed loyal to coursing, while the soft "betting boys forsake the real thing for the safety of the less idiosyncratic electric hare and the comfort of a stadium" (Copold 1996,

18; see also Clapson 1992, chap. 6). Coursing, the BFSS (n.d.) implies, is not only "the true test of a gazehound" but also the test of the mettle of hardy country folk as the soul of Britain.

The hare-coursing protest that occurred in 2005 could not have been imagined during the nineteenth century, when the Waterloo Cup was considered the premier sporting event in Britain and attracted crowds as large as 75,000. Then, as now, *tradition* was a key word. In 1836 when the Cup started, hare coursing was viewed as one of the world's oldest sporting activities (some pamphlets claimed it was *the* oldest field sport), predating the popularity of foxhunting. Beginning with the Swaffham Club in Norfolk, founded by Lord Orford in 1776, coursers organized clubs to maintain the tradition in the wake of social and economic change, especially changes in the cultural landscape brought by enclosure laws (creating larger estates and fewer small farms), industrialization, and urbanization. By 1856, hare-coursing advocates had organized 382 clubs, and in 1858, they established the National Coursing Club as a central sporting authority. By the early twentieth century, the sport had gone into decline, with fewer than 200 active clubs (fewer than 25 were active at the century's end), although large crowds (estimated as high as 39,000) still gathered for the Waterloo Cup prior to World War II. To be sure, hare coursing could be found in other nations (United States, Spain, France, Portugal, Pakistan) in the twentieth century, but Britain remained the sport's hub, where it was linked to other dog-centered activities such as fox and deer hunting.

By the 1930s, animal protection campaigns appealed to the social conscience by suggesting that social welfare for humans should be extended to animals. Activists linked the treatment of animals with attitudes toward the "lower sort" of people—attitudes that were in need of reform. They argued that social justice for humans could not be achieved unless cruelty to animals was curbed. "There is no welfare state for animals," the Blue Cross declared in a fund-raising pitch with a pointed reference to the rise of a welfare state in the United Kingdom (Kean 1998, 198–99). Animal welfare organizations singled out hare coursing as a target of scorn for promoting violence and inequality, but they were countered by pro-hunting organizations linking field sports as exalted traditions with preservation of the countryside. Coursing organizations publicly presented hunting and coursing practitioners as ordinary, beleaguered folk who were using the sports to rid their fields of crop-eating, disease-carrying hares while gaining a sense of needed community. Bolstered by a petition against hunting circulated by the League for the Prohibition of Cruel Sports that attracted a million signatures, Labourite Seymour Cocks introduced an animal protection bill in Parliament in 1949 to abolish both coursing and stag hunting, but it was defeated by a vote of 214 to 101 (Kean 1998, 187). One result of the agitation for stricter animal protection laws was the Labour government's appointment of a commission, chaired by Scott Henderson, to investigate the reported abuse of animals. The commission concluded in 1951, "The degree of cruelty involved in coursing is not sufficient to justify its prohibition." Animal welfare groups criticized the commission's report because its membership did not include persons known to be opposed to blood sports (Pine 1966, 134–35).

Historian Richard Thomas credits the intervention of the minister of agriculture, responding to the ecological and economic concerns of his civil servants that a ban would have detrimental effects, for persuading the Labour front bench to vote against the bill despite their personal convictions against coursing and hunting (1983, 153). Activists from the league stepped up their emotional appeal by using the trauma of mass death in World War II in their arguments. For instance, league president Hamilton Fyfe observed, "I do not see how anyone who considers it justifiable to torment and kill animals for fun can ever really look with horror or shame at the killing and wounding of men in battle, and until those are the feelings aroused by war we shall never be rid of it" (quoted in Kean 1998, 186–87).

Indeed, women involved in the League for the Prohibition of Cruel Sports were quoted as saying that men learned to wage war from the brutal practice of blood sports such as coursing. Leslie Pine, managing editor of *Shooting Times*, supported their case in writing, stating, "Compassion for other living things might do something to heal man's own terrible wars and the evils which he inflicts upon his own kind." He differentiated between shooting sports (which he supported) and blood sports such as coursing (which he did not); the latter promoted what he called a "blood lust" for killing and callousness toward "lower creatures." In the book *After Their Blood*, he reported the following statement by a courser with regard to newborn hares: "'They're waiting for mother,' he said with a smile, 'we haven't the heart to kill them now, but in a few weeks' time when they're running about, we shall mow them down'" (Pine 1966, 56). His insinuation was that the coursers were heartless child killers and, by extension, that coursing contributed to the indoctrination of violence in children by employing young people as beaters to drive the hares into the courses. In a symposium organized in 1960 to defend hunting in Britain, novelist Christopher Hugh Sykes returned a salvo in the gender wars that emerged in the animal welfare debates with a reference to the female-dominated antis: hunting "may even survive the latest threat to its existence: a monstrous regiment of women" (Sykes 1960, 231). His image of a fearsome organized sisterhood disrupting the natural order of things was all the more provocative because of its reference to Scottish religious reformer John Knox's famed 1558 protest of female sovereigns in *The First Blast of the Trumpet against the Monstrous Regiment of Women.*

With coursing fingered as the most barbaric of field sports by animal welfare organizations, abolition rather than regulation became a priority through the 1970s. The assumption was that if the event considered most offensive could be banned, others such as the hunting of stag, otter, fox, and hare would quickly follow. In 1970, the House of Commons voted for legislation banning coursing, but the bill ran out of time when a general election was called. Pressured to respond under this barrage, supporters of coursing made their appeal to an individualistic libertarian premise while linking coursing to a national identity rooted in preservation of the countryside. As late as 2005, spokespersons such as television personality Clarissa Dickson-Wright would repeat the pro mantra that "it's about preserving a very fine old traditional countryside activity," appended to the view that "this is about a freedom, and people's right not to be told what they can do and can't" (Bocquet 2003). The animal rights answer was to refer to a broader sense of modernization and moralism, not to a rural-urban cultural distinction, as expressed by Josie Sharrod of the International Fund for Animal Welfare in a comment about the Waterloo Cup in 2003: "In the twenty-first century, it's appalling that people should be getting their kicks watching small animals being savaged by dogs. It's uncivilised, and it's time it was brought to an end" (Bocquet 2003). Repeating the idea that hares are small, innocent, and lovable, animal rights activists rhetorically connected the aggrieved animal to children and women during a time of heightened media awareness of domestic abuse, women's rights, and social justice.

Historically, hare coursing was a British field sport managed by landowning gentlemen and associated with the aristocracy. The Waterloo Cup, named for the Waterloo Hotel in Liverpool, was in fact run on land owned by the Earl of Sefton, who had organized the Altcar Coursing Club in 1825. A cigarette card featuring the Waterloo Cup, part of a series of famous "Sporting Events and Stars" issued in 1935, corroborated the aristocratic association more than 100 years later with the caption: "The Blue Riband of the Coursing World, competition for which attracts the cream of British nobility, sportsmen and their valuable dogs to Altcar, near Liverpool, every February." Further, the image on the front of the card highlighted the majestic design of the silver cup, suggesting its connection to royalty.

Queen Elizabeth I is usually credited with igniting royal interest in the sport and initiating the first code of rules in 1590; compiled by the Duke of Norfolk, these rules still form the basis of the sport (Prescott 1984, 54). Her animal welfare concern, according to sport historians, was to reverse the dogs' advantage and apply the ethic of "fair chase" by giving the hare more law—at least fifty to eighty yards' head start (Branigan 2004, 152–53). Fifteen years before the duke's rules circulated, English poet George Turberville noted the special fascination with coursing among his countrymen. As a translator of a French tome on hunting, he felt compelled to comment on customs at home: "Bycause I finde nothing in myne Author particularly written of coursing with Greyhounds, it seemeth unto me, that they have not that kind of Venerie so much in estimation in France, as we do hold it here in England" (Casciogne 1575, 244). Of the different kinds of outdoor recreations, he considered hare coursing the most "noble pastime" because, unlike hunting, it can be done "without unmeasurable toyle and payne." He considered coursing with deer and fox detrimental to the hounds, whereas hare coursing was most competitive because of the hare's speed. "Therefore," he concluded, "few men will course a fox unless it be with old greyhounds which are brused dogs, and which they make small account of" (Casciogne 1575, 248). He offered a verse to exalt the image of the sporting hare:

I am an Hare, a beast of little strength,
Yet making sport, of loue and gentle gestes,
For running swift, and holding out at length,
I beare the beil, above all other beastes. (Casciogne 1575, 159–60)

In this verse, then, the hare is fair, feral game, worthy of competition with the regal greyhound of man.

Turberville linked hare coursing to pride in property by noting, "He that seeke a hare muste go overthwart the landes. And every lande that he passeth over, let hym beginner with his eye at his foote, and to looke downe the lande to the furlongs end" (Casciogne 1575, 246). Like many commentators after him, Turberville took pleasure in the sudden, agile motions of the hare (and the action of betting on the greyhound):

> It is a gallant sport to see how the hare will turne and winde to save hyr selfe out of the dogges mouth. So that sometimes even when you think that your Greyhound dothe (as it were) gape to take hyr, she will turne and cast them a good way behind hyr: and so saveth hir self by turning, wrenching, and winding, until she reach some covert and so save hyr life. In coursing at the Hare it is not material which dogge killeth hyr (which hunters call bearing of an Hare) but he that giveth most Cotes, or most turnes, winneth the wager. (Casciogne 1575, 246–47)

In 1615, Gervase Markham, in a treatise on "countrey contentments," pointed out that the English husbandman "preferreth" coursing to other pursuits such as hawking and foxhunting (97). "A very noble and worthy pastime" according to Markham, coursing highlighted the importance of greyhound breeding to the English landowner. His text provides early evidence of betting at coursing matches by explaining how wagers were gained, lost, or annulled. It appears that there was some protest of the events, either the gambling or the chase, for he defends "men's recreations" in the countryside by stating, "what to one is most pleasant, to an other is most offensive." Because the book is entitled *Country Contentments*, one can reasonably presume that this "other" is from the city and perhaps female, since he refers to the "manly and warlike" character of many "recreations" with "beasts" (Markham 1615, 3).

Richard Blome extolled hare coursing in his influential *Gentleman's Recreation* (1686), an encyclopedic work that linked liberal learning to participation in hunting, horsemanship, and agriculture. Comparing coursing with hunting as a noble pursuit, Blome observed, "Coursing with Greyhounds is a Recreation in great esteem with many of the Gentry; it affords greater pleasure than Hunting in some respect; as First,

In regard it is sooner ended. Secondly, It requires less toyl. Thirdly, The Game is for the most part always in sight. And lastly, In respective of the delicate shape, and qualities of a Greyhound" (1686, 97). Blome praised the greyhound as possessing the greatest velocity and most pleasing shape among all dogs and pointed out in considerable detail its attributes of breeding: "long, lean Head, with a sharp Nose, from the Eyes downwards; a full clear Eye, with large Eye-lids, little Ears, a long Neck bending like a Drake, with a loose hanging Weezand, broad Breasted, his Body indifferent long, and reasonable great, with a Back straight and Square, having a rising in the middle, a small Belly, broad Shoulders, round Ribs, with a long space between his Hips, a strong Stern, a round Foot with large Clefts, and his Fore-legs strait and shorter than his hinder" (1686, 95). Blome included an illustration with visual cues to the social significance of coursing: a gentleman sits on horseback while dogs chase the hare in the foreground. In the background, as a sign of his control over the estate, is a panorama of the dignified manor and domesticated land free of the pesky animals. Indeed, Blome emphasized that hare coursing was an exercise in human dominion over the land because the hares were rousted "by walking cross the Lands . . . and casting your Eye up and down" (1686, 97). He also included guidance on eliminating hares from properties by netting and trapping, but he appreciated the "sport" of coursing for the job because it "is pleasing to see the Turns and windings that the Hare will make to save her self, which sometimes prove effectual unto her" (Blome 1686, 97).

Representations of Hare and Hound

Chroniclers document that coursing began in the sixteenth century as battles of pride among landowners, with smooth-haired greyhounds being viewed as royal animals dominating the lowly, trespassing (and, in folk belief, omens of bad luck or evil) hares (Genders 1975, 2). Coursing figures in picturesque literary and pictorial renderings of British noble life, particularly as forests were cleared and proprietary fields created. In Shakespeare's *Love's Labour's Lost* (performed between 1594 and 1595), Biron, a lord attending the king, announces at the beginning of the third scene of the fourth act, "The king he is hunting deer; I am coursing myself." Especially revealing for the emerging symbolism of aggressive English identity is the connection between coursing and men in battle in Shakespeare's *Henry V* (act 3, scene 1; emphasis added):

> And you, good yeoman,
> Whose limbs were made in England, show us here
> The mettle of your pasture; let us swear
> That you are worth your breeding; which I doubt not;
> For there is none of you so mean and base,
> That hath not noble lustre in your eyes.
> *I see you stand like greyhounds in the slips,*
> *Straining upon the start. The game's afoot:*
> Follow your spirit, and upon this charge
> Cry "God for Harry, England, and Saint George!"

The seals of kings Edward VI (1547–1553) and Charles I (1644) featured greyhounds, and the dogs used in hare coursing enjoyed a reputation of being "above all other breeds, fit to be the companion only of those of royal descent," according to chronicles beginning in the eleventh century (Genders 1975, 2–3). Late in the nineteenth century, Harding Cox dedicated his tome on coursing to the Prince of Wales, claiming that his attendance at coursing events "testifies to his being, like most English gentlemen, fond of all manly sports" (1892, vi).

Squires in the eighteenth century often commissioned painters to depict coursing on their properties, showing the extent of their holdings and their dignified appearance. Some painters such as Samuel Howitt, Abraham Cooper, Henry Alken, and Dean Wolstenholme became specialists in these idealized scenes, which often pictured lords overlooking their estates accompanied by their obedient hound companions (Cox 1892, vi). These sporting scenes were widely circulated as prints into the twentieth century and figured prominently in the nostalgia for countryside activities in the interwar period. Player's Cigarettes, for example, issued a series of twenty-five "Old Sporting Prints" in 1924, including Howitt's "Coursing." The reverse of the card quotes Turberville's observation in *The Noble Art of Venerie* (Casciogne 1575) that the "noble pastime, mete for Nobility and Gentlemen," was preferable to hunting. Howitt's image shows a landowning gentleman overlooking an extensive landscape with plowing in the background and a greyhound looking up obediently at his master while a hare scampers away.

The association between field sports—including hare coursing, deer hunting, and foxhunting—and a past way of life based on aristocratic control had a bearing on the political upheaval in Britain caused by bans on hunting in the late twentieth century. Pros expressed their resentment of urban moralists, who represented displacement of their livelihoods and lands. They pointed out that hare coursing, though still primarily an activity of country dwellers in the twentieth century, drew participants from a broad social spectrum and was not restricted to the gentry. Both sides accused the other of elitism. One difference, reflecting the priorities of a social welfare state where victims receive governmental protection, was the dispute over who deserved such protection. The pros claimed that as a marginalized, displaced minority, country dwellers were at risk and had the right to preserve their traditions and way of life centered on the endangered landscape. Antis wanted to extend social protection to animals and justified this intervention by promoting the idea that kindness to animals—living creatures involved in society but unable to speak for themselves—instilled an ethic of nondiscriminatory treatment for all individuals.

Protests of field sports, with references to class struggle and modern or religious ethics, began with the organization of the first coursing club in 1776. Anglican vicar Humphry Primatt published *The Duty of Mercy and the Sin of Cruelty to Brute Animals*, a tract arguing for animal protection on the grounds that animals feel pain. He also observed that hunting symbolizes a master-subject relationship and maintains discriminatory social treatment. He was joined in his protest by notable romantic poets such as Percy Shelley ("Queen Mab"), John Clare ("On Seeing a Lost Greyhound in Winter Lying upon the Snow in the Fields"), and John Keats ("Isabella"). Set against the background of rising industrialization and imperialism, Keats especially viewed animal protection as part of a utopian social vision of the future in which nature, animals, and humans lived in blissful egalitarian harmony (Kean 1998, 26).

In 1781, an anonymous author published a set of letters extolling the hunting of hares and foxes in *Treatise upon Hunting*, reminding readers of the "heroes of antiquity who were taught the art of hunting." As further testimony to its appeal, he commented, "In most countries, from the earliest times, hunting has been a principal occupation of the people, either for use or amusement; and many princes have made it their chief delight" (Beckford 1932, 32). Recoiling from charges of "inhumanity" for promoting cruelty to animals and speculation that he was a fellow clergyman countering Primatt's argument for Christian mercy, the author republished the work in 1796 under his name, Peter Beckford. The new edition included a note that was especially revealing of the central place of hares and hounds in the defense of hunting:

> Since the above was written, hunting has undergone a severe censure (vide Monthly Review for September, 1781) nor will anything satisfy the critic less than its total abolition. He recommends feats of agility to be practised and exhibited instead of it. Whether the amendment proposed by the learned gentleman be desirable or not, I shall forebear to determine; taking the liberty, however, to remind him, that as hunting hath stood its ground from the earliest times, been encouraged and approved by the best authorities, and practiced by the greatest men, it cannot now be supposed to dread criticism, or to need support. Hunting originates in nature itself, and it is in perfect correspondence with this law of nature, that the several animals are provided with necessary means of attack and defence. (Beckford 1932, 23)

Beckford defended hunting as fitting the laws of nature and promoting ecological balance, following the call in Genesis for human dominion over the land and its creatures rather than representing humans' destructive arrogance against nature (see Scully 2002). Though a member of the gentry, Beckford questioned whether a gentleman should actually indulge in the "noble diversion" or merely oversee it. He wrote to his correspondent, "You will say, perhaps, there is something too laborious in the occupation of a huntsman for a gentleman to take it upon himself; you may also think it is beneath him; I agree with you in both—yet I hope that he may have leave to understand it. If he follow the diversion, it is a sign of his liking it; and if he like it, surely it is some disgrace to him to be ignorant of the means most conducive to it" (Beckford 1932, 23). Beckford sought to modernize hunting by rationalizing it, ordering it in a code of conduct, but preserving its continuity by reference to tradition.

Since Beckford was corresponding with someone from outside the country who proposed to take up a homegrown tradition, he was forced to reflect on what was distinctively British. He observed that fox and hare were rarely hunted in France, Germany, and Italy, yet in Britain, these animals were especially worthy of hunting skills. But more than the question of prey, he was drawn to the appeal of the hound in the British imagination. Horses were used widely across Europe, he noticed, but in Britain, no human companion for the hunt was more appreciated than the dog, "that useful, that honest, that faithful, that disinterested, that entertaining animal" (Beckford 1932, 20). He bragged, in fact, that "the hounds which this country produces are universally allowed to be the best in the world," and he found in this trait signs of a national character that had not been trumpeted because it was taken for granted (Beckford 1932, 19).

What was it that Beckford admired in the dog that became a metaphor for British character? Cleanliness, for one thing. "Dogs are naturally cleanly animals; they seldom, when they can help it, dung where they lie: air and fresh straw are necessary to keep them healthy" (Beckford 1932, 51). Dogs appear closer to humans than to animals, in Beckford's view, because they share a domestic (or in psychoanalytic terms, anal-retentive) emphasis on clean space and social order. Human caregiving in a parental role is necessary to ensure that the dog's material surroundings (the kennel) are sweet and clean.[5] The other meaning of cleanliness is one of control, because the dogs "clean up" the countryside of pests and command the field. The implication is that dogs have human qualities, although in terms of agility, sense of smell, and faculty for loyalty, humans are deficient in comparison. As an agent for humans, the dog's cleanliness is crucial to separate the gentleman from contamination by the blood of the kill and confrontation in the dirt.[6] Beckford also admired hounds for being "handy," referring to their faithfulness and instrumentality as a kind of filial piety. He explained: "it respects their readiness to do whatever is required of them; and particularly, when cast, to turn easily which way the huntsman pleases" (Beckford 1932, 95). These traits within the context of a manly pursuit imply esteem for the masculinity of the hound not only as a male companion but also as the gentleman's surrogate and family member. Yet it is a type of restrained masculinity, suggesting the self-consciousness, or redemption, of British aggression and hierarchy based on cunning, neatness, breeding, and agility rather than brutish power. For instance,

Beckford encouraged names anthropomorphizing the animals and expressing "speed, strength, courage" (1932, 72). He pointed out that the feminine name "Madam" accords disrespect to the animal and gave the example of a huntsman who tended to rage against such hounds, hollering frequently, "as loud as he could—'Madam, you d—d bitch!'" (Beckford 1932, 72). Thus he recommended that even females of the species used for hunting be given masculine names.

Beckford underscored the importance of breeding in the hound, evoking a social connection: "hounds are frequently *too ill bred* to be of any service." "There is an active vanity in the minds of men which is favourable to improvement . . . ; you, therefore, will find pleasure in the breeding of hounds. . . . Is it not extraordinary that no other country should equal us in this particular, and that the very hounds procured from hence should degenerate in another climate?" (Beckford 1932, 71, 65). Beckford cited a chauvinistic poem by William Somerville (1675–1742), a devotee of field sports, to confirm his opinion:

In thee alone, fair land of liberty!
Is bred the perfect hound, in scent and speed
As yet unrivall'd, while in other climes
Their virtue fails, a weak degen'rate race. (Beckford 1932, 65)

Indeed, the pursuit of improvement toward the goal of perfection, administered by elites to their faithful "servants," constitutes the "pleasure" Beckford asserted in the breeding of hounds. The racial implication is that superiority is home-bred in the countryside and enacted in the pursuit of prey. Hunting is no mere "trifle," he declared, for in "the chace of a stout noble beast, may be represented the whole art of war, strategems, policy, and ambuscades, with all other devices usually practised to overcome an enemy with safety." He avowed that hunting energizes a people, especially a people weakened by modern conveniences and lack of national purpose, by giving them more than exercise: "ease and laziness can have no room in this diversion" (Beckford 1932, 25–26). He appears to joke in one letter, to criticize upper-class indulgence, by belittling hounds that had been "nursed so much care, were weakly and timid, and had every disadvantage attending private education" (Beckford 1932, 70). Further viewing hunting as a metaphor for the nerve of a nation, he even compared the qualities of a good prime minister to a good huntsman: "a clear head, nice observation, quick apprehension, undaunted courage, strength of constitution, activity of body, a good ear, and a good voice" (Beckford 1932, 21–22).

Another indication of the centrality of hare hunting to the discourse on animal-human relations in Britain comes from William Blane (1788) in *Cynegetica; Or, Essays on Sporting: Consisting of Observations on Hare Hunting*. The title refers to the *Cynegeticus* of Xenophon, who waxed poetic on the method of hunting hare and whom Blane credits as "one of the finest Writers, the bravest Soldiers, the ablest Politicians, the wisest Philosophers, and the most virtuous Citizens of antiquity" (Blane 1788, 11–12). The longevity of the tradition was important to Blane because it bolstered the idea of hunting "the little animal" as a basic human instinct, and it underscored the civilized roots of hare hunting in the Greek classics.[7] Another classical connection is to the Romans, who presumably introduced hare coursing to Britain (Branigan 2004, 72–75). Referring to the anti-hunting sentiments from philosophical and literary quarters, Blane wrote, "I know the literary and speculative part of Mankind are apt to consider these kind of country diversions in a contemptible light; and, perhaps, they may be inclined to despise any person who shall devote his time to the writing, or even the reading, of a single page, on a subject which they may think only deserving the attention of Grooms, Country 'Squires, and Dog-boys. But this opinion is by no means founded on reason" (1788, 2). The discourse he established was about the function of the countryside, and he attacked the view that modern life, represented by the rationalism and cosmopolitanism of rising industrialization, was morally superior or more "civil" than the countryside. He implored readers in his introduction:

But rural diversions, when followed in a liberal manner (for I do not wish to renew the almost extinguished breed of mere hunting 'Squires), are particularly useful in this island, where, from the nature of our Government, no man can be of consequence without spending a large portion of his time in the country, and every additional inducement to this mode of life is an additional security to our freedom and independence. I much question whether our morals, or even our manners, are greatly improved by that style of living, which empties our country seats to fill the metropolis, or the large provincial towns; and whether the

manly character that once distinguished the Englishman has
not suffered more on the side of firmness and integrity, than
it has gained on that of politeness and elegance, by sacrificing
the rough sports of the Field to the softer amusements of the
Assembly and Card Table. (Blane 1788, 4–5)

Citing the wholesomeness and healthfulness of countryside vigor associated with walking, riding, and hunting outdoors, he warned of "the
dreadful consequences which must inevitably attend an entirely sedentary life" in cosmopolitan circles. To arouse sympathy, he gave the
case of

the young and ingenuous Peasant torn from his weeping Parents, and his distracted Bride, and either hurried into a loathsome dungeon, or banished to an unhealthy climate, only for
the murder of a Hare or a Partridge. But I will venture to say,
there is hardly a Day-laborer in the kingdom that may not, in
a reasonable manner, be indulged with the use of these animals
by a proper application; and if he is fond of the diversion they
afford, and chuses to be idly busy rather than industriously so,
he may perfectly satisfy himself by attending the Hounds or
Greyhound of the 'Squire, or assisting the Game-keeper with
his gun. (Blane 1788, 6–7)

Again going on the offensive, he railed against enclosure laws that force
farmers and hunters to leave the land, "which afford a noble and manly
diversion to their Proprietor." His naturalistic answer to Shelley's utopian vision was, "As the beasts of the forest and the fruits of the soil are
equally common in a state of nature, so I see no reason why they may not
be equally appropriated in a state of civil society" (Blane 1788, 6–7).

The Widening Gulf between City and Country

Parliament became involved in the debate over animal protection as
early as 1800, when legislation was introduced to outlaw bullbaiting.
Narrowly defeated by a vote of forty-three to forty-one, this groundbreaking proposal brought up the "barbaric cruelty" of using dogs as
human surrogates to torment other animals, in this case, bulls. But the

social justification was to regulate the behavior of the poor or "lower class of people," as one Whig member of Parliament (MP) stated, with the intention of controlling vice and crime at these events, rather than to target the aristocratic, gentlemanly pursuit of blood sports (for instance, kings and princes engaged in cockfighting and dogfighting at the time) (Kean 1998, 31–32).[8]

The first British law to protect animals was known as Martin's Act, after Richard Martin, an MP from Galway. The 1822 law imposed fines and imprisonment on individuals who "beat, abuse, or ill-treat" horses, cows, steers, and sheep—domesticated animals that were the property of individuals and were visible in the workaday world. Public cruelty in the cities was the particular concern of animal welfare organizations such as the Society for the Prevention of Cruelty to Animals (SPCA), formed in 1824 in London. Indeed, much of the SPCA's attention was focused on civic improvement by eliminating bullbaiting, cockfighting, and dogfighting and showing that these were not gentlemanly or civilized pursuits because of the bloodlust they promoted and the vice they invited. The SPCA testified to Parliament that such sports were in fact attractive to a criminal and degenerate element, even if supported by nobility (and a number of MPs). Although all three activities it pejoratively labeled "blood sports" indicative of urban blight were outlawed by the 1840s, organized campaigns against hare coursing and foxhunting in private clubs were slower to develop, probably because such pursuits evoked the ethical idea of a "fair chase" with a "clean" air of dignity rather than a "fight to the death" trapped in a ring within the wider context of urban filth.

In the countryside, the rural poor could not legally engage in hunting until the Ground Game Act of 1880 allowed tenant farmers to ferret for rabbits. Despite a considerable amount of poaching, coursing and hunting exemplified the social and political dominance of landowners (Thomas 1983, 18). The emphasis in animal welfare campaigns was on fighting cruelty to animals, especially those used for work, by handlers in plain view on city streets, rather than cruelty to animals hunted as "country diversions" (Kean 1998, 69). Lobbying for the extension of protection to private events, clubs, and sports in the countryside was more of a twentieth-century movement emblematic of post–World War I social reform movements aimed at subverting inequalities of class and privilege. At the forefront of this movement was the League for the Prohibition of Cruel Sports, founded in 1925, and countered by the British Field Sports Society, organized in 1930. The league's first editorial declared a focused campaign to outlaw hare coursing, along with the prohibition of fox, deer, and otter hunting (Kean 1998, 186).

Yet hare coursing had already gone into decline without a prohibition. One factor was the Ground Game Act of 1880, which allowed tenants on land to kill hares and eat them without fear of prosecution. The law addressed the social welfare of tenant farmers in the countryside as economic dependence on agriculture diminished and urban industries and wealth increasingly dominated society. As cereal prices dropped (due to imports from the Continent and America), small farmers found that their ground game was more valuable than their crops. Legislation was necessary, however, to reverse the pattern of game and poor laws in effect since the seventeenth century, which were designed to punish offenses against landowners' property, including hunting. It is symbolically significant that one of the actions by tenants seeking to repeal these laws was the killing of dogs, suggesting the hound's role as the landowner's agent and master of the landscape (Thomas 1983, 18). Conservationists reported a drastic reduction in the number of hares in the years following passage of the Ground Game Act, and this had a chilling effect on coursing. By 1892, the number of coursing clubs had dropped from its midcentury high of more than 380 clubs to only 137 (Thomas 1983, 49).

Another factor in the early-twentieth-century decline of hare coursing was the replacement of live hares with mechanical or "dummy" hares. With the mechanical versions, the focus of the sport was on racing and betting, cognitively aligning it more with horse racing than with hare coursing. Use of mechanical hares was first reported in Hendon, England, in 1876, but it did not become standard practice until the 1920s. The commercial expansion of greyhound racing with use of mechanical lures took off after the opening of Belle Vue track in Manchester in 1926 (Genders 1975, 60–62). Opening day attracted only 1,700 people, but it increased tenfold two meetings later. The inauguration of the Mecca of greyhound racing at White City in 1927, with 100,000 in attendance, signaled the betting crowd's switch from countryside coursing to stadium racing.

Although the use of mechanical lures spread at urban greyhound racing tracks, hare coursing still persisted as a countryside activity.

Greyhound racing was more accessible to city folk and attracted an industrial working-class clientele. The countryside no longer dominated socially, but it still held a fascination in the public imagination as a source of heritage. By 1900, the English urban population had risen to 77 percent of the total (by the century's end, the figure stood at 89 percent) (Hicks and Allen 1999, 14). Public opinion appeared to turn against hare coursing in the twentieth century as the urban view spread that coursing was unnecessary for supplying food and that violence against animals could be prevented with mechanical replacements. To be sure, the Waterloo Cup continued to be ritualized as a grand festive event and a symbolic reminder of the sport's heyday, as well as Britain's, until late in the twentieth century. But in a 1978 survey, although respondents recognized the proud tradition of the event, they were less sympathetic with hare coursing and increasingly considered it "anachronistic" if not cruel for a progressive society (Thomas 1983, 187–99).

In the context of the political hegemony of urban interests and the widening cultural gulf between city and country, a nagging question remained: did rural communities have the right to be different and to perpetuate customs associated with their identity, even if those customs did not conform to the ethical views of the urban majority? (see Williams 1973). Problematizing this question was a wave of nostalgia for country life as modernization spread, perhaps driven by collective urban guilt for destroying the rural livelihood or a sense of the lost golden age represented by country life. In a series of popular oral histories of country folklife during the 1960s and 1970s, George Ewart Evans bemoaned the way industrialization and urbanization had "uprooted the family by destroying its attachment to place" (Evans 1966, 18; see also Baker 1974; Evans 1960, 1961, 1970, 1975, 107–22; Hartley 1979). Alexander Fenton, author of *Scottish Country Life* (1976), added, "it is only in the last century and a half that the rate of change due to industrialisation, the growth of towns and cities, rural depopulation, has speeded up to moon-rocket proportions. Possibly awareness of this fact is making our present age an age of conservation, of consciousness of the environment" (Fenton 1985, 42). Whether inspired by nostalgia for a bygone rural heritage or environmental consciousness, there is now cognizance that Britain's soul has suffered from the disappearance of countryside customs. As Roy Palmer expressed in *Britain's Living Folklore:* "There is a need to rediscover something which is more permanent and part of a continuing tradition. By tapping into our heritage of song and story, ritual and celebration, our lives are given shape and meaning" (1991, 8).

Yet this rediscovery also meant a modern reconstruction—some say romanticism or invention—of tradition to conform to images of a prior rural culture as primitive if nonetheless wholesome (Evans 1970, 17–20; Hobsbawm and Ranger 1983; Jenkins 1972, 497–516; Mackay 2000–2001, 25–31). The hunting and coursing debate of the late twentieth and early twenty-first centuries brought the conflicts between the image and the reality of rural practices out into the open, forcing a confrontation between the ethical bases of the "dominion" of rural life and the "modernism" of the urban worldview. The mid-twentieth-century growth of rural museums, folklife surveys, and oral histories in Britain—trying to capture memories of a threatened or bygone way of life—was a sign of the national heritage's roots in the countryside in the context of growing urban and industrial displacement, although representations of hunting and coursing were notably absent.[9] As advocates for tradition, midcentury folklife scholars, without mentioning hunting and coursing, made the case generally that such rural preservation was necessary for the "defence of civilization."[10] Implying an ethical basis for tradition, pioneering folklife scholar Iorwerth C. Peate addressed the British Association for the Advancement of Science in 1959 and editorialized that the machine age (with negative developments such as "the war machine, the finance machine, the industrial machine") represented an "upthrust into barbarism" (with the key movement being an "abandonment of the countryside"). He further stated that the study of rural folklife (particularly the knowledge transmitted from generation to generation) was vital for "our civilization to be saved." "Tradition," he declared, "is the only buffer against the new barbarism." One way to read this rhetoric as a context for the hunting debate is that the ethical basis of tradition (interpreted as the praxis of rural life) was disputed, with both sides claiming to advocate for the progress of civilization and constructing the other (either rural or urban) as barbaric. Recognizing the acceleration of modernity as instigating the discourse on tradition, both sides, with stakes in a future collective and national well-being, had a mission to regain the soul or spirit of living, to find, as Peate pronounced, "a serious meaning and a real purpose in our modern world" (1959, 97–109).

Sexual Symbolism of Hare and Hound

Up to this point, I have historically and philosophically contextualized the debate over coursing, lasting several centuries and climaxing in the Parliamentary deliberation over the Hunting Act 2004, in terms of the role of the countryside amid changing social, political, and environmental conditions in the British experience. Central to the intellectual background of, and subjective stances in, the public confrontations over coursing is advocacy for civilization as essential ethical progress or modernization on the anti side, and concern for the loss of spirit or tradition on the pro side. A host of issues swirls around the conflicts that arose as the two sides attempted at different times to move the discourse to one or the other argument: associations with class and hierarchies in a social welfare state, relations between humans and animals in a civil as well as industrialized society, definitions of cruelty and violence in a feminizing culture, the growing cultural gulf between rural and urban life, divisions over the imaginative perception of British heritage in its rural legacy, loss of British global eminence and self-confidence in its social models, and ethical disputes over the rights of communities to pursue their own practices when they differ from national normative patterns.

Culturally and psychologically, the question remains why the perception of coursing in the British imagination has been so polarized, represented alternatively as a revered and reviled tradition. One answer is that the symbolism of the event evokes different responses arising from the tendency to project human attributes onto animals in competitive sports. Emphasizing the cruelty of coursing, antis in the debate characterize the hare as an "innocent," "little," "terrified" animal pursued by the relentless, overpowering hound. Vera Sheppard, an animal rights campaigner, described the sounds coming from the chased hare as "a heartrending wailing cry like some child in dire distress" (1979, 66–67). Recording artist Maddy Prior drew attention to the image of the hare in the lyrics of "The Fabled Hare" on her popular 1993 album *Year*. There, she symbolized the hare as a woman pursued by the masculinized dog:

Scent of dog, scent of man
Closer closer smell them coming

Hot breath, hot death
Closer closer hard the running

Tongues pant, hearts thump
Closer closer through the fields
Teeth snap, bones crack
Closer closer at my heels.

The hare has thus been infantilized and feminized in the antis' rhetoric to emphasize its image as a defenseless victim. In various unguarded moments, the battle over field sports has erupted into
gender stereotypes, suggesting that members of female-dominated
organizations such as the NSACS have been overly sensitive, while
the male-dominated BFSS has been brutish rather than gentlemanly.
A questionnaire distributed by the BFSS during the 1970s resulted in
many degrading comments describing the NSACS as being composed
of women "who think more of their dogs than their children" (Thomas
1983, 254). Closer to the truth is that many of the activist women used
the metaphor of animals *as* children, extending the concern for animal
rights into the feminist concern for society's patriarchy and the juvenilization of women. Early in the twentieth century, animal welfare activists were linked to suffrage feminism and later with campaigns for child
welfare and domestic abuse protection (Kean 1998, 181–83, 207–10;
Taksel 1992; Thomas 1983, 169–70).[11]

For feminist activists, coursing's use of "beaters" to flush out the
hare referred rhetorically to violence against women, and the accusation that blood sports promote a bloodlust insinuated sexual predation
by the hound, which took a salacious male role over the feminized,
outsized hare. The coursing greyhound, wolfhound, and other gazehounds, given attributes of haughtiness and aggression, were further
categorized as the pursuing male because of their reliance on the consuming gaze, associated with the ogling man. The symbolic connection between staring and men's sexual objectification of women drew
the attention of Freudian psychoanalysts such as Sandor Ferenczi, who
clinically interpreted the protruding eye of the man's gaze as being
unconsciously related to exposed genitals (Ferenczi 1950, 270–75). "I
have no doubt," Ferenczi wrote, "that the sense of embarrassment one
experiences on being stared at, and which keeps one from staring hard

at others, finds its explanation in the sexual-symbolic significance of the parts of the face. . . . I may refer also to the sexual symbolism of ogling, in the bashful drooping of the eyes on someone, etc., further such expressions as 'to cast eyes at someone, to throw sheep's eyes'" (1950, 273–74). On this basis, the use of the gazehound as male surrogate in the frame of the sporting contest overcomes the opprobrium for ogling and encourages conquest of the feminized, chased hare.

The representation of the lustful male is reinforced in the image of the hanging, salivating tongue of the panting dog (particularly the wolfhound and related wolf). *Wolf, hound,* and *dog* are symbolically equivalent slang terms in English for a shady male in pursuit of sex, made famous by Elvis Presley's 1956 hit "Hound Dog" (composed by Americans Jerry Lieber and Mike Stoller). Originally performed by a blues-shouting woman, Big Mama Thornton, in 1952, it includes the admonishment, "You ain't never caught a rabbit and you ain't no friend of mine." The song, reissued in 1978, resonated with British audiences and reached the top twenty-five in the United Kingdom; it has been recorded by musicians as diverse as John Entwhistle and the Royal Artillery (Alanbrooke) Band.

The female sexuality of the hare is suggested by the popular eroticized image of the Playboy bunny, as well as the folk speech equating men with dogs or hounds and their desire for women who have intercourse "like bunnies." Indeed, the nickname "pussy" is commonly applied to hares as well as cats, carrying connotations of the bawdy slang for female genitalia (Smith 1978, 101). Another association between rabbits or hares and female sexuality was the "rabbit test" for pregnancy, common from the 1920s until late in the century (women's urine was injected into female rabbits, which were then checked for signs of ovarian changes). Further linking hare coursing to the violation of women is the characterization I heard of home-produced videos of hare coursing sold over the Internet as "pornography."[12]

More than fox or stag hunting, hare coursing is likened in the antis' rhetoric to rape, particularly in reference to hounds grabbing and mounting the hare, "bringing it down," producing screams, and being rewarded for the score. Moreover, antis typically see coursing as more objectionable than hunting because the very idea of a course evokes the feeling of entrapment related to rape, and the juvenilized image of the hare suggests the molestation of little girls (Smedley 1990, 9). Protest signs at the Waterloo Cup 2005, for instance, complained of the "perversion" of the sport, suggesting abnormal sexual obsessions enacted through coursing. Protesters' outcries against hares being dispatched by wringing their necks can be linked to a fear of strangulation during sexual attack and a belief that men derive perverted, dominative pleasure in choking (Allen 1985; Buzash 1989; Hall 1899, 561; 1914, 333, 349; see also Hall 1897, 163). Activists' negative response to neck wringing as a way to dispose of animals was echoed in women's protest of pigeon shoots in America during the 1990s (discussed in the previous chapter) and earlier in Scotland, where pigeon shoots were outlawed in the 1920s. The characterization of the hare as innocent and infantilized, coupled with the frequent reference to blood in the chase, may be psychologically despicable to antis because of the connection between blood and the loss of virginity (Meyer 2005, 86–107). Perhaps symbolically related are narratives connecting hares to virgins; Wirt Sikes reports in *British Goblins* (1880) a Welsh legend of the prince of Powys pursuing a hare into a great thicket, where he "was amazed to find a virgin of surprising beauty engaged in deep devotion, with the hare he had been pursuing under her robe, boldly facing the dogs, who retired to a distance, howling, notwithstanding all the efforts of the sportsmen to make them seize their prey. . . . The legend is perpetuated by some rude wooden carvings of the saint, with numbers of hares scuttling to her for protection" (162–63). The image of the predatory hound as violating virgins is probably based on the association of the small, furry hare as young yet possessing a sexually receptive "tail." The hound, in contrast, is phallicized by having an extended neck; in coursing, its long muzzle appears to be penetrating the pursued hare.

In coursing events, the ganging behavior of the crowd, urging the hounds to dominate the hare, reinforces the image of sexual predation. One anti observer reported in disgust, "In practice, as soon as the hare passed the slipper the crowd bayed like mad for the greyhounds to be released. Beer swigging supporters shouted: 'Let the bloody dogs go! What's the bastard up to? Can't he see the f . . . hare?' . . . In one course a dog bowled the hare over. Over and over she tumbled, with fur flying, before darting off again to escape" (Huskisson 1983, 133). Antis' frequently mentioned objection to the "tug-of-war" between hounds, with the hare acting as the rope, can be read as a battle of male possessiveness resulting in the hare's treatment as a trophy of domination.

"Preparations for a Day's Coursing in Ireland." *Illustrated Sporting and Dramatic News*, February 23, 1884.

According to Mike Huskisson's narrative, "One dog had hold of her shoulders, the other her back feet. She squeaked and squealed. The dogs tussled for possession and, in an instant, one dog won. As the mounted judge and pickers-up approached he ran off triumphantly, still clutching her by the shoulder. Still she squealed, and still the crowd cheered and jeered" (1983, 134).

Betting among the crowd also drew the ire of antis, because money was made at the expense of suffering animals. At a deeper level, in line with the perception of coursing as sexual predation, gambling can be construed as a symbolic substitute for masturbation, particularly in blood sports in which a masculinized animal dominates or feminizes another animal. The excited use of the hands, building up as the chase ensues, and the vocal encouragement to provide satisfaction and release to the gambler have been likened to autoerotic gratification in interpretations of male-dominated sports such as cockfighting (Dundes 1994, 262–64; Lindner 1950, 93–107). Linguistic evidence comes from the British slang word *flutter* for a small gamble at sporting events. Behaviorally, it invokes the masturbatory image of moving the hands back and forth quickly before the bet is placed and refers to the momentary excitement of taking a risk. It also can be used colloquially to refer to sexual gratification for pleasure rather than passion (Partridge 1970, 291). From the anti viewpoint, the cognitive connection of gambling with coursing events is further evidence of "depravity"; this term, common in the animal rights rhetoric, also suggests that the tradition is driven not by culture but by psychological compulsion.

Restoration and Regeneration of the Land

Common mass media images in the twentieth century of hares as cuddly bunnies, often infantilized and feminized, have contributed to the perception of coursing as rapacious. A literary influence may well be the character of Peter Rabbit, introduced by Beatrix Potter in popular children's books beginning in 1902. In the first story *The Tale of Peter Rabbit*, Potter characterizes Peter sympathetically as he is hounded by Mr. McGregor for wandering into his garden looking for food. British author A. A. Milne created the cutesy, if obsessive gardener figure Rabbit in the Winnie-the-Pooh novels beginning in 1926 (Disney bought the film rights in 1961 and produced several films through the 1980s). The popularization of the cute, cuddly Easter bunny, often feminized by the color pink and associated with the fertility of spring, also undoubtedly had an influence. Animated movies commonly demonize hunters and romanticize their prey, most notably in Walt Disney's global hits *Bambi* (1942), which also has a rabbit character named Thumper, and *Bugs Bunny Rides Again* (1948). In the twenty-first century, the popular movie *Over the Hedge* (2006) features a crazed exterminator's heartlessness, symbolized by the image of a rabbit being pounded on the head adorning his truck, drawing the audience's sympathy for animals in their confrontation with humans. Of the animals in Sony Pictures' *Open Season* (2006)—about woodland creatures taking revenge against hunters—rabbits show up in the greatest number, often to the annoyance of the other animals, and they also take the most abuse. This seems to explain their skittish, frenetic ways, since in the movie they live in a constant state of fear.

The hare has more of a destructive image in agricultural folklife.

Considering the prevalence of open fields in British agriculture, the quickly reproducing hare was cursed for causing damage to crops and plants close to the ground. The animals use their incisors to make a distinctive diagonal cut when clipping off woody twigs, buds, and flower heads. They commonly feed on cereal grains, turnips, and high-value garden crops and kill newly planted saplings and shrubs. Hare populations reportedly multiplied significantly in the mid- to late nineteenth century as increased agricultural efficiency, resulting in higher, more nutritious yields, enabled them to thrive. Before the Ground Game Act allowed tenant farmers to kill hares and rabbits on their land to protect crops, coursing was viewed as a form of pest control. Hare numbers declined after the act was passed but peaked again after World War II, resulting in renewed calls for hunts and courses to reduce the population. These efforts were effective in bringing the numbers back down, and the hare population had stabilized in the United Kingdom at the end of the twentieth century at approximately 800,000, three times greater than the fox population (Committee 2000).

With the high status given to property ownership and the lack of natural barriers in open fields, farmers demonized the hare as a parasitical scourge on the land. Unlike other wildlife that complied with farmers' agrarian dominion, died out, or left for other feeding grounds, hares were like squatters on farmers' fields, feeding on the fruits of human labor. The fear was that if hare reproduction was left unchecked, the animals would devour the landscape and therefore destroy the properties (Evans and Thompson 1972, 127–99). More than other pests, the hare in farm lore is characterized as brazenly defying human control, even mocking landowners with the personae of tricksters or other more fearsome characters. Indicative of this view are British and Irish rural folktales in which witches take the form or are the companions of hares (Evans and Thompson 1972, 142–99; Black 1883, 86–87). According to folklorist Stith Thompson's international motif index, the narrative element of the witch in the form of a hare is confined to British-American sources (Thompson 1975, 3:287). The wizened witch works against fertility and seeks to deplete the life source, such as blood and milk, of other animals; for instance, in Thompson's motif D655.2, the witch transforms herself into a hare to suck cows' milk (Newall 1971, 35–36; Opie and Tatem 1989, 189–90; Simpson and Roud 2000, 166). The natural enemy of the dreaded witch is the dog, and narratives describe witches who agree to participate in coursing because they belittle the dog's power to defeat them (see Baughman 1966, 240–41; Briggs 1991, 2:664–66; Ballard 1991, 75; Lysaght 1991, 43–44).

The apparent invincibility of the witch-hare (also referred to as *monstrous* hare) owes to farmers' frustrations in trying to eradicate the pests from their fields (Smith 1978, 97–102). Other dire consequences connected with sighting or passing a hare that persist in the twenty-first century include producing a harelip in the fetus of a pregnant woman and portending fire (Ballard 1985, 70; Opie and Tatem 1989, 190, 193; Eberly 1991, 230).[13] In rural folk speech, *hare* or *rabbit* is a taboo word; Iona Opie and Moira Tatem reported that as late as 1953, young boys told them, "So powerful is the animal supposed to be [as an ill omen] that people will not even say the word. They refer to it as a 'Wilfred' or 'one of them furry things.' But if one person is very angry with another and really wishes them bad luck he will say 'Rabbits to you'" (Opie and Tatem 1989, 193). This cognitive categorization of hares and rabbits as taboo and ill omens fits into the folk idea of witchlike or monstrous (or lunar) characteristics attached to nonnormative or uncontrollable behavior. Hares, for example, are considered bizarre and excludable rather than domesticated and integrated. Signs of ominous behavior include the "madness" expressed by the hare's springtime nocturnal activity, tooth grinding, foot thumping, and wailing.

Related to the characterization of the hare as prey is the hunting or chasing game of "Hare and Hounds" associated with British folklife. The game is usually described as a boys' game played primarily in the country (Opie and Opie 1969, 176–78; Gomme 1964, 1:191; Sutton-Smith 1972, 200–201). "Hares" are chosen for their running ability and are given a head start before the "hounds" go after them. The game is related to coursing because the players generally agree on the direction taken and the bounds for the chase; they also may designate a "home" to which the hares must return. Enjoyment of the game, according to players, comes not only from the thrill of the "hunt" (or escape) but also from the playing field covered. Children use the context, or pretext, of play to enter otherwise off-limits areas such as private property, including gardens and fields. Hares are encouraged to use deception as well as fleetness as they evade their pursuers; they may double back on their tracks, alter the route, or even hide until the hounds have passed (Gomme 1964, 1:191; Brewster 1953, 77). Playing the game as dusk approaches makes the chase more challenging, straining the use of sight. The game is male dominated, according to folklorists Iona and Peter Opie, because it can get "rough," in their words, when the boys in the role of hares are captured. "If the hounds catch the hares, the hounds give them any punishment they like," a boy explained to the Opies. Smacks on the head are common, and the Opies also heard that the victors may pretend to eat the prey (Opie and Opie 1969, 177). Reflecting on his boyhood pursuits, one informant in Northern Ireland remembered: "I mentioned some of the games we played at school. One of the favourite ones was 'Hounds and Hares.' Now I think we mentioned the tradition of people walking on foot, and hunting all round the countryside. And that was, we imitated that in the school, because you had the hare, was appointed, and the hare got a few minutes to hide, and then the hounds all started out after, so there was a wild chase, and eventually the hare was caught, and another hare was found. So we just imitated what was around in real life" (Ballard 2006).

Besides the enactment of hare coursing in this children's game, its other significant feature is the reflection of countryside praxis in its reference to control of property. The dramatic structure that drives the game is the hounds' removal of the hares from the "home" presumed to belong to the hounds; although the hares are being chased away, they nonetheless seek to return (Bronner 1990; Dundes 1964). They disregard the concept of proprietorship by roaming freely over hill and dale. Brian Sutton-Smith even reported, "Players were not loath to go in the front door of a house and out the back," and it was common to take shortcuts across private gardens (1972, 200). School officials noticed that the harshness of this field play carried over to the playgrounds, and according to Sutton-Smith, many supervisors were under pressure, especially in the critical period of social reform and anti-coursing efforts between 1900 and 1920, to decrease the number of "rougher games and practices of earlier years" (1972, 12).

Defenders of the game point out the physical exertion gained from participation. Arguably, the running is motivated by a goal. Symbolic expulsion of undesirable elements drives the game rather than exercise or even capture. The pursuit should take an extended time, informants told the Opies: "to have a good game you want an hour at least because you might run for miles. We go all across the country, round the school, over the rivers, across bogs" (Opie and Opie 1969, 176). The action of the game invites trespass over property. The hounds' job is to restore order by eliminating the unruly hare, using skills of sight and persistence as well as anticipation of the devilish hares' duplicity. But even if the hounds are triumphant in capture, they learn that the pesky hares find a way to return—and the chase resumes on other occasions. In some play, captured hares become hounds rather than going "out," suggesting that action against the hares will restore order, symbolized by the landowner-surrogate hounds (Bronner 1988, 180). One indication of the order based on property is the layout of the course itself, since it is common for the hares to defy the previously agreed-upon route. These features suggest the game's meaning for countryside praxis, underscoring the need to eliminate hares from the land if the order of farm and property is to be maintained.

To be sure, not all coursers played Hare and Hounds as children, regarded *hare* as taboo speech, or spouted beliefs about bad omens associated with hares, but my point is that their perception of the hare as pernicious, justifying its elimination by dogs cast in the role of hero, draws on agrarian experience and lore. Rather than viewing hares as innocent and defenseless, coursers consider them harmful and powerful. Symbolically, the destruction of hares appears justified not just as an eradication of a pest but also as a restoration, or even regeneration, of the land. The confrontation enacted between hare and hound is a contest for control of the land and the imposition of human dominion.

Child's plate with a coursing scene.

Historically, a material culture of fancy dishes and decorative arts that depict coursing scenes of hounds pursuing hares can be read as verification of the sanctity of the property by removing its violators. Although they may seem strange kitchen decorations to modern onlookers, coursing scenes suggest the bounty that comes from the imposition of dominion (Prescott 1984, 55–56). Many of the decorated bowls, dishes, and tureens are oversized and suggest the communal sharing of hardy soups and stews. Indeed, coursing trophies such as the Waterloo Cup look more like bulging, often gaudy, containers than cups. Viewers can appreciate the skills of the hounds touted in their triumph over the pesky, potent hares (stamina, agility, persistence). They can grasp these objects as reminders of the human mastery that is considered essential to success and status in the fields, defined by property.

In this agrarian worldview, property overseen by sighthounds gazing out over the fields is also an extension of the value of the patriarchal family. Contributing to dogs' association with Britishness is their common depiction on coats of arms. The greyhound is the most common heraldic dog, often connected to good breeding, aggressive power, fidelity, stability, and affection (Branigan 2004, 101–4). Hounds as male surrogates are highly regarded because of their regal associations, the suggestion of being first in rank. In animal welfare campaigns throughout the twentieth century, dogs were thought to receive better treatment than feminized animals such as cats and hares. Female activists' attempt to improve the public's regard for cats, in fact, was a social statement about changing gender roles in the family as well as in society. In the context of the present discussion, suffice it to say that dogs were represented with the male heads of families in portraiture more frequently than cats were. Whereas dogs were viewed overlooking fields as the landowner's domain, cats appeared in domestic pursuits (regulating mice in the kitchen) and were associated with working-class strata. Many antis saw dogs, in fact, as predatory; this view has been around since the nineteenth century, when it was claimed that "no boy . . . would dream of passing a cat without throwing at it, setting a dog on it, or chevying it in some way" (Kean 1998, 160). In relation to coursing, antis viewed the campaign to protect hares as a successor to the earlier attempt to raise the status of cats (as female surrogates), while pros extolled the heroic qualities of the hound as the foundation of British family and countryside tradition.

In the wake of the ban, coursers vowed to continue the fight to maintain their sport, while animal rights advocates turned their attention to extending the ban to Northern Ireland, where coursing is still legal ("Way Ahead" 2006). The National Coursing Club advised members in Great Britain how to stay within the limits of the law and still use dogs to pursue prey by applying the guidelines of "stalking" and "flushing out" hares with a maximum of two dogs ("Dogs" 2006). Other huntsmen turned to falconry, although many coursers insisted that they were not ready to abandon their hounds, which are central to the tradition and to their sense of identity (Bowcott 2005). But more than the question of how to facilitate or abolish the pursuit of prey, the aftermath of the ban brought to the fore the signification of the ways of life represented by traditional practices in the "modern world" or "civilization." At stake in this inquiry is the relative value of city and country, men and women, animal and human, and the ethics and metaphors that humans live by.

Future Shot

"I'll tell you why I'm the future of hunting," eighteen-year-old Meredith Odato said after winning the Pennsylvania Game Commission's youth essay contest. "Hunting is not only a tradition," she continued, "but also a remarkable way of life; a lifelong process devoted to the establishment of character and knowledge, unique qualities known exclusively to those who hunt. Indisputably, I am the future of hunting because I acquired so much from predecessors, including one vital responsibility: to prolong the legacy of hunting" (Odato 2005). Game Commission officials beamed because they had promoted the contest as a way to focus attention on "passing along the legacy of hunting from one generation to the next." This definition of tradition gained importance because they had read the latest statistics from the U.S. Fish and Wildlife Service and knew that the media would report another decline in the number of hunters. Their design of the contest placed much of the blame for this decline on a lack of fidelity to tradition by youngsters and their hunting parents, lured away by mass-mediated culture.

An unnamed conspirator in hunting's woes is the animal rights movement, although by diminishing its adherents as a radical fringe of wacko tree huggers, hunting advocates do not avow the movement's full impact on cultural norms. But hunters sense their presence; they are the enemy. Worry fills the faces of hunting advocates, and they see a glimmer of hope in the words of a bright-eyed girl who learned her skills from her father. Advocating more concerted initiatives to encourage her youthful cohort, Bud Pidgeon of the U.S. Sportsmen's Alliance warned, "If we don't start replenishing hunters now, we could let our heritage slip away" (quoted in "Young Hunters" 2005). The rhetorical emphasis on tradition and heritage lets people know that whether they hunt or not, the values represented by hunting in America are theirs. Hunting is not just for hunters, he intimated; it is a symbol for all people who care about family, community, and nation. To his thinking, as the future of hunting goes, so goes the national culture.

Heidi Prescott of the Humane Society of the United States, leader of the "enemy camp," agrees, but in her mind, if hunting does not decline, society will devolve. Her explanation for the slipping numbers is that hunting is a relic of the past, when people gained their provisions from the wild; it is detestable as a recreational pursuit because its enjoyment depends on killing and abuse. Her message echoes that of a century earlier when the British predecessor of the Humane Society, the Humanitarian League, declared, "In a civilised community, where the services of the hunter are no longer required, blood-sports are simply an anachronism, a relic of savagery which time will gradually remove" (Salt 1915, vii). Pragmatically and ethically speaking, according to spokesman Henry Salt, "not only the cruelty, but the wastefulness of the practice of breeding and killing animals for mere amusement, should be made clear" (1915, vii). In the twenty-first century, animal rights advocates call for moral strength by comparing their work to nineteenth-century abolitionist movements to eradicate slavery, for a key issue in both is the unconscionable treatment of life as property—abused, dispensable, killed property (see Spiegel 1996). Resentful of the notion that animal rights is a single-issue or fringe movement, some leaders see the campaign against hunting as a broad-based battle against prevailing exploitative social and economic structures. They use the rhetoric of "liberation" to signal that revolutionary change is the goal, going beyond welfare or even rights for animals. Gary Francione (1996) of the Rutgers University School of Law, for instance, trumpeted the view to an American audience: "The plain fact is that this country and other industrial countries are deeply dependent on animal exploitation to sustain their present economic structures. The plain fact is that we are more dependent on animal exploitation than were the states of the southern United States on human slavery. . . . Now is the time to develop a radical—nonviolent but radical—approach to animal rights as part of an overall program of social justice." Even for those activists who do not go so far and want to mainstream animal rights as part of modern liberal politics, the hunter is a destructive killer, plain and simple, if not a slaveholding tracker.

In the twenty-first century, hunting advocates obviously have a different image of the recreational hunter: in an era of urban sprawl and concern for the environment, the modern hunter is a conservationist, a last line of defense against an industrial and corporate scourge on nature. Young Meredith Odato, in her message about the future of hunting, thinks of herself that way. "As a student of nature," she wrote, "I developed into a young steward, one who encourages ethical management and conservation of wildlife and wild places" (Odato 2005). Various "hunting heritage" bills passed in state legislatures iterated the appealing ring of wildlife management and conservation. The Hunting Heritage Protection Act introduced at the federal level by Senator Saxby Chambliss of Georgia in 2005 underscored the point in six of his seven congressional "findings":

(1) recreational hunting is an important and traditional recreational activity in which 13,000,000 people in the United States 16 years of age and older participate;

(2) hunters have been and continue to be among the foremost supporters of sound *wildlife management and conservation practices* in the United States;

(3) persons who hunt and organizations relating to hunting provide direct *assistance to wildlife managers and enforcement officers* of the Federal Government and State and local governments;

(4) purchases of hunting licenses, permits, and stamps and excise taxes on goods used by hunters have generated billions of dollars for *wildlife conservation, research, and management;*

(5) recreational hunting is an essential component of *effective wildlife management* by—
    (A) reducing conflicts between people and wildlife; and
    (B) providing incentives for the *conservation of—*
        (i) wildlife; and
        (ii) habitats and ecosystems on which wildlife depend;

(6) each State has established at least 1 agency staffed by professionally trained *wildlife management* personnel that has legal authority to manage the wildlife in the State; and

(7) recreational hunting is an *environmentally acceptable activity* that occurs and can be provided for on Federal public land without adverse effects on other uses of the land. (S.1522; emphasis added)

Again, tradition enters the rhetoric as justification, with the implication that hunting's status as a traditional activity in a modernizing society makes it deserving of protection—and value laden.

The politicized rhetoric was also proclaimed by Pennsylvania Governor Tom Ridge (who went on to head Homeland Security) when he urged attendees of his national Governor's Symposium on North America's Hunting Heritage to develop a strategy to "revitalize and reinvigorate the *tradition of hunting*." Hunting, he baldly proclaimed, "is part of our culture, part of our history, part of our economy and, hopefully, part of our future" (Schneck 1998, A16).

Prescott was skeptical. Addressing another hunting heritage conference, she observed that the negative images of hunting undermine the claims of hunting advocates that hunters are great wildlife managers and conservationists. She noted the irony of an animal rights spokesperson speaking at a hunting heritage conference being picketed by her compatriots. Given the opportunity to explain her position, she did not hold back. She told the hunting advocates, "When abusive hunting events are exposed, the image of hunting goes down one peg further in the eyes of the viewer. You know we will be right there to make sure the situation gets maximum exposure. That is one way hunters play right into our hands, and one way hunters are their own worst enemies. Believe me, the hunters give us constant ammunition to use in our campaigns against hunting" (Prescott 1995, 3). Prescott's prime example was the Hegins pigeon shoot. She urged hunters to sign a petition against it, even if, in her words, it meant "getting in bed with the enemy." If hunters refused to stop hunting, they should at least clean up their act, she insisted, and they could start by eliminating activities like the pigeon shoot. To those who answered that pigeon shoots do not fall under the praxis and ethic of hunting, Prescott pronounced, "As long as hunters continue to defend these practices, it will remain hunting in the minds of the public and in our minds and we will continue to refer to it as hunting" (1995, 5). She predicted that if the route to ending hunting is to eliminate one egregious example at a time—prairie dog shoots, cockfights, dogfights, coyote killing contests, pheasant tower shoots, "canned hunts," the use of bait or hounds to hunt black bears—the debate over hunting and animal-related recreation will last for many years, but inevitably, killing for sport will end if society seeks ethical progress.

From Prescott's viewpoint, the hunters' claim to be conservationists is infuriating. Her organization makes the case that hunters trample on the environment as well as extinguish wildlife. Animal rights groups, as part of environmental activism, work toward the preservation of natural habitats and the protection of threatened and endangered species. They create sanctuaries for animals, such as Cleveland Amory's Black Beauty Ranch in Texas or the Rabbit Sanctuary in South Carolina. Unlike zoos that imprison and distress animals for a twisted human sense of enjoyment, these sanctuaries, according to Amory's vision, are places "where animals are looked after, not looked at" ("Cleveland" 2007). They seek "humane approaches to your wild neighbors," such as using noise to scatter pigeons or using bright and flashy objects to repel crows rather than shooting them. With a self-promoted environmental protection agenda and altruistic, humane motives, animal rights groups felt assaulted when the federal Animal Enterprise Terrorism Act (AETA) was signed into law in 2006. Animal activists protested that by outlawing acts of "damaging or interfering with the operations of an animal enterprise," the law criminalized constitutionally protected free speech and civil disobedience. They attributed its passage to a backlash against the implications of social and economic structural changes as animal rights victories mounted, as well as a post-9/11 hysteria that labeled aboveground advocates dangerous ecoterrorists.

How have life and hunting changed as a result of the animal rights movement? One obvious consequence is the growth of vegetarianism and veganism since the late twentieth century. More than 6 percent of the American population is now vegetarian, and restaurants and caterers regularly offer vegetarian menus to their customers. Although this change can be attributed in part to health consciousness, self-described vegetarians and vegans commonly cite moral or ethical reasons as the prime motivation for not eating animals ("Information Sheet" 2007). Vegetarianism in the United Kingdom has fared less well; meat consumption is on the rise again after vegetarianism's peak in 1997, when more than 3 million people declared themselves vegetarians in the wake of the scare over mad cow disease. Nonetheless, overall since 1973, meat consumption is sharply down. Many citizens who do not identify themselves as vegetarian nonetheless avoid eating red meat, not only for health concerns but also because of the cognitively disturbing bestial or carnivorous image of consuming bloody flesh. Consumers are also adversely inclined toward companies that use animals to test their products, and animal rights groups have pressured companies to pull the plug on product development with animals. One victory came in 2007 when the world's leading soft-drink manufacturers, Coca-Cola and Pepsi, both agreed to stop funding research using animals. Another signal of animal rights consciousness is that Hollywood filmmakers routinely assure viewers that no animals were harmed in the making of their pictures.

In a 2007 Gallup survey of American values and beliefs, 38 percent of respondents thought it was morally wrong to buy or wear clothing made of fur (Saad 2007). Animal rights campaigns were successful in outlawing cockfights nationwide when the last state where it was legal—Louisiana—agreed to ban the practice in 2007. Bolstered by this success, animal rights groups moved on to pigeon shoots, lobbying state legislatures to pass official bans. In Great Britain, a critical victory was the virtual shutdown of Huntingdon Life Sciences near Cambridge, Europe's largest vivisection laboratory, after animal rights groups publicized the plight of suffering dogs, monkeys, and rabbits. Campaigner Greg Avery of Stop Huntingdon Animal Cruelty promised, "When Huntingdon closes we won't just go on to another company. We will go on to a whole area of animal abuse. And look to knock out big chunks— puppy farming, factory farming, circuses and zoos. All these could be finished. We're becoming bigger, even more intelligent and even more determined not just to take companies down but to finish whole areas of animal abuse" (Cox and Vadon 2004). Emboldened by such victories, the Calgary Animal Rights Coalition announced its intention "to challenge long held *folkloric* attitudes towards those with whom we share this planet; to stop the abuse and exploitation of non-human animals," and protests escalated against circuses, rodeos, and horse races (Animal Rights Canada 2007; "About SHARK" 2007; "Activists" 2002). Its deep-seated "folkloric attitudes" being what they are, the American public has been less receptive to assaults on cultural institutions such as circuses, rodeos, and horse races than on corporate testing of commercial products or bloody sports of ill repute such as cockfights and dogfights (Beers 2006). It appears that the symbolic association of these institutions with community and nineteenth-century roots of a pioneer or ascendant America sways people to support them despite sometimes graphic exposés (Allen 1998; Cormack 2007; Davis 2002).

Where does that leave recreational hunting? Because hunting covers a wide swath of experiences, the animals being pursued rather than hunting as a praxis are important to the public in making ethical decisions. For example, protests of rattlesnake hunts generate less sympathy than protests of baby seal hunts, and predatory bobcats are less sympathetic than mourning doves or whales. As I have shown, the stalking and killing of deer, pigeons, and rabbits receive mixed reviews and cause ambivalent feelings, which has added to the controversies over hunting these animals. In Great Britain, the Hunting Act of 2004 that banned hare coursing and foxhunting was probably less about the status of hares and foxes and more about the urban welfare state's shift in attitude against the property-owning aristocracy rooted in the countryside, despite protests that this view did not accurately portray participants.

Could an equivalent ban occur in America? A 2003 Gallup poll found that an overwhelming 73 percent of respondents somewhat opposed or strongly opposed a ban on all types of hunting, while a substantial minority of 22 percent somewhat or strongly supported such a ban. Yet when Americans were asked whether they favored hunting animals for sport, they were less supportive. A majority of 53 percent said they opposed hunting, 42 percent supported hunting, and 5 percent did not know. The strongest support came from men (54 percent, versus 30 percent of women) and whites (47 percent of whites, versus 23 percent of blacks, 29 percent of Hispanics, and 22 percent of Asians). Support for hunting was consistent across all four regions of the country, but the two that "strongly" favored hunting were the Midwest and East, with 24 and 22 percent, respectively. Despite the popular characterization of hunters as ignorant and lower class, the poll showed that support for hunting was highest in the three highest income ranges, and those with a high school diploma or college degree were more likely to be favorably inclined than those less educated. One perception that seemed to hold was that the "older generation"—those older than forty—viewed hunting more favorably than the "younger generation." The weakest support was among eighteen- to twenty-nine-year-olds. As far as political culture goes, the margin between conservatives and liberals was not as large as I expected: 45 percent of conservatives favored hunting, compared with 33 percent of liberals.

It could be that direct-action protests of hunting turned people off to the idea of a ban. In a 1990 poll, 72 percent of respondents were strongly opposed to the tactic of activists going into the woods during hunting season to harass hunters and scare away wildlife, whereas only 3 percent lent their support. Hunting's association with heartland or grassroots traditions also figured into public opinion. The view that animal rights undermined tradition was evident in widely publicized campaigns against indigenous groups resurrecting ancient customs, including whale hunting, to recapture their heritage (Sullivan 2000; Weinbaum 2004). Observers noted a backlash against the animal rights movement as a small, irritating cadre of professionally trained extremists seemed hell-bent on taking away ordinary folks' choices—from eating meat to wearing leather shoes. Indeed, looking to the future, one of the movement's leaders acknowledged, "We need to reshape the movement as one of grassroots activists, and not 'professional activists' who populate the seemingly endless number of animal rights groups" (Francione 1996).

Though willing to be convinced on the ills of corporate and scientific culture, ordinary people seemed less receptive to the wholesale end of a long-standing vernacularized tradition. Qualitatively, in story and image, people relate hunting to heritage and traditional values of father-son bonding, the pioneer wilderness, and rough-hewn self-reliance. Say what you will about over-the-top rocker-hunter Ted Nugent, but he struck a responsive nerve in the public with his best-selling *God, Guns, & Rock 'N' Roll* (2000) when he wrote, "at deer camp a unified focus envelops the family unit, and a combination of individualism and team effort takes on a life of its own that epitomizes what should be, and is, family. Water is carried, wood is stacked, fires are stoked, food is prepared, dishes are washed, and trash is handled. . . . Certainly a grand and easily grasped lesson in reality; all but missing in today's crazed and scattered household" (233–34). To be sure, animated depictions of ruthless hunters are less than complimentary in movies ranging from *Bambi* (1942) to *Open Season* (2006). Yet hunters also appear to be leaders and competitors, judging from the seemingly requisite images of presidential candidates venturing out to hunt since the 1980s. Are they trying to be role models in the incarnation of some biblical Nimrod or heroic Boone and Crockett? In the 2004 presidential campaign between George W. Bush and John Kerry, a lively debate ensued as to who was the true sportsman and who supported hunters (and the Second Amendment right to bear arms) more (Evans and Marshall 2004). Bush expressed admiration for Theodore Roosevelt as the kind of hardy leader "who understood that hunting and fishing are a very important part of the American scene," whereas Kerry said that hunting made him physically vigorous and environmentally conscious. In his words, "I hunt and fish and climb mountains—I've been an outdoors person all my life and have an enormous respect for our relationship to the balance that's necessary to preserve that enjoyment" (Evans and Marshall 2004, 54). After the election, Vice President Dick Cheney suffered public disapproval after he accidentally shot a companion during a quail hunt in Texas and delayed disclosure of the incident. The subject of countless blogs, talk shows, and comedians' barbs, Cheney's capabilities and ethical responsibilities as a hunter, and a national leader, were frequently questioned in the discourse (Mignot 2006; Leibovich 2006).

In an analog of the "Lucky Shot" tall tale (see tale type 1890 in Uther 2004, 2:478–79; motif X1110 in Reaver 1972, 370), presidential hopeful Hillary Clinton in 2008 tried to endear herself to "Joe Sixpack" by telling this story: "I've hunted. My father taught me how to hunt. I went duck hunting in Arkansas. I remember standing in that cold water, so cold at first light. I was with a bunch of my friends, all men. The sun's up, the ducks are flying and they are playing a trick on me. They said, 'We're not going to shoot, you shoot.' They wanted to embarrass me. The pressure was on. So I shot, and I shot a banded duck and they were as surprised as I was" (Suarez 2008). Her rival for the Democratic nomination Barack Obama was not amused and fired back by questioning Clinton's genuineness using pioneer imagery: "She's talking like she's Annie Oakley! Clinton's out there like she's on the duck blind every Sunday, she's packing a six-shooter! C'mon!" (Miller 2008). Was Obama insinuating that Clinton did not fit the hunter ethos because she was a woman, affluent, or cosmopolitan?

Talking to people and listening to their stories, I have found that a tipping factor in attitudes toward hunting is a libertarian streak in Americans. Even if they do not want to hunt, they believe that hunters have the right to maintain their tradition as a proud legacy if it does not impede others. They think of hunting as a noncommercial, individualistic or family custom pitting the adventurous hunter against imposing nature. Ethically, this seems to elevate hunting above spectator sports that cheer competitive killing on an artificial stage, such as pigeon shoots, prairie dog shoots, and snake roundups, and commercial exploitation, such as seal and whale hunts. They find, in fact, something admirable about the fortitude involved in a primal activity conducted in the woods or wilderness, and they respect its rejection of the trappings of modern technological and massified culture. One component of their allowance for hunting is that they do not directly encounter the activity, or the guns it entails, because it is pursued away from home in remote wilderness locations. In addition, the animals constituting hunters' prey are generally thought of as dangerous or in need of control, so hunters might be seen as performing a service requiring pluck as well as developed skills and traditional, handed-down wisdom. Accordingly, many perceive hunting to be a redemptive, romantic endeavor that preserves the values of fidelity to family and nature and respect for tradition. As famed aviator Chuck Yeager put it, "To me, hunting brings out all that is good in our country. I really enjoy meeting people who like to hunt because they are, for the most part, truly honest and caring people. These are the kind of people who teach their kids to hunt and fish, the way I taught my children and grandchildren. These are people whose values are sound and ethics are solid. The future of hunting depends on our young people and with what I've seen of the quality of young people getting involved today, I believe that future is bright" (2001, xiv).

A few signs bear out Yeager's optimism. One reason for hope, according to hunting heritage advocates, is the rise in the number of women taking up hunting. The proportion of women hunters in America has grown from 4 percent to 12 percent in less than ten years. Betty Lou Fegely, chairperson of the board of the Outdoor Writers Association of America, explained the trend as feminist empowerment in the wake of the dissolution of the two-parent family. "Millions of women today find themselves alone and facing the challenge of leading their children to more meaningful lives. Hunting is something of lifetime value," she said (Schneck 1998). According to a survey by *Field and Stream*, the majority of women hunters were guided by men; they were introduced to hunting as children by their fathers (42 percent) or as adults by their boyfriends or husbands (39 percent). Defying the image of the docile honey at home, these modern-day Calamity Janes cited "excitement and adventure" as the prime reason for going hunting. Their prime target, as for men, is deer (Hiss 2007; Hurst 2007).

Cultural critics have worried that, driven by the liberating desire to invert the image of the pursued sexual object or caged wife at home, these women have fetishized guns so that their purpose of protection is turned into aggressive, antisocial impulse (Browder 2006; Stange 1997; Stange and Oyster 2000).

Mary Zeiss Stange, a hunter and author, resists the categorization that when women stalk animals in the woods they are following in men's footsteps or becoming she-devils. Invoking the Roman mythic figure of Diana (Artemis in Greek mythology) as huntress, nurturer of children, and feminine protector of the weak and vulnerable, she insists that a metaphorical refocusing occurs for women hunters that renders the symbolism of blood and pursuit differently. Not mere hunting companions to their male counterparts, women are less concerned about male bonding or being "one of the guys" than about experiencing nature as feminine and comprehending life-and-death issues (Hurst 2007). She claims that "Woman the Hunter gives the lie to conventional gender categories, in another—having to do with the heart of the matter, with blood-knowledge, she transforms them." Of particular value on both a spiritual and a physical level, Stange finds that when she goes out hunting, "the dual functions of giving and taking life are fused; hence the frequent comparison of hunting to childbirth, and the complex symbols and rituals attaching to Artemis." "Blood is a fact of female life," she emphasizes, "a continual reminder of our rootedness in the life-death-life process. By virtue of the interplay of biological identity and socially imposed role, the manifold implications of killing in order to live are for women necessarily very close to the surface of consciousness" (Stange 1997, 188).

Another trend that hunting and anti-hunting groups have been monitoring is the liberalization of state restrictions on young hunters. To encourage youth hunts, various states have proposed lowering the legal age for hunting and trapping to as low as ten years. Another strategy is to allow youth exemptions on antler restrictions and to offer discounted combination licenses that join standard hunting license privileges with archery, muzzle loading, and fur trapping. In Pennsylvania, the state had a financial incentive to encourage youth hunting: regaining lost revenue. Junior license sales dropped 40 percent from 1976 through 1999, and the combination license program resulted in a rebound (Kittrell 2003). Supporters emphasized hunting's coming-of-age function in pushing for such programs. For example, Ed Wentzler, a spokesman for United Bowhunters of Pennsylvania, commented, "I can't think of a better way to put a child into a position where he rises to a level of maturity" (Lewis and Murphy 2001, A12). To compensate for the fathers who are not passing the tradition down, the Game Commission also initiated a mentoring program focused on special youth hunting seasons such as squirrel, waterfowl, and antlerless deer (Schneck 2001b, 2007). In an effort to expand hunting time on weekends for nine-to-five, Monday-through-Friday wage earners and their children, various proposals have been floated to allow hunting on Sunday.

Game commission measures to expand hunting among youth have been criticized by animal advocacy groups as exploitation of children and, worse, a danger to them. Prescott linked the "national crisis" of violence committed by children to the maltreatment of animals, and she accused hunting of nurturing abuse. In a press release opposing a Pennsylvania bill to join thirteen other states that allow ten-year-olds to hunt, Prescott stated, "Putting guns and steel-jawed leghold traps in the hands of a 10-year-old is irresponsible for many reasons. Children should be taught kindness and compassion for other creatures, not taught to injure and kill them for fun" (Fund 2001).

One skirmish in the debate occurred during deer season when a Harrisburg newspaper printed a front-page picture of a three-year-old carrying a foreleg ripped from a 130-pound doe being butchered by her grandfather (Klaus 2004, A1). Family tradition was part of the story. Theodore Lupey bragged that he was part of a four-generation hunting family. His father had started him out hunting rabbits as a child, until he eventually graduated to deer. Now his four sons hunt, but his daughter does not. Invoking the tall tale of the "Lucky Shot" (see tale type 1890 in Uther 2004, 2:478–79; motif X1110 in Reaver 1972, 370), he told the reporter that he brings only two shells with him when he goes out at the start of deer season. "For 13 years in a row, I got a deer with one shot. I'm feeling lucky today" (Klaus 2004, A1). What sparked letter writers, however, was the photograph, raising questions about the welfare of the child. Some readers were outraged that the paper had printed such a horrible sight; others pointed to the animal's dismemberment as evidence of how the hunting culture desensitizes children to violence; still others defended the scene as teaching the realities of country life.

Three-year-old Aryanna Lupey removes a deer's foreleg from her grandfather's butcher shop while her twin sister, Alexis, tries to help Theodore Lupey, who bagged a 130-pound deer on his Pennsylvania property. (Photo by Christopher Millette for the *Patriot-News*, Harrisburg, Pennsylvania)

Tania Wolf wrote in immediately to say, "This image has to be one of the most horrifying things I've ever seen on the front page of a newspaper." What disturbed her was "that a man would actually let his granddaughter walk around with it as if it was the same as the latest Barbie" (Wolf 2004). The mother of the child replied, declaring that she had no problem with her daughter's actions. She wrote that her girls look forward to hunting season when her relatives bring in a deer. "This serves as a tradition as well as a bonding experience," she emphasized, and she observed that her children had matured as a result of being involved in the butchering. Then she pointed a scolding finger at mass culture represented by Barbie when she wrote, "I would rather have them engrossed in learning activities such as this, than playing video games (much of which contain unnecessary violence) and watching TV. . . . At least my children know the process by which meat is made before it heads to the supermarket" (Lupey 2004). She had support from another mother who wrote that the real violence is on the nightly news, not in the woods. Implying a critique of the fragmentizing effect of modern, mass-mediated culture, she pointed out a positive consequence of the girl's involvement: "At least their family is spending time together" (Sheldon 2004).

Some readers protested the depiction of a butchered animal and criticized hunting and exploitation by humans in general. "I was shocked, disgusted and infuriated," Caroline Simpson (2004) complained to the editors. She challenged them by asking, "You would never run a photo with an animal carrying a human being's leg; why run a photo of a young child carrying a poor deer's leg?" Outraged that the picture glorified the "yearly slaughtering of these gentle animals," Susan Afflerbach (2004) proclaimed, "I pity the children who are being taught that horror scenes like this are normal. And I pity the adults who take pleasure in this so-called sport." One boy wrote in to have his say, lest the grownups think kids are being forced to hunt against their will. Fourteen-year-old Tim Martin (2004) exclaimed in his letter, "Please, just hear me out on this one, and grow up." He continued, "Hunting is a tradition thousands of years old . . . , but as soon as someone does something like this [give a three-year-old a deer leg], it's time to shut the whole operation down." He felt "disgusted," he wrote, "with how all these people shun myself and millions of other Americans because we enjoy hunting."

The Pennsylvania bill to lower the hunting age was defeated, leading some commentators to wonder whether, by the time children are teenagers, they are already too addicted to mass media or alienated from family to take up hunting. Forty-something bow hunter Finn Anthony told one reporter that children are "missing that time with the family, out in the woods with their parents or uncles or aunts. You don't really get time with your family today—either Dad's working too much or the kids are glued to the television or the computer. Then it's bedtime and the next day you do it all over" (Lewis and Murphy 2001, A12).

Although viewed as being from different worlds, hunting and media have joined in a host of video and computer games. Even though the games do not result in the death of animals, they have generated controversy because they portray simulated hunting as the ultimate entertaining thrill. In 2006, a coin-operated video game called Big Buck Hunter Pro became the hottest-selling, biggest-moneymaking video game in bars and arcades across America. It received notoriety because it was popular outside of traditional hunting regions and, according to MSNBC, "has become surprisingly popular in liberal bastions like New York City that have strict gun laws and where the idea of real hunting repulses many residents" (Goldman 2006). The game epitomizes the "first-person shooter" perspective, in which the player lifts a gun and shoots at the screen. Big Buck players are "virtually" transported to Montana, Idaho, Nevada, and Wyoming to stalk elk, antelope, bighorn sheep, and moose in addition to bucks. They score points for accuracy, distance, and the animal's weight. A head or neck shot instantly brings down the animal; gut shots take two or three rounds. The game's designers worked in ethical considerations by assigning penalties to players who take shots at ewes or does, portrayed as innocent. Death for the computer-generated animals is dramatic. As Adam Goldman reported, "When blasted, the deer tumble to the ground; the birds explode into billows of feathers, the bunny rabbits into a cloud of fur. Bonus rounds include shooting frenetic turkey, rampaging boar, thick cow paddies, whiskey jugs and ducks. The machines spit out endearing lines like this one: 'That's some nice shootin'' and other catchy commentary" (2006). The ease of killing in the game has sounded an alarm in post-Columbine America, where there is a fear that shooting play is a prelude to violent reality (Boal 2000–2001; Budra 2004, 1–12; Poole 2000). Although real animals are not killed in the game, animal advocates such as Lucy Knight find it "disturbing for people to get so much pleasure out of it," especially since many players are not hunters or people who would ever take up hunting, yet they are still titillated by killing animals (Goldman 2006). Another safety concern is the linkage between drinking and shooting, because this kind of arcade entertainment is especially prevalent in bars and casinos.

The line between media-generated fantasy and reality became even more blurred with the development of "Internet hunts." Hailed by promoters as the digital future, where hunting thrills can be experienced without stepping into the wild, Internet hunting has attracted criticism as a combination of the worst traits of mass-mediated culture and the bloodlust of hunting. It started in January 2005 when entrepreneur John Lockwood let a friend become the first hunter to kill a confined animal with a computer click rather than the pull of a trigger. The digital hunter sat in his home forty-five miles from Lockwood's hunting preserve in the Texas hill country and, with digicam technology, fixed the animal in his sights before clicking his mouse to signal a shot. A rifle mounted in a blind back on Lockwood's ranch then fired a bullet at a wild hog hunched over a feeding station. From that auspicious or audacious beginning, depending on your point of view, Live-Shot.com was launched. For a basic monthly fee plus a charge for every ten rounds of ammunition, subscribers can fire at inanimate targets. For considerably more money, members can buy a two-hour slot and use a joystick to take a crack at a live animal; they then pay extra to process its meat, have its head mounted, and ship it to any location.

Decrying the operation as "desktop killing," "hi-tech atrocity," and "pay-per-view slaughter," animal rights activists and hunting heritage advocates have joined forces to lobby legislators for a ban on remote-control hunting. Finally, there is common ground between the enemy camps, although for somewhat different reasons. The National Rifle Association (NRA) cites hunters' folk law: "The NRA believes the element of a fair chase is a vital part of the American hunting heritage. Shooting an animal from three states away would not be considered a fair chase." For Kirby Brown, executive director of the pro-hunting Texas Wildlife Association, Internet hunting does not qualify as hunters' praxis: "The idea of sitting at a computer screen playing a video game and activating a remote-controlled firearm to shoot an animal is not hunting. It's off the ethical charts." He found it disturbing that the person at the computer needs no shooting skills, and there is no environmental context. Lockwood made the case that Internet hunting allows the disabled and shut-ins to enjoy hunting, but opponents were not buying that argument. The Humane Society of the United States warned that "Lockwood's real-life video game has real-life consequences for animals—and perhaps for people, if the remote-control rifle software lands in the wrong hands. . . . This is disembodied killing in which the hunter experiences no consequences: He sees no blood, hears no cries, feels nothing but the joy of the kill, like a kid with a violent video game" (Humane Society 2005). In fact, other protesters on both sides made comparisons to the stupefying effects of fantasy video games such as Grand Theft Auto, DOOM, and Duke Nukem (Humane Society 2005; Budra 2004). In the same year that Live-Shot.com was introduced, seven states banned Internet hunting, and Representative Tom Davis of Virginia introduced a federal bill making participation in

Internet hunting a felony. Internet hunting sparked a firestorm of reaction, signaling that in an age of virtual praxis, hunters are redefining hunting as real-life behavior and ethics.

This is not to say that hunting has not gone high-tech. Each new and improved piece of equipment draws more protests from animal rights groups. One gadget singled out by the Fund for Animals as outrageous is a radio directional tracking system for hunting dogs. Hunters attach collars outfitted with transmitters on their dogs, and they carry the small, portable receivers with them in the field (Barber 2007). Radio signals from the dogs can be monitored as far as twelve miles away. Critics claim that the device tempts hunters to stay in the warm confines of their trucks until the prey has been cornered, detracting from the ethic of the sporting chase and leaving open the question of what constitutes a fair fight. In response, promoters of the equipment point out its value in finding lost or even stolen dogs. With advancements in satellite communications technology, the cell phone and global positioning system (GPS) have increasingly been applied to hunting purposes. Many hunters who embrace the primal spirit of hunting as a preindustrial tradition that enacts the pioneer experience resist the use of such technology and seek to preserve hunting as a pre- or antimodern bastion. Some deer camps I attended exhibited this preservationist tendency by banning cell phones and even eschewing electrification, whereas others reveled in having the latest gadgetry. As a matter of principle, I found that, as a tradition-centered group, hunters seriously contemplate the potentially disruptive effects of new technology on the hunting cultural experience, as well as the financial burden of using such equipment to hunt in the future. But one accessory remains sacrosanct: the gun, which most hunters feel is in danger of being "taken away" by misguided gun-control fanatics in cahoots with animal rights activists and freedom-robbing government "suits." Bumper-sticker slogans that have been around since the 1970s convey the libertarian message in no uncertain terms: "I'LL GIVE YOU MY GUN WHEN YOU TAKE IT FROM MY COLD, DEAD HANDS" and "IF GUNS ARE OUTLAWED, ONLY OUT-LAWS [THE GOVERNMENT] WILL HAVE GUNS" (Levinson 1989, 650; White 1997, 8–10).

Despite the decline in the number of hunters, a substantial amount of financial capital has gone into building a modern consumer culture for them. Hunters have gained renewed visibility as a result of several

A sculpture by Vic Payne sits outside the entrance to Cabela's, Hamburg, Pennsylvania, October 2003. (Photo by Simon Bronner)

superstores, including Cabela's, Bass Pro Shops, and Gander Mountain, which forecast future expansion. These stores have had a hand in casting hunters as outdoorsmen and -women and luring nonhunters into the undomesticated world of grit, freedom, and tradition. Gander Mountain's slogan is "We Live Outdoors," and Bass Pro Shops proudly claims to be "The World's Leading Supplier of Premium Outdoor Gear." Looking inside the stores or through their catalogs, it is clear that hunting is at the center of the outdoor life. In unprecedented expanses filled with hunting-related gear, they bring the breathtaking vista of the outdoors inside and promise humans a way to control the untamed environment. In display and rhetoric, these superstores project the value of exerting dominion over the flora and fauna. These stores have a stake in ensuring that hunting does not become a relic of the past, even if that means redefining it for the future.

Bass Pro Shops, a privately held company founded in 1972, does not report sales and earnings figures, but it claims to have invented the

Conservation Mountain in Cabela's, Hamburg, Pennsylvania, November 2007. (Photo by Simon Bronner)

"A Proud Pennsylvania Tradition," declares a sign in the hunting section of Bass Pro Shop, Harrisburg, Pennsylvania, January 2008. (Photo by Simon Bronner)

giant outdoor store concept. It operates a chain of fifty-seven stores in the United States and Canada, paralleling the rapid growth of Cabela's, established in 1961. Dow Jones Newswires reported that Bass's sales had climbed to $1.6 billion in 2005, whereas competitor Cabela's edged close to $2 billion in the same year (Dochat 2006, C1). Although Gander lagged behind with sales of $804 million, it had the most outlets, with more than eighty stores. Michael C. May, spokesman for the Sporting Good Manufacturers Association, observed that these superstores have the effect of boosting consumer interest in hunting activities and the intention of turning the "non-outdoorsman into an outdoorsman" (Seward 2005). Although Cabela's has fewer stores than its competitors, each store's large interior space has been described as "jaw-dropping" (Cabela 2001, 155). Stores contain up to a quarter million square feet of retail space and work to be destinations for travelers, including tourist gawkers as well as clothing shoppers. Visitors can spend large blocks of time there—eating at the restaurant, taking target practice, shopping for supplies, and even arranging hunting trips (Braunschweiger 2008). With all this volume, Cabela's is not basing its draw primarily on discounting; rather, it wants to be the brand associated with the outdoor lifestyle and related advice, wisdom, and heritage (Heavey 2007). Unlike other retail superstores, Cabela's and Bass Pro Shops have the feeling of an exhibition hall, trade show, and museum devoted to the promotion of hunting, fishing, and camping.

At trade shows such as the Eastern Sports and Outdoor Show, hailed as America's largest exhibition of hunting and fishing organizations and stores, tradition is a key word that connects the labyrinth of booths. The mammoth show, which is sometimes more of a pep rally than a shopping experience, blared its 2008 theme of "Pass on the Tradition" alongside a logo of a father and son walking together, guns and game in hand. T-shirts with the requisite camouflage patterns showcase bucks and turkeys, the animals drawing the most attention at the show. More than noting the longevity of hunting as a reflection of tradition, the slogan uses an imperative phrase to impel elders to teach youth to take up hunting. The Rocky Mountain Elk Foundation varied the phrase to tap into hunters' fondness for storytelling by declaring, "Pass It On!" One gimmick to underscore the show's theme was a multigeneration ticket that offered a discount to a senior, adult, and child attending the show together. Showgoers learned about the launch of *Outdoor Kids Club Magazine*, with its mission to "excite, educate, and engage kids in the outdoors and the wonderful sports of hunting and fishing." Why? Because "these wonderful activities are part of our rich heritage" and they provide a way for parents to "share more quality time together" with their children (Miami Valley Outdoor Media 2008).

Besides distributing anti–gun-control bumper stickers, the NRA is promoting a new magazine called *Gone Huntin'*, with an appeal to defend "hunters rights" by defeating "the increasingly well-organized and well-financed anti-hunting, animal-'rights' forces" (Robinson 2007). Those forces are responsible for the decline in hunting, the NRA insists, not hunting's inappropriateness for the times. After all, the organization's executive director writes, "Powerful forces aligned against one of America's *oldest, proudest traditions* have reduced hunter numbers by the millions" (Robinson 2007; emphasis added). The NRA vows to secure open, public hunting lands as a conservation measure and recruit new hunters through youth and women's programs. Chev-

T-shirts with messages such as "DEER HUNTERS GET ALL THE BIG RACKS" and "HUNTERS LIVE FREE AND HUNT HARD." Eastern Sports and Outdoor Show, Harrisburg, Pennsylvania, February 2008. (Photo by Simon Bronner)

rolet, a prime sponsor of the show, invites hunters to get deeper into the wild in their off-road vehicles and identify with the toughness and go-anywhere freedom of their pickup trucks.

These trade shows feature special events and political lobbying that stores like Cabela's and Bass Pro Shops generally do not have. Deer are brought in to demonstrate how to process wild game. On another day, a culinary group offers up dishes made with moose, alligator, and trout. Attendees can bring in antlers for measuring and get a certified score. Most of all, in keeping with promotion of the sporting life, various contests are organized, from elk calling to taxidermy. In 2008, the local newspaper got in the spirit by sponsoring an essay contest, with the winners awarded a free family pack of tickets to the show. Contestants had to write essays about how one's family "passes on the traditions and heritage of hunting and fishing" (Schneck 2008). The content of the ten winning entries was like a psychological word-association test: what do hunters think of when they hear the word *tradition?* Nine of the ten essayists focused on learning to hunt with fathers and the hand-

Demonstration of how to process deer in the field. Eastern Sports and Outdoor Show, Harrisburg, Pennsylvania, February 2008. (Photo by Simon Bronner)

U.S. Army recruiting display at the Eastern Sports and Outdoor Show makes the connection between hunters and soldiers as adventurers and outdoorsmen. Harrisburg, Pennsylvania, February 2008. (Photo by Simon Bronner)

ing down of wisdom and lore not available in books. "I was extremely fortunate to not only have shared so many great outdoor experiences with my dad, but for my first 20 seasons I got to share them with both of my grandfathers," one contestant wrote, then added, "I look back on all those trips into Penn's Woods with these three men and know that no book or magazine will ever teach me as much as I learned during those days afield" ("Readers" 2008). Tradition in this sense is a counter to the disruptive effect of mass culture on family bonding, several entries confirmed. One father asserted, for example, "Spending time with my children is the best way of passing the traditions and heritage of hunting and fishing. With the many things pulling kids away, from electronic gadgets to sports, if I don't make time it will be lost" ("Readers" 2008). The contestants often reflected on the need for a concerted effort to maintain continuity in passing on traditions to their children. Back in the day, they did not have to think about it because it was built into the patterns of everyday life, but today, they observed, it is more difficult to make time, given so many modern distractions. Mass culture is epitomized by the enervating comforts of the technologized home, they intimated, and society would benefit from a dose of tradition—"the greatest gift of all," according to writer Thomas Harned. He beseeched readers, "Take the time. You'll be the better for it." He pointed out, "When you share the experience on your favorite trout stream, high on a ridge top or posting up on a special deer stand, you're carrying on our outdoor traditions" ("Readers" 2008).

The children who are taking up hunting, if the contest entries constitute a valid sample, are more likely to be girls than in years past. One essay came from fourteen-year-old Danielle Leiby, who signaled a change in the patrilineal pattern. "I'm . . . following in the hunting and fishing footsteps of my father," she wrote, and "whether it's catching your first fish or shooting your first trophy, we are establishing a great tradition" ("Readers" 2008). A woman who does not hunt recalled that her father had hunted "faithfully year after year." "Now," she wrote, "I'm proud to say that I married a man who has been passing the tradition on to our daughter, Jordan, age 11, for many years." She indicates the power of narrative as well as the hunt: "From tagging along at a very young age while he is trapping, to just being in the pictures when he comes home from a successful hunt, [Jordan's] always excited to hear the story of how the hunt progressed and ended" ("Readers" 2008).

The essays as imaginative expressions downplay the technological advances of hunting. The image they project is one of escaping the neutering appliance-filled home and the sanitized office and retreating to the rough outdoors. As one writer underscored, "a small log cabin in the woods" seemed an especially appropriate place to learn hunting from his father ("Readers" 2008). Part of the draw of the trade shows, though, is to see what is new in hunting and fishing gear. Especially important to the commodification of the outdoors, these shows highlight all manner of gadgetry, despite the perception of hunting as going primitive. They are a reminder that the technology improves the hunter's effectiveness to notch a kill, leading some critics to question whether this gives the hunter an unfair advantage over the animal, if hunting is meant to be a sports contest. One can see canoes, a familiar image in pioneer lore, decked out with stereo and GPS, interior LED lights, and solar power sources. That old bow and arrow now boasts a machined-aluminum riser, cam system, speed bearings, and Teflon-coated cable guard. It can even be outfitted with a video camera to record the release of the arrows, whose carbon-composite fiber construction is laser-inspected for ultimate straightness. An ear insert can amplify sounds below forty decibels up to five times, and illuminated rifle scopes with fiber optics and tritium allow windage and elevation adjustments (Schneck 2008). The traditionally minded can pick up a flintlock harking back to the Pennsylvania or Kentucky rifle of pioneer days, used today during muzzle-loader season. Vendors displaying an array of firearms use the connection to American heritage in their advertising and promote the challenge of "one shot, one kill," which appeals to many hunters. For souvenirs that underscore hunting's cultural continuity, attendees can take away belt buckles, T-shirts, key chains, and underwear declaring, "HUNTING—AN AMERICAN TRADITION."

Cabela's in particular has embraced the promotional concept in media as well as material culture. Having returned from an ethnographic sojourn in Penn's woods, I explored Cabela's in Hamburg, Pennsylvania, where I had the feeling that I was conducting fieldwork in a cultural scene all its own. Before one even enters the store, there is a huge sculpture by artist Vic Payne paying tribute to America's pioneer heritage. A Native American sits in the rear of a canoe while a buck-skin-clad white adventurer stands at the front, taking aim with a cocked musket. In between them is a covered mound with nature's bounty, including a bagged buck. Once inside, the dominant feature is Conservation Mountain, measuring thirty-six feet high by eighty-eight feet wide by ninety-eight feet deep. It contains prime specimens of pursued wild game against a natural background, including a waterfall and a small pond with live trout. It emphasizes human triumph over the rugged pinnacle and its unsubdued wildlife as the ultimate sign of adventure. Its conservation message justifies the death of these animals as part of the sage wildlife management by hunters. Off to the side is a gallery of mounted animal heads—a kind of hall of fame for animal combatants. Walking farther down, the human dimension of hunting is displayed with a simulated deer camp featuring a Disneyesque mechanical hunter who regales passersby with stories of the thrill of the hunt. On the other side is a display of African safari animals that can be bagged on hunting trips arranged through Cabela's travel service. By Cabela's count, store designers have scattered more than 700 animals throughout the showroom to create an atmosphere of "the wilderness come to life indoors" (Cabela 2001, 127). An aquarium built into the site also draws notice because one walks through it.

If browsers get the itch to try their hand at hunting in the "great outdoors," they can go to the Wilderness Creek Shooting Gallery or archery range. The in-store shooting gallery has twenty-seven guns and seventy laser-activated targets set in a prospector's cabin scene somewhere in the Old West. Killing off the pesky varmints in the scene enacts a rags-to-riches mythology for self and nation and ensures that gold and manifest destiny can be achieved for folksy types panning for the American dream. If all this adventure works up an appetite, one can go to the restaurant romantically named the High Plains Cache for some unusual fare that includes wild boar wrap and venison bratwurst. From the balcony seating area, one overlooks the expanse of the store, which is like taking a bird's-eye view of a wondrous nineteenth-century world's fair. I looked around and realized that couples were here on dates, families came for a day-long outing, and connoisseurs were attracted to a secured inner sanctum where rare firearms were curated. Children, convinced that the store was a combination theme park and nature center, could go over to an area and play with old-fashioned pop guns or plastic fishing rods. They might glimpse the production of a television show on the premises, broadcast on WildTV and the Outdoor Channel. Or they could pick up video games tailor-made for this clientele, such as Cabela's Big Game Hunts, Cabela's Dangerous Hunts 1 and 2, and Cabela's Outdoor Adventures.

In Cabela's twenty-first-century version of a crystal palace, hunters reign over a consumer culture that builds on the vernacular image of their customs. It is not enough for customers to survey hundreds of guns on the wall and camouflage attire. They can also create a hunter's world in their own homes by purchasing furnishings embodying the rugged legacy of the outdoors, including "hand-hewn Rocky Mountain aspen" beds and tables, a footstool in the shape of a black bear, and children's camouflage loungers. Antler chandeliers hang overhead in public areas, and for the privacy of the bathroom, one can order a buck's head toilet seat or a freestanding bear toilet-paper holder. Plastic animals can be bought to create a wildlife assemblage on the manicured front yard; wall mountings and sculptures are available for the interior, including mythical jackalopes and hand-scrimshawed ostrich eggs.

Reminiscent of vintage Sears and Montgomery-Ward catalogs, those offered by Cabela's hold a revered place in the home or cabin, just as those old consumer bibles once did (Howard 2004). Cabela's special catalog for deer hunting in 2006 was emblazoned with an old-time photograph of gritty men bedecked in flannels and overalls, proudly standing around their bagged buck. On the cover was a painting of a man on snowshoes facing down a huge buck in a romanticized pioneer scene that could have been issued by Currier and Ives. Historian Thomas Schlereth's comment about revolutionary department-store catalogs promising country folks the ability to participate in the consumer "good life" also applies to this new generation of outdoor gear. He notes that when something people could easily make at home became available as a manufactured product, those "who prided themselves on being producers increasingly became consumers. In this long process, people who thought of themselves as advocates of the traditional increasingly became participants in the modern" (Schlereth 1989, 375).

There is a postmodern twist, of course, in the option of ordering gear to brave the wilderness over the Internet. Bass Pro Shops makes shopping online easy by offering the "Adventure Credit Card" with its logo. Its Web site features the standardized rustic wooden entrance of its chain stores, with huge signage carrying the words "Outdoor World" on top of an arch, funneling customers inside. The Cabela's Web site also uses an image of its entrance to give customers the impression of going inside its huge frontier full of goods. Its dominant theme is also vernacular, with cobblestone columns appearing even broader than they are in real life thanks to wide-angle photography. When I visited Harrisburg's Bass Pro Shops in 2007, the come-on image was a camouflage-covered hunter gazing out intently from behind a tree with a bow that seemed more machine than craft. The message in bold letters announced, "Take Aim . . . Shop Our Archery Gear."

Beneath Gander Mountain's online catalog heading "Gear Up for Deer" are several items: LED Lighted Logo Camp, Reversible Hot Seat, and Tinks #69 Doe-in-Rut Buck Lure. If all this seems to take away from the primitive aspect of making do with the resources at hand, Cabela's assures customers that their gear will allow them to venture deeper into the woods or spend more quality time with family. Set beside a picture of a family cookout in its catalog, for instance, is the slogan, "Weekends were made for adventure—not yardwork." Cabela's sells itself as a way to unbind from the enervating effects of suburban postmodernism. Like Cabela's, Bass Pro Shops has simulated a mountain with wild game on its cliffs. To reach the hunting and gun section at Bass, one climbs the escalator surrounded by a woods motif and gains a superior vantage overlooking the floor devoted to fishing. Like Cabela's, it has firing ranges open to all ages and a children's section with hunting-themed toys, including "Shotgun Sam," a figure that, with the touch of a button, swivels in different directions and makes gun blasting sounds. At Bass Pro Shops, customers can try their hand at a climbing wall, conveying the message that the outdoors means action and is not for the faint of heart or the couch-potato type.

Appearing to some viewers like a wilderness version of a wondrous Oz rising up and commanding the horizon, to animal rights activists, Cabela's looks more like a giant morgue for hundreds of dead animals. Animals in Print, an animal rights organization advocating a vegan lifestyle, put out an action alert warning of the megastore's business model, based on squeezing tax incentives and enterprise grants out of localities where it builds. That organization sees Cabela's not as a natural history museum worthy of the name but as an indoctrination center for a consumerism of animal extinction and abuse (Animals in Print 2005). And it is right, for Cabela's is not a natural history museum nor really a museum of hunting; it is more reminiscent of a world's fair exhibition in which mechanically outfitted humans exercise dominion over the land and its living creatures. I realized the strong emotions the store engendered when my dean suggested a faculty retreat in one of its generous community meeting rooms. I understood the dean's thinking. It was an inviting structure of cultural interest that provided food, meeting space, and distractions away from campus. She was not prepared for the angry response from several faculty members who refused to patronize an institution dedicated to the celebration of killing. They said they would feel violated as women in a place surrounded by decapitated bodies that had been stalked, captured, and kept as trophies in the mode of rape. Others sent e-mails complaining of the public threat intrinsic in the store's mass display of weapons in a society despoiled by gun violence. Upon reflection, Cabela's can appear menacing: it displaces the sedate, controlled, commercial, interior-centered environment of malls (as agents of a homogeneous mass culture characterized by self-restraint and domestication) with an invitation to partake of rejuvenating adventure and danger "out there," even if it is covered by a roof (Bronner 1989; Farrell 2003; Zukin 2005). If hunting has a future, megastores can participate in its maintenance by metaphorically refocusing hunting as the good life outdoors—a life given meaning by tradition and untethered from modern corporate routine. Hunter rolls may be down, but the megastore parking lots are full. The good life conveyed by the megastores shares the consumer cultural vision of providing tools for increased leisure, but these tools are not for domestication. The good life is represented as feeling one's inner wildness and vitality by embracing the challenges of the outdoors. The megastores respond to anxiety about the deadening effect of modernity by providing gear for every adventure, a camouflage pattern for every apparel; they even offer wild game as fast food to allow one to resist being tamed.

Both hunting heritage advocates and animal rights activists promise futures in which their message will broaden, using modernity as a common oppugnant force. For animal rights groups, modernity is shaped by greedy corporate types who promote exploitative capitalism and entertainment using the lower sort who cannot speak for themselves. In the heartland, they try to convince hunters that in upholding their traditions, they are being duped by a larger system that will not benefit them. Hunting heritage advocates, meanwhile, yearn to show that the redemptive and regenerative functions of hunting extend to the traditional values and institutions troubled by the mass culture version of modernity: family, community, and environment. Animal rights groups build on previous campaigns, pointing to the exploitative dark side of hunting as an impediment to social progress, security, and justice. Rather than targeting specific practices, it is likely that the systems and structures that support these practices will receive critical attention. The challenge is to convince people that the widely accepted egalitarian goals of eliminating violence and discrimination begin with animals. In the words of Gary Francione (1996), preaching to the converted, "We should recognize that there is a necessary connection between the animal rights movement and other movements for social justice. Animal exploitation involves species bias or speciesism, and is as morally unacceptable as other irrelevant criteria such as race, sex, sexual orientation, or class, in determining membership in the moral universe. But if we maintain that speciesism is bad because it is like racism, sexism, or homophobia, then we have necessarily taken a stand on those other forms of discrimination." Animal rights advocates have as much of an image problem as hunters do. They understand the need to strip themselves of the terrorist label and to distance themselves from the stereotype of spoiled, rich, urban do-gooders with a misplaced mission.

The mass of the public is willing to hear animal rights on the stump because of their own uncertainty about caring for what seem to be increasingly vulnerable children and the rapidly shrinking environment. Perhaps as more pets become members of the family and people hear more stories about serial killers kicking cats in their childhood, it will be less of a stretch for them to see a link between the treatment of animals and the treatment of people (Lockwood and Ascione 1998; Grier 2006). Whereas animal rights campaigns appeal to people's compassion for animals as a path to social justice and ethical progress, promised by the idea of a moral evolution as people fast-forward into the future, hunting heritage advocates pull at the public's heartstrings by asking about the root, grounding, and meaning of the past as a key to belonging. Hunting has emerged in the debate as more metaphor than sport, more praxis than pursuit. Through the rhetoric of the various controversies of the last few decades, hunting has taken on the image of a preserve for the wild, a bastion of tradition, or a constructed backwoods version of it. Tradition is what people do that connects them as communities and families to a heritage conveyed from generation to generation, and it wrests identity from folk-wrought expressions in story, song, craft, and ritual. The press intently covers animal rights protests of hunting, and we watch for their exaggerated tussles. We fathom the images and interpret the rhetoric they present for their polarized sides because we want to balance tradition and modernity for our nation and ourselves.

Notes

1. Ritual and Controversy at Deer Camp

1. There is evidence that the sportsmen's campaign to revive youths' interest in hunting with combination permits has been working, at least in Pennsylvania. Reports for 1996 and 2001 show that the number of hunters fifteen years or younger actually increased from 75,000 to 96,000.

2. A substantial number of hunters reported having their first hunting experiences as very young children—8 percent before the age of six.

3. Conversation recorded November 28, 2003, near Lewistown, Mifflin County, Pennsylvania. Camp Hunter does not have electricity, and its heat is provided by a fireplace. The first floor, where this conversation occurred, is one open room; bunk beds are distributed throughout another open room on the second floor. With the focus around the fireplace, conversations tend to be open for all to hear rather than held between two people. My host also belonged to another camp and described Camp Hunter as more "traditional." About twenty men gathered that night for dinner. Most of the men were in their forties. I counted four youths who came to the camp with their fathers.

4. In *Following Tradition* (1998), I argue that this neglect of hunting as tradition owes to the modern folkloristic motive of showing tradition as adored art in exhibited form or as an emotional, sympathetic response to groups and events threatened by modernity. Even if they are widespread as folk practices, hunting and shooting are avoided because they raise conflicts in the folkloristic presumptions about tradition as vernacular art in step with progressive causes. Some notable folkloristic exceptions are Russell 2002; Dundes 1997; Hufford 1992; Ives 1988; Bronner 1986, 162–78; Newall 1983; Abernethy 1971; Boyle 1969; Koch 1965. Most of these studies identify folk genres such as beliefs, rituals, songs, and narratives associated with hunting rather than the processes of hunting as cultural practice. Russell and Ives are distinctive for their consideration of the political context of the regulation of or protest against hunting; Dundes and Hufford offer symbolist interpretations, with Dundes proposing a psychoanalytic explanation of male ritual combats and Hufford interpreting the social

structural implications of narrative performance following Geertz (1994) and Bateson (1972). My 1986 study of turtle hunting considered the social status of hunting in a community and its psychological relation to public rituals of consumption. Drawing attention in the early twentieth century to the collection of hunting stories and beliefs in Pennsylvania was Henry Shoemaker, the nation's first "state folklorist" (see Shoemaker 1992, 1993). Labeled a popularizer, he never received much appreciation for his work among academic folklorists (see Bronner 1996b). Today, popular awareness of hunting and shooting as traditions is evident in the *Outdoor Life* cable network (see www.olntv.com) and mass-market magazines such as *Field and Stream* and *Outdoor Life*.

5. In Mifflin County where I conducted fieldwork, however, the drives are more characteristic of the communitarian Amish than the individualistic men from modern society gathered at camps on Jacks Mountain and the Kishacoquillas Creek Valley in the county.

6. Recorded December 1, 2003, near Lewistown, Mifflin County, Pennsylvania. Shirttail cutting for new hunters is also documented in an archival project for the Center for Pennsylvania Culture Studies at Penn State Harrisburg (see Guerriero 1994). Huffman in *Ten Point* (1997, 97) includes a photograph of a shirttail-cutting ritual in which a board similar to the one at Camp Hunter is visible with displayed shirttails.

7. Boyle (1969, 14) also notes differences between the British versions of blooding and the central European practice of the hunter dipping a twig or leaf in the animal's blood and sticking it in his hatband. Though apparently related to the initiatory function of blooding, the dipping practice does not involve the direct experience of fusion with, or domination over, the animal. Still, there is a parallel in creating a connection between man and animal, since a common custom is to give the deer a "last bite" by putting grass, twigs, or leaves in its mouth. Sterba (1947, 424) refers to the hunter's three-pronged twig, dipped in the deer's blood, as a phallic symbol.

8. Of folkloristic interest is the performance element of the tag line, "Now that's a good testicle!" It shows the eater's unwillingness to acknowledge the distaste of the dish, implicitly a manly trait. One can compare this humorous ending to the narrative of "moose-turd pie," made famous by raconteur and singer Utah Phillips (1935–2008) and interpreted by Saul Broudy (1982):

The worst job I ever had was working for the Pacific Railroad, doing a thing called "gandy-dancing." Now most of you know the railroad was built partially by Irish labor. Well, back then the workers would use this long handled shovel, made by the Gandy Shovel Company of Great Neck, New York. Well, they'd shove one end of the shovel under a railroad tie, and then run out to the other end of the shovel, when they could find it, and do a little jig on it, and they called it "gandy-dancin'." This would lift the tie up so they could shove gravel under it, which would level the roadbed, so when the train came along, it wouldn't tip over, which would be a real drag for everyone. Well, nowadays, they run three cars out on the rail: a bunk car, an equipment car, and a mess car. The only thing they don't give you is a cook. The bosses figure you'll find out who the best cook is, and use him. Well, they were wrong. Y' see, they just find out who complains the loudest about the cooking, and he gets to be the cook. Well, that was me, see. Ol' alligator mouth. That was the worst food I'd ever had, and I complained about it. Things like "dog bottom pie" and "pheasant sweat." I thought it was garbage. So I complained. And everyone said, "alright, you think you can do better? You're the cook." Well, that made me mad, see? But I knew, that anyone who complained about my cooking, they were gonna have to cook. Armed with that knowledge, I sallied forth, over the muddy river. I was walking along, and I saw just this hell of a big moose turd, I mean it was a real steamer! So I said to myself, "self, we're going to make us some moose turd pie." So I tipped that prairie pastry on its side, got my shit together, so to speak, and started rolling it down towards the cook car: flolump, flolump, flolump. I went in and made a big pie shell, and then I tipped that meadow muffin into it, laid strips of dough across it, and put a sprig of parsley on top. It was beautiful, poetry on a plate, and I served it up for dessert. Well, this big guy come into the mess car, I mean, he's about 5 foot forty, and he sets himself down like a fool on a stool, picked up a fork and took a big bite of that moose turd pie. Well he threw down his fork and he let out a bellow, "My God, that's moose turd pie!" *"It's good though."* ("Utah's Page" [Utah Phillips], http://www.utahphillips.org/utah.html).

Related to my argument concerning the connection of the liver and testes and the double meanings of waste and genitalia is the symbolic equivalence of the "turd" in Phillips's railroad camp setting and the "testes" served up as a hunter's dish in deer camp.

9. "Deer Antler Plus," drawing on folk medicine and belief, is found in many locations, including a site labeled "Male Sexual Enhancement" (http://www.deerantlerplus.com/?aid=759774) in June 2004. According to

the site, it is rated the "No. 1 Sexual Performance Enhancer on the Market." The site explained the folk practice as follows:

Deer Velvet has been used for thousands of years in the Orient for impotence in men. It has been referred to as one of the top sexual performance enhancers in the world. It has been said to produce strong sexual desires, stamina and strength. The royal houses of the emperors are thought to have made the finest advancements through the energy and insights of great Chinese herbalists. Deer Velvet is believed to balance and normalize negative conditions and imbalances. Many have referred to Deer Velvet as an aphrodisiac; an agent that stimulates sexual desire. It is said to increase physical stamina, sperm volume and sexual vitality. Deer velvet has been referred to as one of the top herbal aphrodisiacs in the world. It has been noted that deer velvet appears to strengthen the body as it is balancing the hormones needed for peak sexual function. . . . The velvet from the deer antlers is harvested at peak mating season, when the testosterone levels in the blood that circulates throughout the cartilage of the antler are high. There are volumes of documented research on the benefits of deer velvet antler in China, Russia, Korea and Japan. From these reports, here are some excerpts which relate directly to its sexual benefits: Recover sexual functioning and experience a return of potency and libido. Strong kidney function, strengthen the heart, increase blood circulation, strengthen the mind and the central nervous system and to have a positive mood. Directly controlling the reproductive hormone production of the gonads.

10. According to data gathered in 1995–1996, the average hunter spent $754 on hunting-related activities and fifteen days hunting. The study showed that 73 percent of that money was spent on equipment. Hunters aged sixteen and older spent $691 million in Pennsylvania in 1996; five years later, the figure rose to over $941 million. See Pennsylvania State Data Center 2000, 2002; "Future Hunting" 2004.

2. The Pigeon Shoot Controversy

1. I am grateful to Jay Mechling of the University of California at Davis for his many contributions to the project and insights into the event. He joined me at the 1991 shoot and participated in a preshoot conference on animal rights tactics while I worked with Hegins shoot supporters. Jacqueline Thursby of Brigham Young University also added valuable comments as chair of an American Folklore Society panel where this research was first

presented. Ken Thigpen of the New York Institute of Technology, who participated in the panel, also shared his experiences in Pennsylvania with animal rights activists and hunting culture. Janet Davis of the University of Texas kindly sent me her historical files on pigeon shoots from the American Society for the Prevention of Cruelty to Animals, and Marjolein Efting Dijkstra of the Department of Ethnology at Meertens Institute in the Netherlands provided information on comparative European traditions. At a presentation at Indiana State University, Alan Dundes and Ron Baker offered insightful comments on my psychological interpretations. Elaine Lawless and Lisa Rathje of the University of Missouri provided constructive editorial notations. Back in Pennsylvania, Vicki Terwilliger of the *Pottsville Republican* and Jennifer Miller, a local historian from the Hegins Valley and a descendant of Fred Coleman, provided valuable materials on the history of the Coleman Memorial Shoot and the Coleman family. Robert Tobash, chair of the Labor Day Committee, and Bud Angst, columnist for the *Citizen Standard* in Valley View, Pennsylvania, kindly shared their files on the Hegins shoot with me. On the animal rights side, I am grateful to Heidi Prescott, national director of the Fund for Animals, for allowing me access to the fund's archives on its Hegins campaign and to Ingrid Newkirk, president of People for the Ethical Treatment of Animals (PETA); Steve Hindi, founding president of Showing Animals Respect and Kindness (SHARK); and Doris Gitman, animal rights activist in Schuylkill County, Pennsylvania, for sharing their private materials on the shoot.

2. PETA, one of the organizations involved in the Action for Life conferences, had a special interest in speaking out against meat consumption, protecting wildlife by thwarting hunters (using bullhorns to scare away animals), and protesting trapping as well as the wearing of fur. During the 1980s, its activities in the heartland included picketing rodeos and circuses. It attracted publicity when an activist wearing a pig costume hit the Iowa pork queen in the face with a pie during the World Pork Expo; PETA also placed an advertisement in the *Des Moines Register* in August 1991 comparing Jeffrey Dahmer's serial murders in Milwaukee to the slaughter of livestock (Guither 1998, 48–50). Trans-Species Unlimited (later called Animal Rights Mobilization, or ARM!), founded in 1981, also protested fur trapping and wearing before the Hegins shoot, but its main effort was in an intense campaign against barbiturate addiction studies in cats at Cornell University in 1988 (Guither 1998, 50–52; Finsen and Finsen 1994, 81–84).

3. As an extension of this argument, Mechling (1989, 320–21) points out the possibility of interactive routines forming cultural systems between humans and inanimate objects—such as the play between a child and a

stuffed animal or adults' interactions with their automobiles—and between humans and imaginary others—such as the play between a child and an imaginary friend.

4. A list of contestants for the shoot between 1934 and 1984 was published privately by the Hegins Labor Day Committee (1984). In the five years between 1979 and 1983, there were 1,562 contestants; of those, 16 were women, constituting 1 percent of all contestants.

5. Residents named the traditional match shoot held at the Valley View Gun Club the Warren Klinger Memorial Shoot after his death in 1987 (see Zemencik 2003). The name rhetorically connected the match shoot to the Coleman Memorial Shoot by honoring a local sportsman.

6. In *Following Tradition* (1998), I argue that this neglect of hunting as tradition owes to the modern folkloristic motive of showing tradition as adored art in exhibited form or as an emotional, sympathetic response to groups and events threatened by modernity. Even if they are widespread as folk practices, hunting and shooting are avoided because they raise conflicts in the folkloristic presumptions about tradition as vernacular art in step with progressive causes. Inspired largely by animal rights challenges to the traditions of hunting and fishing in places such as Utah, the first scholarly folkloristic journal to devote an entire issue to traditions of, and debates over, hunting and fishing was *Western Folklore* 63, nos. 1–2 (winter–spring 2004), edited by Jacqueline Thursby of Brigham Young University. Popular awareness of hunting and shooting as traditions is evident in the *Outdoor Life* cable network (see www.olntv.com) and mass-market magazines such as *Field and Stream* and *Outdoor Life*.

7. The song appeared on the CD *Street Cinema* (Ruffhouse/Columbia, 1999), with composer credits to K. Briggs, K. Howell, M. Bryan, and S. Ford. The transcribed lyrics are available at http://www.geocities.com/SunsetStrip/Venue/9769/rap/n/no_pigeons.html. The background of the song is that it was intended as a masculinist answer to "No Scrubs" on *Fanmail* by the women in the rap group TLC (1999).

8. To show the influence of the biblical passage in the discourse of animal rights, I used the text from the chapter entitled "God Created Man in His Own Image" in Tom Regan and Peter Singer's *Animal Rights and Human Obligations* (1976, 58–59). The material from the Bible is the first chapter in the section "Animal and Human Nature." It is followed by philosophical excerpts from Aristotle, St. Thomas Aquinas, Descartes, Voltaire, Hume, and Darwin. My inclusion of "creature" in brackets refers to modern translations such as *The Tanakh*, edited by Jaroslav Pelikan (1992, 14). It also changes the category of food to an action: "Every creature that lives shall be yours to eat."

9. State senator Frank Shurden, a Democrat from Henryetta, Oklahoma, explained that the muffs, described by reporters as "tiny boxing gloves," can be worn over the cocks' spurs. The cocks are also outfitted with lightweight vests containing electronic sensors to record hits and keep score rather than allowing the roosters to slash and peck each other to death while human spectators bet on the outcome. Janet Halliburton, president of the Oklahoma Coalition against Cockfighting, which led the drive for the 2002 law, resisted the compromise, saying, "What this is going to do is make a platform for him to continually try to amend the existing ban" ("Gamecock" 2005). The significant point of this exchange, in light of my analysis, is that making the contest less cruel or less bloody would not satisfy the animal rights advocates because it was the *idea* of the cockfight, with its symbolism of male combat, that needed to be abolished. A related controversy arose in the state over the men's folk practice of "noodling," the catching of freshwater fish (usually large catfish) with one's bare hands. Noodling is legal only in Oklahoma, Tennessee, Mississippi, and Louisiana. A film entitled *Okie Noodling* directed by Bradley Beesley and distributed by the Public Broadcasting System in 2002 drew attention to the activity and the protest of the noodling tournaments in Oklahoma.

3. The Hare-Coursing Controversy

1. Survey results on attitudes toward hare coursing and foxhunting are reported in Thomas 1983, 187–99. According to the poll, 75 percent of respondents were opposed to hare coursing, and 60 percent were against foxhunting.

2. Although Thomas focuses primarily on the ecological, economic, and ethical arguments, he recognizes that "the feeling that hunting is 'characteristically English' and that parliament 'should not interfere with the traditional life of this country' is deep-rooted in the hunting community." He adds, "The argument appears in most hunting debates and even coursing has been praised as an 'ancient and rather esoteric pastime'" (Thomas 1983, 240). An appeal to the Englishness of hunting with dogs is made by the Duke of Beaufort (1960, 55) in the frontispiece to his chapter "Masters and Huntsmen" in *In Praise of Hunting*. The unattributed verse states, "What lay behind / Was English character and mind, Great kindness, delicate sweet feeling (Most shy, most clever in concealing Its depth) for beauty of all sorts / Great manliness and love of sports."

3. My hope is that this commentary at least gets the message across that folklorists should more actively consider public disputes over animal-human practices as reflections of critical cultural conflicts and anxieties in the understanding of the dynamics of tradition. Despite the fact that hunting is

one of humans' most persistent global customs in the modern age, folklorists who claim tradition as their scholarly domain have generally avoided the subject. My explanation for this hesitation is an intellectual legacy emphasizing purportedly "artistic" expressions *within* a bounded group rather than disputed customs *between* emergent groups or identities. Thus, in my literature search, reports of beliefs and stories *about* hares were far more abundant than interpretations *of* coursing traditions and their protests. See Bronner 1998, 461–74; 2004; 2005a. The work of folklorist Jay Mechling is particularly illuminating, especially his social-psychological observation of traditions enacted between humans and animals as the basis of groupness and the representation of animals as metaphors for social structure (see Mechling 1987, 1989; Mechling and Wilson 1988). With regard to the cultural significance of animal-human relations in Britain, foxhunting has received more scholarly attention than hare coursing, although folkloristic and ethnological consideration is still surprisingly rare. Some exemplary folkloristic and ethnological treatises on foxhunting in Britain are Dannemann 1978; Howe 1981; Newall 1983; Fukuda 1997; Eliason 2004.

4. In an e-mail I received from Fionna Smyth, Northern Ireland campaigner, League against Cruel Sports, on November 5, 2006, she stated "We almost achieved a ban under an amendment to the game preservation act but the previous assembly was dissolved before it could be enacted. Since then we have attempted to get it banned on conservation grounds, because the Irish hare is a declining species. There have been a number of temporary protection orders and we are campaigning to make these permanent." For the distinction of the Irish hare among British species, see Evans and Thompson 1972, 41–49.

5. For a contrast to the "ejective" function of anality associated with lower-class agrarian groups, especially symbolized by the chicken immersed in its own feces, see Bronner 2006b, 2007; Dundes 1984.

6. For the theory of male contamination by "outside" blood that is shed by "getting down in the dirt," see Meyer 2005, 38–45. Earlier, Rudolf Steiner (1997, 43) connected the social separation from blood by theorizing in psychoanalytic terms that the ego is the "above" and the blood belonging to the physical body is "below." I also discuss the separation of pigeon shooting as a less bloody male shooting sport pursued by gentlemen in "Contesting Tradition" (2005a, 409–52).

7. Cox (1892) also uses this rhetorical argument for the classical roots of hare coursing when he cites the appreciation of hare coursing by Greek chronicler Arrian during the Roman period (A.D. 150).

8. For primary texts, see Blome, "A Short Treatise of Cock-fighting" 1686, 277–80, and Markham, "Of the Fighting Cock" 1615, 81–97.

9. See Hines 1972; McManus 2000; Evans 1969; Owen 1981; Glassie 1983. British folklife surveys that represent hunting in the praxis of rural life are Owen 1959, 34–35; Grant 1961, 337–39. Methodologically, Seán Ó Súilleabháin suggested an interview protocol for hunting and coursing in *A Handbook of Irish Folklore* (1942, 24–25, 697).

10. The quote comes from the title of Peate's "The Study of Folk Life; and Its Part in the Defence of Civilization" (1959). It should be pointed out that in contrast to this British view, American folklorists expanded the idea of folklife from the continuous traditions of the past in rural communities to emergent expressions found in all groups. See Dorson 1978; Dundes 1980; Oring 1986; Toelken 1996.

11. For general discussions of the connection between women's movements and animal rights campaigns, see Adams and Donovan 1995; Donovan and Adams 1996; Gaard 1993; Midgley 1983.

12. For discussions of the relation of hunting to pornography and rape, see Adams 1995, 2000, 2003; Comninou 1995; Luke 1998; Bergman 1996; Clifton 1990. The metaphor of rape also vividly appears in the title of Andrée Collard with Joyce Contrucci's book *Rape of the Wild: Man's Violence against Animals and the Earth* (1988).

13. Linda-May Ballard shared with me an interview she conducted in Northern Ireland with a tradition-bearer identified as "RM" for the Ulster Folk and Transport Museum in 2006. The interviewee said, "Hares were supposed to have special, special powers. I can't put my finger exactly on it, but I know that my, in my father's family, there was one child born with a hare lip, and eh, it was put down to the fact that a hare ran into the kitchen, and the child was born with a hare lip."

References

Abernethy, Francis Edward. 1971. "The East Texas Communal Hunt." In *Hunters and Healers*, ed. Wilson M. Hudson, 3–10. Austin, Tex.: Encino Press.

"About SHARK: Who We Are, What We Do, Where We Are Going." 2007. SHARK (Showing Animals Respect and Kindness) Web site. http://www.sharkonline.org/?P=0000000582 (accessed July 19, 2007).

Abrahams, Roger D. 1986. "Ordinary and Extraordinary Experience." In *The Anthropology of Experience*, ed. Victor W. Turner and Edward M. Bruner, 45–72. Urbana: University of Illinois Press.

"Activists Plan Grand National Protest." 2002. BBC Sport Web site, March 26. http://news.bbc.co.uk/sport2/hi/other_sports/horse_racing/1894346.stm (accessed July 19, 2007).

Adams, Carol J. 1995. "Woman-Battering and Harm to Animals." In *Animals and Women: Feminist Theoretical Explorations*, ed. Carol J. Adams and Josephine Donovan, 55–84. Durham, N.C.: Duke University Press.

———. 2000 [1990]. *The Sexual Politics of Meat: A Feminist-Vegetarian Critical Theory*. New York: Continuum.

———. 2003. *The Pornography of Meat*. New York: Continuum.

Adams, Carol J., and Josephine Donovan, eds. 1995. *Animals and Women: Feminist Theoretical Explorations*. Durham, N.C.: Duke University Press.

Afanas'ev, A. N. 1976. "Poetic Views of the Slavs Regarding Nature." In *Vampires of the Slavs*, ed. Jan L. Perkowski, 160–70. Cambridge, Mass.: Slavica.

Afflerbach, Susan. 2004. "Sickening Photo." *Patriot-News* (Harrisburg, Pa.), December 3, A13.

Aftandilian, Dave, ed. 2007. *What Are the Animals to Us? Approaches from Science, Religion, Folklore, Literature, and Art*. Knoxville: University of Tennessee Press.

Akeley, Carl Ethan. 1923. *In Brightest Africa*. New York: Doubleday, Page.

Allen, Jeanne. 1985. "The Representation of Violence to Women: Hitchcock's 'Frenzy.'" *Film Quarterly* 38:30–38.

Allen, Michael. 1998. *Rodeo Cowboys in the North American Imagination*. Reno: University of Nevada Press.

Allen, William H., Jr. 1975. *How to Raise and Train Pigeons.* Rev. and enlarged ed. London: Sterling.

American Boy's Book of Sports and Games: A Practical Guide to Indoor and Outdoor Amusements. 2000 [1864]. New York: Lyons Press.

Ames, Kenneth L. 1992. *Death in the Dining Room, and Other Tales of Victorian Culture.* Philadelphia: Temple University Press.

Angst, Bud. 1999. "Passing of a Classic." *Citizen-Standard* (Valley View, Pa.), August 18. http://www.citizenstandard.com/columns/nipped/99nip/nip0818.htm.

Animal News Center. 2004. "Appeal to Halt Cruel Pigeon Shoots Rejected." *Buzzle.com: Intelligent Life on the Web,* January 17. http://www.buzzle.com/editorials/1-17-2004-49555.asp (accessed July 19, 2007).

Animal Rights Canada. 2007. "Online Resources for Canadian Activists." http://www.animalrightscanada.com/groups/ (accessed July 19, 2007).

Animals in Print. 2005. "Cabela's Dead Animals Worthy of a Museum." *Animals in Print: The On-Line Newsletter,* November 30. http://www.all-creatures.org/aip/alert-20051130.html (accessed July 20, 2007).

Ardener, Edwin. 1980. "Some Outstanding Problems in the Analysis of Events." In *Symbol as Sense: New Approaches to the Analysis of Meaning,* ed. Mary LeCron Foster and Stanley H. Brandes, 301–21. New York: Academic Press.

Arkansas Duck Hunter Company. 2008. "Hunting Gift Ideas." http://www.arkansasduckhunter.com/hunting_gift_ideas.asp (accessed January 30, 2008).

Arluke, Arnold, and Clinton R. Sanders. 1996. *Regarding Animals.* Philadelphia: Temple University Press.

Armstrong, Robert Plant. 1971. *The Affecting Presence: An Essay in Humanistic Anthropology.* Urbana: University of Illinois Press.

Arnold, Richard. 1956. *Pigeon Shooting.* London: Faber and Faber.

Baker, Margaret. 1974. *Folklore and Customs of Rural England.* Trowbridge, England: David and Charles.

Baker, Ronald L. 1986. *Jokelore: Humorous Folktales from Indiana.* Bloomington: Indiana University Press.

Ballard, Linda-May. 1985. "'Just Whatever They Had Handy': Aspects of Childbirth and Early Child-Care in Northern Ireland, prior to 1948." *Ulster Folklife* 31:59–72.

———. 1991. "Fairies and the Supernatural on Reachrai." In *The Good People: New Fairylore Essays,* ed. Peter Narváez, 47–93. Lexington: University Press of Kentucky.

———, interviewer. 2006. Transcript of fieldwork with Roy Murray

(CD2006.5). Cultra, Northern Ireland: Ulster Folk and Transport Museum.

Barber, Ken. 2007. "Bird Dogs and Radio Tracker Q&A." Gun Dog Supply Web site. http://www.gundogsupply.com/tracker-radio-article.html (accessed July 20, 2007).

Bateson, Gregory. 1972. *Steps to an Ecology of Mind.* New York: Ballantine.

Batley, John. 1996. *The Pigeon Shooter: A Complete Guide to Modern Pigeon Shooting.* Shrewsbury, England: Swan Hill Press.

Baughman, Ernest W. 1966. *Type and Motif-Index of the Folktales of England and North America.* The Hague: Mouton.

Beattie, John. 1966. "Ritual and Social Change." *Man* (n.s.) 1:60–74.

Beaufort, Duke of. 1960. "Masters and Huntsmen." In *In Praise of Hunting*, ed. David James and Wilson Stephens, 55–72. London: Hollis and Carter.

Beck, Jane. 1992. "Afterword." In *Deer Camp: Last Light in the Northeast Kingdom* by John M. Miller, 125–27. Cambridge, Mass.: MIT Press.

Beckford, Peter. 1932 [1796]. *Thoughts upon Hare and Fox Hunting in a Series of Letters to a Friend.* New York: Jonathan Cape.

Beers, Dian L. 2006. *For the Prevention of Cruelty: The History and Legacy of Animal Rights Activism in the United States.* Athens: Swallow Press/ Ohio University Press.

Beesley, Bradley, dir. 2002. *Okie Noodling.* DVD. Minneapolis: Redline.

Bell, Catherine. 1992. *Ritual Theory, Ritual Practice.* New York: Oxford University Press.

———. 1997. *Ritual: Perspectives and Dimensions.* New York: Oxford University Press.

Ben-Amos, Dan. 1984. "The Seven Strands of *Tradition:* Varieties in Its Meaning in American Folklore Studies." *Journal of Folklore Research* 21:97–131.

Bensman, Todd. 1998. "Loaded Issue: Dallas Gun Club Planning Live Pigeon Shoot, Sources Say; Animal Group Vows to Stop Event." *Morning News* (Dallas, Tex.), August 21, 1, 16.

Bentham, Jeremy. 1882. *The Theory of Legislation*, trans. R. Hildreth. London: Trübner.

Bergman, Charles. 1996. *Orion's Legacy: A Cultural History of Man as Hunter.* New York: Penguin.

Bernstein, Richard. 1971. *Praxis and Action: Contemporary Philosophies of Human Activity.* Philadelphia: University of Pennsylvania Press.

Berry, Wendell. 2003. "The Agrarian Standard." In *The Essential Agrarian Reader: The Future of Culture, Community, and the Land*, ed. Norman Wirzba, 23–33. Lexington: University Press of Kentucky.

Bethke, Robert D. 1976. "Storytelling at an Adirondack Inn." *Western Folklore* 35:123–39.

———. 1981. *Adirondack Voices: Woodsmen and Woods Lore.* Urbana: University of Illinois Press.

Bettelheim, Bruno. 1962. *Symbolic Wounds: Puberty Rites and the Envious Male.* New York: Collier.

BFSS. N.d. *This Is Coursing.* London: British Field Sports Society.

Biedermann, Hans. 1994. *Dictionary of Symbolism: Cultural Icons and the Meanings behind Them.* New York: Penguin.

Black, William George. 1883. "The Hare in Folk-Lore." *Folk-Lore Journal* 1:84–90.

Blagojevich, Governor Rod R. 2004. "Governor Signs Illinois Hunting Heritage Protection Act Legislation Encourages Maintaining and Enhancing Recreational Hunting Opportunities on Public Lands in Illinois." Press release, July 29. http://www.illinois.gov/PressReleases/ShowPressRelease .cfm?SubjectID=3&RecNum=3242 (accessed July 10, 2007).

Blane, William. 1788. *Cynegetica; Or, Essays on Sporting: Consisting of Observations on Hare Hunting.* London: John Stockdale.

Blechman, Andrew D. 2006. *Pigeons: The Fascinating Saga of the World's Most Revered and Reviled Bird.* New York: Grove Press.

Blome, Richard. 1686. *The Gentleman's Recreation.* London: S. Roycroft.

Blunt, Matt. 2007. "Blunt Signs Legislation Protecting Missouri Flood Plain from TIF Development." Press release, July 3. http://gov.missouri .gov/press/FloodPlain070307.htm (accessed July 10, 2007).

Boal, Mark. 2000–2001. "Winning the Blame Game: In the Wake of the Columbine Killings the Media Blamed Violent Videogames, and the President Vowed to Investigate the Industry." *Brill's Content*, December/January, 138–39.

Bocquet, Kevin. 2003. "Waterloo Cup: The Final Stand?" BBC News, February 25. http://news.bbc.co.uk/1/hi/uk/2798493.stm (accessed June 28, 2006).

Boone and Crockett Club. 2008. "Fair Chase Statement." http://www .boone-crockett.org/huntingEthics/ethics_fairchase.asp?area= hunting Ethics (accessed February 9, 2008).

Bowcott, Owen. 2005. "An Eagle on the Arm, and the Hunt Is On." *Guardian* (London), September 17, 3.

Boyle, John. 1969. "A Eurasian Hunting Ritual." *Folklore* 80:12–16.

Brady, Erika. 1990. "Mankind's Thumb on Nature's Scale: Trapping and Regional Identity in the Missouri Ozarks." In *Sense of Place: American Regional Cultures*, ed. Barbara Allen and Thomas J. Schlereth, 58–73. Lexington: University Press of Kentucky.

————. 1994. "'The River's Like Our Back Yard': Tourism and Cultural Identity in the Ozark National Scenic Riverways." In *Conserving Culture: A New Discourse on Heritage*, ed. Mary Hufford, 138–51. Urbana: University of Illinois Press.

Braley, Berton. 1919. *Buddy Ballads: Songs of the A. E .F.* New York: George H. Doran.

Brandes, Stanley. 1985. *Forty: The Age and the Symbol.* Knoxville: University of Tennessee Press.

Branigan, Cynthia A. 2004. *The Reign of the Greyhound: Popular History of the Oldest Family of Dogs.* Hoboken, N.J.: Howell.

Braunschweiger, Amy. 2008. "To the Hunter Go the Spoils." *New York,* February 4, 49.

Brewster, Paul G. 1953. *American Nonsinging Games.* Norman: University of Oklahoma Press.

Briggs, Katharine M. 1991. *A Dictionary of British Folk-Tales in the English Language,* 2 vols. London: Routledge.

Bringéus, Nils-Arvid. 1988. "Pictures of the Life Cycle." *Ethnologia Scandinavica,* 5–33.

Bronner, Simon J. 1983. "The Paradox of Pride and Loathing, and Other Problems." In *Foodways and Eating Habits: Directions for Research,* ed. Michael Owen Jones, Bruce Giuliano, and Roberta Krell, 115–24. Los Angeles: California Folklore Society.

————. 1985. "What's Grosser than Gross?: New Sick Joke Cycles." *Midwestern Journal of Language and Folklore* 11:39–49.

————. 1986. *Grasping Things: Folk Material Culture and Mass Society in America.* Lexington: University Press of Kentucky.

————. 1987. *Old-Time Music Makers of New York State.* Syracuse, N.Y.: Syracuse University Press.

————. 1988. *American Children's Folklore.* Little Rock, Ark.: August House.

————. 1989. "Reading Consumer Culture." In *Consuming Visions: Accumulation and Display of Goods in America, 1880–1920,* ed. Simon J. Bronner, 13–54. New York: W. W. Norton.

————. 1990. "'Left to Their Own Devices': Interpreting American Children's Folklore as an Adaptation to Aging." *Southern Folklore* 47:101–15.

————. 1996a. *The Carver's Art: Crafting Meaning from Wood.* Lexington: University Press of Kentucky.

————. 1996b. *Popularizing Pennsylvania: Henry W. Shoemaker and the Progressive Uses of Folklore and History.* University Park: Pennsylvania State University Press.

————. 1998. *Following Tradition: Folklore in the Discourse of American Culture.* Logan: Utah State University Press.

———. 2000a. "The American Concept of Tradition: Folklore in the Discourse of Traditional Values." *Western Folklore* 59:87–104.

———, ed. 2000b. "The Meanings of Tradition." Special issue, *Western Folklore* 59 (2): 87–195.

———. 2002. "Questioning the Future: Polling Americans at the Turn of the New Millennium." In *Prospects: An Annual of American Cultural Studies*, vol. 27, ed. Jack Salzman, 665–85. New York: Cambridge University Press.

———. 2004. "'This Is Why We Hunt': Social-Psychological Meanings of the Traditions and Rituals of Deer Camp." *Western Folklore* 63:11–50.

———. 2005a. "Contesting Tradition: The Deep Play and Protest of Pigeon Shoots." *Journal of American Folklore* 118:409–52.

———. 2005b. "Menfolk." In *Manly Traditions: The Folk Roots of American Masculinities*, ed. Simon J. Bronner, 1–60. Bloomington: Indiana University Press.

———. 2006a. *Crossing the Line: Violence, Play, and Drama in Naval Equator Traditions*. Amsterdam: Amsterdam University Press.

———. 2006b. "'Heile, Heile, Hinkel Dreck': On the Earthiness of Pennsylvania German Folk Narratives." In *Preserving Heritage: A Festschrift for C. Richard Beam*, ed. Joshua R. Brown and Leroy T. Hopkins, 77–100. Lawrence, Kans.: Society for German-American Studies.

———. 2007. "Analyzing the Ethnic Self: The *Hinkel Dreck* Theme in Pennsylvania-German Folk Narrative." *Columbia Journal of American Studies* 8:20–54.

Broudy, Saul. 1982. "The Effect of Performer-Audience Interaction on Performance Strategies: 'Moose-Turd Pie' in Context." PhD diss., University of Pennsylvania.

Browder, Laura. 2006. *Her Best Shot: Women and Guns in America*. Chapel Hill: University of North Carolina Press.

Brown, Mary Ellen, and Bruce A. Rosenberg, eds. 1998. *Encyclopedia of Folklore and Literature*. Santa Barbara, Calif.: ABC-CLIO.

Brunvand, Jan Harold, ed. 1996. *American Folklore: An Encyclopedia*. New York: Garland.

———. 1999. *Too Good to Be True: The Colossal Book of Urban Legends*. New York: W. W. Norton.

———. 2001. *Encyclopedia of Urban Legends*. Santa Barbara, Calif.: ABC-CLIO.

Budra, Paul. 2004. "American Justice and the First-Person Shooter." *Canadian Review of American Studies* 34:1–12.

Bureau of Land Management. 2000. "Statement of Henri Bisson, Assistant Director for Renewable Resources and Planning, Bureau of Land

Management, on H.R. 4790 Hunting Heritage Protection Act before the House Resources Committee, Subcommittee on Fisheries Conservation, Wildlife and Oceans." Bureau of Land Management News, July 20. http://www.blm.gov/nhp/news/legislative/pages/2000/te-000720HB.htm (accessed July 11, 2007).

Burke, Ronald, and Susan Black. 1997. "Save the Males: Backlash in Organizations." *Journal of Business Ethics* 16:933–42.

Burkert, Walter. 1996 [1983]. "The Function and Transformation of Ritual Killing." In *Readings in Ritual Studies*, ed. Ronald L. Grimes, 62–71. Upper Saddle River, N.J.: Prentice-Hall.

Burrison, John A. 1989. *Storytellers: Folktales and Legends from the South*. Athens: University of Georgia Press.

Buzash, George E. 1989. "The 'Rough Sex' Defense." *Journal of Criminal Law and Criminology* 80:557–84.

Cabela, David. 2001. *Cabela's, World's Foremost Outfitter: A History*. Forest Dale, Vt.: Paul S. Eriksson.

Calvert, Karin. 1992. *Children in the House: Material Culture of Early Childhood, 1600–1900*. Boston: Northeastern University Press.

Camp, Elwood W., and Harris C. Hartman. 1937. "C.C.C. Speech." *American Speech* 12:74–75.

"Camp Rules." 2003. *Field and Stream* 108 (November): 74.

Campbell, Hugh, Michael Mayerfeld Bell, and Margaret Finney. 2006. "Masculinity and Rural Life: An Introduction." In *Country Boys: Masculinity and Rural Life*, ed. Hugh Campbell, Michael Mayerfeld Bell, and Margaret Finney, 1–22. University Park: Pennsylvania State University Press.

Canfield, Patrick M. 1992. *Growing Up with Bootleggers, Gamblers and Pigeons*. Wilmington, Del.: Interlude Enterprises.

Cannon, Anthon S., coll. 1984. *Popular Beliefs and Superstitions from Utah*, 2 vols., ed. Wayland D. Hand and Jeannine E. Talley. Salt Lake City: University of Utah Press.

Carpenter, Tom, ed. 1999. *The Great American Deer Camp*. Minnetonka, Minn.: North American Hunting Club.

Cartmill, Matt. 1993. *A View to a Death in the Morning: Hunting and Nature through History*. Cambridge, Mass.: Harvard University Press.

Casciogne, George. 1575. *The Noble Art of Vernerie or Hunting*, trans. George Turberville. London: Henry Bynneman for Christopher Barker.

Castle Argghhh! 2006. "The Home of Two of Jonah's Military Guys." Blog, November 23. http://www.thedonovan.com/archives/006717.html (accessed January 30, 2008).

Cavalieri, Paola. 2003. "For an Expanded Theory of Human Rights." In

The Animal Ethics Reader, ed. Susan J. Armstrong and Richard G. Botzler, 30–32. New York: Routledge.

Center for Rural Pennsylvania. 1998. *Economic Values and Impacts of Sport Fishing, Hunting and Trapping Activities in Pennsylvania.* Harrisburg: Center for Rural Pennsylvania.

Chambliss, Sen. Saxby. 2007. "Introducing S. 408." *Congressional Record,* January 26. http://www.govtrack.us/congress/record.xpd?id=110-s20070126-24&person=300021 (accessed July 11, 2007).

Chudacoff, Howard P. 1999. *The Age of the Bachelor: Creating an American Subculture.* Princeton, N.J.: Princeton University Press.

Clapson, Mark. 1992. *A Bit of a Flutter: Popular Gambling and English Society, c. 1823–1961.* Manchester: Manchester University Press.

"Cleveland Amory's Black Beauty Ranch." 2007. Fund for Animals Web site. http://fundforanimals.org/ranch/about/ (accessed July 19, 2007).

Clifton, Merritt. 1990. "Killing the Female: The Psychology of the Hunt." *Animals' Agenda* 7:26–30, 57.

———. 1994. "Hunters and Molestors." *Animal People* 3:7–9.

Clough, Caroline, and Barry Kew. 1993. *The Animal Welfare Handbook.* London: Fourth Estate.

Coats, Archie. 1970. *Pigeon Shooting.* London: Andre Deutsch.

Cohen, Carl. 2003. "Reply to Tom Regan." In *The Animal Ethics Reader,* ed. Susan J. Armstrong and Richard G. Botzler, 25–29. New York: Routledge.

Cohen, Percy S. 1980. "Psychoanalysis and Cultural Symbolization." In *Symbol as Sense: New Approaches to the Analysis of Meaning,* ed. Mary LeCron Foster and Stanley H. Brandes, 45–68. New York: Academic Press.

Coleman, Joseph. 2007. "Whaling Tradition Slowly Sinking." *Miami Herald,* November 18, 23A.

Collard, Andrée, with Joyce Contrucci. 1988. *Rape of the Wild: Man's Violence against Animals and the Earth.* Bloomington: Indiana University Press.

Committee of Inquiry into Hunting with Dogs in England and Wales. 2000. "Final Report: The Brown Hare: A Game Animal or Pest Species?" Norwich, England: Stationery Office. http://www.defra.gov.uk/rural/hunting/inquiry/mainsections/report.pdf.

Commonwealth v. A. N. Lewis. 1891. Supreme Court of Pennsylvania, No. 407, 140 Pa. 261, 21A.396 (February 23).

Comninou, Maria. 1995. "Speech, Pornography, and Hunting." In *Animals and Women: Feminist Theoretical Explorations,* ed. Carol J. Adams and Josephine Donovan, 126–48. Durham, N.C.: Duke University Press.

Compassionate Action Institute. 2000–2002. "Things That Kids Can Do to Help: Save the Whales." http://pleasebekind.com/whales.html (accessed January 30, 2008).

Cooper, James Fenimore. 1963 [1841]. *The Deerslayer, or The First Warpath*. New York: New American Library.

———. 1964 [1823]. *The Pioneers*. New York: Signet.

Cooperative Games, Ken and Jann Kolsbun. 2008. "Save the Whales." http://www.cooperativegames.com/1002_childrens_board_games .html (accessed January 30, 2008).

Copold, Steve. 1996. *Hounds, Hares and Other Creatures: The Complete Book of Coursing*. Wheat Ridge, Colo.: Hoflin.

Cormack, Malcolm. 2007. *Country Pursuits: British, American, and French Sporting Art from the Mellon Collections in the Virginia Museum of Fine Arts*. Charlottesville: University of Virginia Press.

Cox, Harding. 1892. *Coursing*. London: Longmans, Green.

Cox, Simon, and Richard Vadon. 2004. "How Animal Rights Took on the World." BBC News, November 18. http://news.bbc.co.uk/go/pr/fr/-/1/hi/magazine/4020235.stm (accessed July 19, 2007).

Creighton, Helen. 1950. *Folklore of Lunenburg County, Nova Scotia*. Ottawa: National Museum of Canada.

Dahles, Heidi. 1991. "Performing Manliness: On the Meaning of Poaching in Dutch Society." *Ethnologia Europaea* 21:19–32.

———. 1993. "Game Killing and Killing Games: An Anthropologist Looking at Hunting in a Modern Society." *Society and Animals* 1:169–84.

Dannemann, Manuel. 1978. "Fox Hunting: A Form of Traditional Behaviour Providing Social Cohesiveness." In *Folklore Studies in the Twentieth Century*, ed. Venetia Newall, 167–69. Totowa, N.J.: Rowman and Littlefield.

Davis, Janet M. 2002. *The Circus Age: Culture and Society under the American Big Top*. Chapel Hill: University of North Carolina Press.

De Angelis, Richard. 1998. "The Vicious Circle." *Animal Guardian* 11:8–9, 14.

Diamond, Cora. 2004. "Eating Meat and Eating People." In *Animal Rights: Current Debates and New Directions*, ed. Cass R. Sunstein and Martha C. Nussbaum, 93–107. Oxford: Oxford University Press.

Dickson, Paul. 2004. *War Slang: American Fighting Words and Phrases since the Civil War*, 2nd ed. Washington, D.C.: Brassey's.

Dillard, Courtney L. 1997. "Oppositional Argument, Civil Disobedience, and 'Norms of Appearance' in the Animal Rights Movement." Master's thesis, University of North Carolina.

———. 2002. "Civil Disobedience: A Case Study in Factors of Effectiveness." *Society and Animals* 10:47–62.

Dizard, Jan E. 1994. *Going Wild: Hunting, Animal Rights, and the Contested Meaning of Nature.* Amherst: University of Massachusetts Press.

———. 1999. *Going Wild: Hunting, Animal Rights, and the Contested Meaning of Nature.* Rev. and expanded ed. Amherst: University of Massachusetts Press.

———. 2003. *Mortal Stakes: Hunters and Hunting in Contemporary America.* Amherst: University of Massachusetts Press.

Dochat, Tom. 2006. "In Their Sights: Gander Mountain Takes Aim at Big Competitors' Subsidies." *Patriot-News* (Harrisburg, Pa.), August 27, C1, 8.

"The Dogs." 2006. *National Coursing Club News.* National Coursing Club Web site. http://www.nationalcoursingclub.org/maintain/news.htm (accessed July 9, 2006).

Donnell, Rich, and May Lamar. 1987. *Hunting: The Southern Tradition.* Dallas: Taylor Publishing.

Donnelly, Frank. 1999. "Into the Woods: Hunters Head out as Deer Herd Hits a 100-Year High." *Patriot-News* (Harrisburg, Pa.), November 29, A1, 12.

Donovan, Josephine. 2003. "Animal Rights and Feminist Theory." In *The Animal Ethics Reader,* ed. Susan J. Armstrong and Richard G. Botzler, 45–49. New York: Routledge.

Donovan, Josephine, and Carol J. Adams, eds. 1996. *Beyond Animal Rights: A Feminist Caring Ethic for the Treatment of Animals.* New York: Continuum.

Dorson, Richard M. 1968. *The British Folklorists.* Chicago: University of Chicago Press.

———. 1972. *Folklore: Selected Essays.* Bloomington: Indiana University Press.

———, ed. 1978. *Folklore in the Modern World.* The Hague: Mouton.

———. 1982a. *Man and Beast in American Comic Legend.* Bloomington: Indiana University Press.

———. 1982b. "Material Components in Celebration." In *Celebration: Studies in Festivity and Ritual,* ed. Victor Turner, 33–57. Washington, D.C.: Smithsonian Institution Press.

Douglas, Ann. 1977. *The Feminization of American Culture.* New York: Avon.

Duda, Mark Damian. 1997. "Why Do We Hunt?" *North American Hunter* (September): 30.

Dugan, William G. 1993. "Tradition in Transition: The Hegins Pigeon Shoot." Master's thesis, Pennsylvania State University.

Dukes, Edmond Craig, ed. 2005. *The Memoirs of Ernest Franklin Dukes, Jr.* Privately printed.

Dunayer, Joan. 2004. *Speciesism.* New York: Lantern Books.

Dundes, Alan. 1964. "On Game Morphology: A Study of the Structure of Non-Verbal Folklore." *New York Folklore Quarterly* 20:276–88.

———. 1966. "Here I Sit—A Study of American Latrinalia." *Papers of the Kroeber Anthropological Society* 34:91–105.

———. 1972. "Folk Ideas as Units of Worldview." In *Toward New Perspectives in Folklore,* ed. Américo Paredes and Richard Bauman, 93–103. Austin: University of Texas Press.

———. 1975. *Analytic Essays in Folklore.* The Hague: Mouton.

———. 1978. *Essays in Folkloristics.* Meerut, India: Folklore Institute.

———. 1980. *Interpreting Folklore.* Bloomington: Indiana University Press.

———. 1984. *Life Is Like a Chicken Coop Ladder: A Portrait of German Culture through Folklore.* New York: Columbia University Press.

———. 1987a. "The American Game of 'Smear the Queer' and the Homosexual Component of Male Competitive Sport and Warfare." In *Parsing through Customs: Essays by a Freudian Folklorist* by Alan Dundes, 178–94. Madison: University of Wisconsin Press.

———. 1987b. "Couvade in Genesis." In *Parsing through Customs: Essays by a Freudian Folklorist* by Alan Dundes, 145–66. Madison: University of Wisconsin Press.

———. 1989a. "April Fool and April Fish: Towards a Theory of Ritual Pranks." In *Folklore Matters* by Alan Dundes, 98–111. Knoxville: University of Tennessee Press.

———. 1989b. "Defining Identity through Folklore." In *Folklore Matters* by Alan Dundes, 1–39. Knoxville: University of Tennessee Press.

———. 1994. "Gallus as Phallus: A Psychoanalytic Cross-Cultural Consideration of the Cockfight as Fowl Play." In *The Cockfight: A Casebook,* ed. Alan Dundes, 241–84. Madison: University of Wisconsin Press.

———. 1997. *From Game to War and Other Psychoanalytic Essays on Folklore.* Lexington: University Press of Kentucky.

———. 1998. "The Vampire as Bloodthirsty Revenant: A Psychoanalytic Post Mortem." In *The Vampire: A Casebook,* ed. Alan Dundes, 159–78. Madison: University of Wisconsin Press.

———. 2002a. "Bloody Mary in the Mirror: A Ritual Reflection of Pre-Pubescent Anxiety." In *Bloody Mary in the Mirror: Essays in Psychoanalytic Folkloristics* by Alan Dundes, 76–94. Jackson: University Press of Mississippi.

———. 2002b. *The Shabbat Elevator and Other Sabbath Subterfuges: An Unorthodox Essay on Circumventing Custom and Jewish Character.* Lanham, Md.: Rowman and Littlefield.

Dundes, Alan, and Carl R. Pagter. 2000. *Why Don't Sheep Shrink When It*

Rains? A Further Collection of Photocopier Folklore. Syracuse, N.Y.: Syracuse University Press.

Eberly, Susan Schoon. 1991. "Fairies and the Folklore of Disability: Changelings, Hybrids, and the Solitary Fairy." In *The Good People: New Fairylore Essays*, ed. Peter Narváez, 227–50. Lexington: University Press of Kentucky.

Edmondson, Joni R., and Shawn A. Hessinger. 1999. "Pigeon Shoot Canceled: Court's Decision Doomed Tradition." *Pottsville Republican*, August 18. http://archives.pottsville.com/archives/1999/Aug/18/E253031.htm.

Edwards, John. 1985. "Hunting Camps." *Pennsylvania Sportsman* (December): 28–29.

Ehrenreich, Barbara. 1997. *Blood Rites: Origins and History of the Passions of War.* New York: Henry Holt.

Eliade, Mircea. 1987 [1959]. *The Sacred and the Profane: The Nature of Religion.* San Diego: Harcourt.

———. 1991. *Images and Symbols: Studies in Religious Symbolism.* Princeton, N.J.: Princeton University Press.

Eliason, Eric A. 2004. "Foxhunting Folkways under Fire and the Crisis of Traditional Moral Knowledge." *Western Folklore* 63:123–67.

Elliott, William. 1859 [1846]. *Carolina Sports, by Land and Water.* New York: Derby and Jackson.

El-Shamy, Hasan, and Jane Garry, eds. 2005. *Archetypes and Motifs in Folklore and Literature: A Handbook.* Armonk, N.Y.: M. E. Sharpe.

Epstein, Richard A. 2004. "Animals as Objects, or Subjects, of Rights." In *Animal Rights: Current Debates and New Directions*, ed. Cass R. Sunstein and Martha C. Nussbaum, 143–61. Oxford: Oxford University Press.

Eshelman, Nancy. 2007. "8-Year-Olds Hunt with Guns?" *Patriot-News* (Harrisburg, Pa.), November 29, A1.

Essin, Emmett M. 1997. *Shavetails and Bell Sharps: The History of the U.S. Army Mule.* Lincoln: University of Nebraska Press.

Evans, George Ewart. 1960. *The Horse in the Furrow.* London: Faber and Faber.

———. 1961. *Ask the Fellow Who Cut the Hay.* London: Faber and Faber.

———. 1966. *The Pattern under the Plough: Aspects of the Folk-Life of East Anglia.* London: Faber and Faber.

———. 1969. "Folk Life Studies in East Anglia." In *Studies in Folk Life: Essays in Honour of Iorwerth C. Peate*, ed. Geraint Jenkins, 35–46. London: Routledge and Kegan Paul.

———. 1970. *Where Beards Wag All: The Relevance of Oral Tradition.* London: Faber and Faber.

———. 1975. *The Days That We Have Seen.* London: Faber and Faber.

Evans, George Ewart, and David Thompson. 1972. *The Leaping Hare.* London: Faber and Faber.

Evans, Sid, and Bob Marshall. 2004. "A Sporting Debate." *Field and Stream* (October): 50–55.

Eveland, Tom. 1992. "Pigeon Shoot, Hunting Are Two Different Things." *Pocono Record,* September 13, E1.

Farrell, James J. 2003. *One Nation under Goods: Malls and the Seductions of American Shopping.* Washington, D.C.: Smithsonian Institution Press.

Faulkner, William. 1994 [1955]. *Big Woods: The Hunting Stories.* New York: Vintage.

Fegely, Tom. 1999. "Deer Camps of Pennsylvania." In *The Great American Deer Camp,* ed. Tom Carpenter, 140–69. Minnetonka, Minn.: North American Hunting Club.

Fenton, Alexander. 1976. *Scottish Country Life.* Edinburgh: John Donald.

———. 1985. *The Shape of the Past: Essays in Scottish Ethnology.* Edinburgh: John Donald.

Ferenczi, Sandor. 1950. *Sex in Psychoanalysis.* New York: Basic Books.

Field and Stream. 2004. "The 2003 National Hunting Survey." *Field and Stream: The World's Leading Outdoor Magazine.* http://www .fieldandstream.com/fieldstream/hunting/article/0,13199,458217,00. html (accessed July 9, 2007).

Fine, Gary Alan. 1979. "Cokelore and Coke Law: Urban Belief Tales and the Problem of Multiple Origins." *Journal of American Folklore* 92:477–82.

Finsen, Lawrence, and Susan Finsen. 1994. *The Animal Rights Movement in America: From Compassion to Respect.* New York: Twayne.

Fleece, Jeffery A. 1946. "Words in -FU." *American Speech* 21:70–72.

Foley, Barbara. 1995. "What's at Stake in the Culture Wars." *New England Quarterly* 68:458–79.

Foster, Mary LeCron. 1980. "The Growth of Symbolism in Culture." In *Symbol as Sense: New Approaches to the Analysis of Meaning,* ed. Mary LeCron Foster and Stanley H. Brandes, 371–97. New York: Academic Press.

Francione, Gary. 1996. "Animal Rights: The Future." World Prout Assembly Web site. http://www.worldproutassembly.org/archives/2005/04/ animal_rights_t.html (accessed July 20, 2007).

French, John C. 1919. *The Passenger Pigeon in Pennsylvania.* Altoona, Pa.: Altoona Tribune.

Freud, Sigmund. 1919. *Totem and Taboo: Resemblances between the Psychic Lives of Savages and Neurotics,* trans. A. A. Brill. London: George Routledge and Sons.

————. 1994 [1913]. "Foreword." In *The Portable Scatalog: Excerpts from Scatalogic Rites of All Nations* by John G. Bourke, ed. Louis P. Kaplan, 5–9. New York: William Morrow.

————. 1995. *The Basic Writings of Sigmund Freud*, ed. A. A. Brill. New York: Modern Library.

Frye, Bob. 2006. *Deer Wars: Science, Tradition, and the Battle over Managing White-tails in Pennsylvania.* University Park: Pennsylvania State University Press.

Fuchs, Rabbi Stephen. 2003. "Enhancing the Divine Image." In *The Animal Ethics Reader*, ed. Susan J. Armstrong and Richard G. Botzler, 224–26. New York: Routledge.

Fudge, Erica. 2002. *Animal.* London: Reaktion Books.

Fukuda, Kaoru. 1997. "Different View of Animal and Cruelty to Animals: Cases of Fox-Hunting and Pet-Keeping in Britain." *Anthropology Today* 13:2–6.

Fund for Animals. 1997. *Killing Their Childhood: How Public Schools and Government Agencies Are Promoting Sport Hunting to America's Children.* New York: Fund for Animals.

————. 1998. "Cruelty Comes to California: Live Pigeon Shoot Begins Today in Sierra County." Press release, May 14.

————. 2000. "'Pigeon Shoots' Illegal Rules California Attorney General." Press release, April 4.

————. 2001. "Fund for Animals Urges Pennsylvania Legislators to Protect Children and Animals by Opposing House Bill 1510." Press release, June 28.

"Future Hunting: Sprawl, Lack of Interest Team up against Pennsylvania's Heritage." 2004. Editorial, *Patriot-News* (Harrisburg, Pa.), December 16, A18.

Gaard, Greta, ed. 1993. *Ecofeminism: Women, Animals, Nature.* Philadelphia: Temple University Press.

"Gamecock." 2005. Associated Press wire story. http://www.sunherald.com/mld/sunherald/news/state/10738996.htm.

Gaster, Moses. 1915. *Rumanian Bird and Beast Stories.* London: Sidgwick and Jackson.

Geertz, Clifford. 1973. "Deep Play: Notes on the Balinese Cockfight." In *The Interpretation of Cultures: Selected Essays* by Clifford Geertz, 412–54. New York: Basic Books.

————. 1994 [1973]. "Deep Play: Notes on the Balinese Cockfight." In *The Cockfight: A Casebook*, ed. Alan Dundes, 94–132. Madison: University of Wisconsin Press.

Genders, Roy. 1946. *Modern Greyhound Racing.* London: Sporting Handbooks.

———. 1975. *The Greyhound and Greyhound Racing: A History of the Greyhound in Britain from Earliest Times to the Present Day*. London: Sporting Handbooks.

Gillespie, Angus K., and Jay Mechling, eds. 1987. *American Wildlife in Symbol and Story*. Knoxville: University of Tennessee Press.

Girard, René. 1996 [1977]. "Violence and the Sacred: Sacrifice." In *Readings in Ritual Studies*, ed. Ronald L. Grimes, 239–56. Upper Saddle River, N.J.: Prentice-Hall.

Glassie, Henry. 1968. *Pattern in the Material Folk Culture of the Eastern United States*. Philadelphia: University of Pennsylvania Press.

———. 1983. "The Moral Lore of Folklore." *Folklore Forum* 16:123–52.

"Goldfinger—Free Me." 2007. YouTube. http://www.youtube.com/watch?v=7rRWLTGSNvg (accessed February 13, 2008).

Goldman, Adam. 2006. "Deer Hunting Game Is a Surprise Hit." MSNBC.com, July 25. http://www.msnbc.msn.com/id/14030610/ (accessed July 20, 2007).

Gomme, Alice Bertha. 1964 [1894]. *The Traditional Games of England, Scotland and Ireland*, 2 vols. New York: Dover.

Goodheart, Eugene. 1997. "Reflections on the Culture Wars." *Daedalus: Journal of the American Academy of Arts and Sciences* 126:153–75.

Gordon, Neal A. 2001. "The Implications of Memetics for the Cultural Defense." *Duke Law Journal* 50:1809–34.

Gould, Dudley C. 1999. *You Tremble Body*. Paducah, Ky.: Turner.

Grant, I. F. 1961. *Highland Folk Ways*. London: Routledge and Kegan Paul.

Gray, John. 1988. *Pigeon Shooting*. Wiltshire, England: Crowood Press.

Green, Thomas A., ed. 1997. *Folklore: An Encyclopedia of Beliefs, Customs, Tales, Music, and Art*. Santa Barbara, Calif.: ABC-CLIO.

Grier, Katherine C. 2006. *Pets in America: A History*. Chapel Hill: University of North Carolina Press.

Guerriero, Frank S. 1994. "Hunting and Its Association with a Child's Rite of Passage from Childhood to Adolescence." Archives of Pennsylvania Folklore and Ethnography, Center for Pennsylvania Culture Studies, Pennsylvania State University, Harrisburg.

Guither, Harold D. 1998. *Animal Rights: History and Scope of a Radical Social Movement*. Carbondale: Southern Illinois University Press.

Hall, Edward T. 1976. *Beyond Culture*. Garden City, N.Y.: Doubleday.

Hall, G. Stanley. 1897. "A Study of Fears." *American Journal of Psychology* 8:147–249.

———. 1899. "A Study of Anger." *American Journal of Psychology* 10:516–91.

———. 1914. "A Synthetic Genetic Study of Fear: Chapter II." *American Journal of Psychology* 25:321–92.

Hall, Jean Houston, ed. 2002. *Dictionary of American Regional English*, vol. 4. Cambridge, Mass.: Harvard University Press.

Hall, Peter. 1995. *Practical Pigeon Shooting*. Wiltshire, England: Crowood Press.

Hand, Wayland, ed. 1961. *The Frank C. Brown Collection of North Carolina Folklore*, vol. 6, *Popular Beliefs and Superstitions from North Carolina*. Durham, N.C.: Duke University Press.

Hand, Wayland, Anna Casetta, and Sondra Thiederman, eds. 1981. *Popular Beliefs and Superstitions: A Compendium of American Folklore from the Ohio Collection of Newbell Niles Puckett*. 2 vols. Boston: G. K. Hall.

Hanna, Brian L. 1986. "The Folklore of Central Pennsylvania Deer Hunting Camps." Archives of Pennsylvania Folklore and Ethnography, Center for Pennsylvania Culture Studies, Pennsylvania State University, Harrisburg.

Haraway, Donna. 1993. "Teddy Bear Patriarchy: Taxidermy in the Garden of Eden, New York City, 1908–1936." In *Cultures of United States Imperialism*, ed. Amy Kaplan and Donald E. Pease, 237–91. Durham, N.C.: Duke University Press.

"Hare Coursing and Fox Hunting in Northern Ireland." 2006. League against Cruel Sports Web site. http://www.league.uk.com/campaigns/ni/index.htm (accessed July 5, 2006).

Harms, Fred P. 1999. "A Unique Tradition." *Aviation Safety Newsletter* (October). http://www.mopilots.org/stlouis/oct99nws.htm (accessed July 9, 2007).

Hartley, Dorothy. 1979. *Lost Country Life*. New York: Pantheon.

Hartog, Hendrik. 1994 [1985]. "Pigs and Positivism." In *Folk Law: Essays in the Theory and Practice of Lex Non Scripta*, 2:711–52. Madison: University of Wisconsin Press.

Heavey, Bill. 2007. "Always on Call." *Field and Stream* (September): 98–103.

Hegins Labor Day Committee. 1984. *Hegins Labor Day Shoot, Hegins, Pennsylvania: 50th Anniversary, 1934–1984*. Valley View, Pa.: Astro Press.

Heller, Peter. 2007. *The Whale Warriors: The Battle at the Bottom of the World to Save the Planet's Largest Mammals*. New York: Free Press.

Hemingway, Ernest. 2001. "Remembering Shooting-Flying: A Key West Letter—*Esquire*, February 1935." In *Hemingway on Hunting*, ed. Seán Hemingway, 179–86. New York: Scribner.

Hendricks, George D. 1958. "Voodoo Powder." *Western Folklore* 17:132.

Hennessey, Tom. 2004. "Sportsmen Loaded for Bear." *Bangor Daily News*,

April 7. http://bangordailynews.com/news/t/default.aspx?a=115&template
=print-article.htm (accessed July 11, 2007).

Herman, Daniel Justin. 2001a. "Hunting." In *Boyhood in America: An Encyclopedia*, ed. Priscilla Ferguson Clement and Jacqueline Reinier, 347–
51. Santa Barbara, Calif.: ABC-CLIO.

———. 2001b. *Hunting and the American Imagination*. Washington, D.C.:
Smithsonian Institution Press.

Hicks, Joe, and Grahame Allen. 1999. "A Century of Change: Trends in
UK Statistics since 1900." Research paper 99/111, House of Commons Library, London.

Hines, Donald M. 1972. "The Development of Folklife Research in the
United Kingdom." *Pennsylvania Folklife* 21 (spring): 8–20.

Hiss, Kimberly, ed. 2007. "The American Huntress (2007)." *Field and
Stream* (July): 70–77.

Hobsbawm, Eric, and Terence Ranger, eds. 1983. *The Invention of Tradition*. Cambridge: Cambridge University Press.

Hodge, Guy R. 1985. "The Bird Wars." *Humane Society News* (spring): 4–8.

Hoffmann, Frank. 1973. *Analytical Survey of Anglo-American Traditional
Erotica*. Bowling Green, Ohio: Bowling Green State University Popular Press.

Howard, Manny. 2004. "At Cabela's, Shop Now, Hunt Later." *New York
Times*, March 26, F1–2.

Howe, James. 1981. "Fox Hunting as Ritual." *American Ethnologist* 8:278–300.

Hruska, Robert R. 1999. *Humorous Stories from the U.P. Hunting Camps*.
Saline, Mich.: McNaughton and Gunn.

Huffman, Alan. 1997. *Ten Point: Deer Camp in the Mississippi Delta*. Jackson:
University Press of Mississippi.

———. 2001. "Ten Point Club." In *Legendary Deer Camps*, ed. Robert Wegner, 178–93. Iola, Wis.: Krause.

Hufford, Mary T. 1987. "The Fox." In *American Wildlife in Symbol and
Story*, ed. Angus K. Gillespie and Jay Mechling, 163–202. Knoxville:
University of Tennessee Press.

———. 1992. *Chaseworld: Foxhunting and Storytelling in New Jersey's Pine
Barrens*. Philadelphia: University of Pennsylvania Press.

———. 1996. "Hunting." In *American Folklore: An Encyclopedia*, ed. Jan
Harold Brunvand, 379–81. New York: Garland.

Humane Society of the United States. 2005. "The Latest Fad in Internet
Animal Cruelty: Pay-per-View Hunting." Humane Society of the
United States Web site, April 8. http://www.hsus.org/wildlife/wildlife_
news/pay_per_view_slaughter.html (accessed July 20, 2007).

———. 2007. "Shooting Pigeons and Calling Yourself a Sportsman Is Like

Hiring an Escort Service and Calling Yourself a Ladies' Man." Advertisement. *Patriot-News* (Harrisburg, Pa.), September 24, A9.

Hummel, Richard. 1994. *Hunting and Fishing for Sport: Commerce, Controversy, Popular Culture.* Bowling Green, Ohio: Bowling Green State University Popular Press.

Hunt, Frazier. 1918. *Blown in by the Draft: Camp Yarns Collected at One of the Great National Army Cantonments by an Amateur War Correspondent.* Garden City, N.Y.: Doubleday, Page.

Hunter, James Davison. 1991. *Culture Wars: The Struggle to Define America.* New York: Basic Books.

"Hunting Jokes." 2004. *Manly Jokes for Manly Men.* http://manlyjokes.tripod.com/hunt.html.

Hurst, Julie. 2007. "Woman Hunters in Penn's Woods: Experiences of Nine Pennsylvania Hunters." Master's thesis, Pennsylvania State University.

Huskisson, Mike. 1983. *Outfoxed.* London: Michael Huskisson Associates.

"Information Sheet: Statistics." 2007. Vegetarian Society Web site. http://www.vegsoc.org/info/statveg.html (accessed July 19, 2007).

Ingersoll, Ernest. 1923. *Birds in Legend, Fable, and Folklore.* London: Longmans, Green.

Isaac, Rhys. 1980. "Ethnographic Method in History: An Action Approach." *Historical Methods* 13:43–61.

Ives, Edward D. 1988. *George Magoon and the Down East Game War: History, Folklore, and the Law.* Urbana: University of Illinois Press.

Jackson, Bob, and Bob Norton. 1987. "Hunting as a Social Experience." *Deer and Deer Hunting* 11:38–51.

James, David, and Wilson Stephens, eds. 1960. *In Praise of Hunting.* London: Hollis and Carter.

Jasper, James M., and Dorothy Nelkin. 1992. *The Animal Rights Crusade: The Growth of a Moral Protest.* New York: Free Press.

Jenkins, J. Geraint. 1972. "The Use of Artifacts and Folk Art in the Folk Museum." In *Folklore and Folklife: An Introduction,* ed. Richard M. Dorson, 497–516. Chicago: University of Chicago Press.

Johnson, Darragh. 1997. "Whether 'Slaughter' or Sport, Pigeon Shoot Goes On." *Sarasota Herald-Tribune,* February 21, 1, 10.

Johnston, Richard F., and Marián Janiga. 1995. *Feral Pigeons.* New York: Oxford University Press.

Jones, Ernest. 1971. *On the Nightmare.* New York: Liveright.

Jones, Michael Owen. 2000. "What's Disgusting, Why, and What Does It Matter?" *Journal of Folklore Research* 37:53–71.

Kammen, Michael. 1987. "Changing Perceptions of the Life Cycle in

American Thought and Culture." In *Selvages and Biases: The Fabric of History in American Culture* by Michael Kammen, 180–221. Ithaca, N.Y.: Cornell University Press.

Kean, Hilda. 1998. *Animal Rights: Political and Social Change in Britain since 1800.* London: Reaktion Books.

Keeley, Mary Paxton. 1930. "A. E. F. English." *American Speech* 5:372–86.

Keenan, Dan. 2005. "Hare Coursing Events Refused." *Irish Times*, December 26–27. http://www.indymedia.ie/article/73604?print_page=true (accessed July 5, 2006).

Kemmerer, Lisa. 2004a. "Hunting Tradition: Treaties, Law, and Subsistence Killing." *Animal Liberation Philosophy and Policy Journal* 2:1–20.

———. 2004b. "Killing Traditions: Consistency in Applied Moral Philosophy." *Ethics, Place and Environment* 7:151–71.

Kenealy, A. J. 1894. "The New York Yacht Club: A Sea-dog's Yarn of Fifty Years." *Outing, an Illustrated Monthly Magazine of Recreation* 24 (August): 388–404.

Kheel, Marti. 2003. "The Killing Game: An Ecofeminist Critique of Hunting." In *The Animal Ethics Reader*, ed. Susan J. Armstrong and Richard G. Botzler, 390–99. New York: Routledge.

Kimmel, Michael. 1996. *Manhood in America: A Cultural History.* New York: Free Press.

Kittrell, Irvin. 2003. "Number of Young Hunters Rebounds Slowly: Combo Permit Seems to Limit Lure of Malls, Video Games." *Patriot-News* (Harrisburg, Pa.), December 1, A1, 8.

Klaus, Mary. 2004. "Armed with Confidence, Veteran Hunter Needs Just One Shot." *Patriot-News* (Harrisburg, Pa.), November 30, A1, 16.

Kligerman, Jack. 1978. "'Pigeon Mumblers' of Brooklyn Wage *Guerra* in the Skies." *Smithsonian* 9:74–82.

Knox, John. 1558. *The First Blast of the Trumpet against the Monstrous Regiment of Women.* Geneva: J. Poullain and A. Rebul.

Koch, William. 1965. "Hunting Beliefs and Customs from Kansas." *Western Folklore* 24:165–75.

Krider, John. 1966 [1853]. *Krider's Sporting Anecdotes.* New York: Abercrombie and Fitch.

Lawrence, Elizabeth Atwood. 1997. *Hunting the Wren: Transformation of Bird to Symbol.* Knoxville: University of Tennessee Press.

Leach, Edmund. 1968. "Ritual." *International Encyclopedia of the Social Sciences*, 19 vols., ed. David L. Sills, 13:520–26. New York: Macmillan.

Leach, Maria, ed. 1949. *Funk and Wagnalls Standard Dictionary of Folklore, Mythology, and Legend*, 2 vols. New York: Funk and Wagnalls.

League against Cruel Sports. 2005. "Scotland 2002 Hunting and Coursing Banned; England and Wales 2004 Hunting and Coursing Banned; Northern Ireland? Cruelty Continues." Flyer issued in London.

Lears, Jackson. 2003. *Something for Nothing: Luck in America*. New York: Penguin Putnam.

Leary, James P., ed. 2001. *So Ole Says to Lena: Folk Humor of the Upper Midwest*, 2nd ed. Madison: University of Wisconsin Press.

Lee, Harper. 1960. *To Kill a Mockingbird*. Philadelphia: Lippincott.

Lefes, William S. 1953. "The Sociology of Deer Hunting in Two Pennsylvania Counties." Master's thesis, Pennsylvania State College.

Leffingwell, William Bruce. 1967 [1895]. *The Art of Wing Shooting*. New York: Arno Press.

Leibovich, Mark. 2006. "After Cheney's Shooting Incident, Time to Unload." *Washington Post*, February 14. http://www.washingtonpost.com/wp-dyn/content/article/2006/02/13/AR2006021301303_pf.html (accessed July 20, 2007).

Levi, Wendell Mitchell. 1957. *The Pigeon*. Sumter, S.C.: Levi.

Levinson, Sanford. 1989. "The Embarrassing Second Amendment." *Yale Law Journal* 99:637–59.

Lewis, Jim, and Jan Murphy. 2001. "State Keeps Hunters' Age Limit." *Patriot-News* (Harrisburg, Pa.), September 29, A1, 12.

Lincoln, Bruce. 1979. "The Hellhound." *Journal of Indo-European Studies* 7:273–85.

Lindahl, Carl, ed. 2004. *American Folktales from the Collections of the Library of Congress*. Armonk, N.Y.: M. E. Sharpe.

Lindahl, Carl, Maida Owens, and C. Renée Harrison, eds. 1997. *Swapping Stories: Folktales from Louisiana*. Jackson: University Press of Mississippi.

Lindner, Robert M. 1950. "The Psychodynamics of Gambling." *Annals of the American Academy of Political and Social Science* 269:93–107.

Linzey, Andrew. 2003. "The Bible and Killing for Food." In *The Animal Ethics Reader*, ed. Susan J. Armstrong and Richard G. Botzler, 227–34. New York: Routledge.

Lockwood, Randall, and Frank R. Ascione, eds. 1998. *Cruelty to Animals and Interpersonal Violence: Readings in Research and Application*. West Lafayette, Ind.: Purdue University Press.

Lounsberry, Mr. 1946. "Hunting Story." Manuscript, Louis C. Jones Folklore Collection, New York State Historical Association, Cooperstown.

Luke, Brian. 1998. "Violent Love: Hunting, Heterosexuality, and the Erotics of Men's Predation." *Feminist Studies* 24:627–55.

———. 2007. *Brutal: Manhood and the Exploitation of Animals*. Urbana: University of Illinois Press.

Lupey, Susan. 2004. "Girls Look Forward to Hunting and Life." Letter to the editor, *Patriot-News* (Harrisburg, Pa.), December 7, A19.

Lynn-Allen, E. H. 1942. *Rough Shoot: Some Thoughts for the Owner-Keeper.* London: Hutchinson.

Lysaght, Patricia. 1991. "Fairylore from the Midlands of Ireland." In *The Good People: New Fairylore Essays*, ed. Peter Narváez, 22–46. Lexington: University Press of Kentucky.

Maas, David R., ed. 1999. *Member Hunting Camps: A Gallery.* Minnetonka, Minn.: North American Hunting Club.

Macafee, Caroline. 1996. *The Concise Ulster Dictionary.* Oxford: Oxford University Press.

Mackay, Andrew. 2000–2001. "My Roots? Why and How Should We Make Rural Life Museums More Relevant to Our Visitors?" *Folk Life* 39:25–31.

Mackinnon, Catharine A. 2004. "Of Mice and Men: A Feminist Fragment on Animal Rights." In *Animal Rights: Current Debates and New Directions*, ed. Cass R. Sunstein and Martha C. Nussbaum, 263–76. Oxford: Oxford University Press.

March, Jenny. 2001. *Cassell's Dictionary of Classical Mythology.* London: Cassell.

Markarian, Michael. 1997. "Pigeons in the Crossfire: A Decade of Debate." *Animals' Agenda* 17 (November/December): 33–35.

Markham, Gervase. 1615. *Country Contentments.* London: I. B. for R. Iackson.

Marks, Stuart A. 1991. *Southern Hunting in Black and White.* Princeton, N.J.: Princeton University Press.

Marsh, Ben. 1987. "Continuity and Decline in the Anthracite Towns of Pennsylvania." *Annals of the Association of American Geographers* 77:337–52.

Martin, Laura C. 1993. *The Folklore of Birds.* Old Saybrook, Conn.: Globe Pequot Press.

Martin, Tim. 2004. "Get over It." Letter to the editor, *Patriot-News* (Harrisburg, Pa.), December 10, A17.

McCabe, Katie. 1986. "Who Will Live and Who Will Die." *Washingtonian* 21 (August): 112–18, 153–57.

McCormick, Charlie. 1996. "Eating Fried Rattler: The Symbolic Significance of the Rattlesnake Roundup." *Southern Folklore* 53:41–54.

McCurry, Justin. 2007. "Killing Whales Is Our Tradition, Say Hunters." *Sydney Morning Herald*, June 25. http://www.smh.com.au/news/environment/killing-whales-is-our-tradition-say-hunters/2007/06/24/1182623745475.html (accessed July 12, 2007).

McDonald, Country Joe. 1994 [1976]. *Paradise with an Ocean View*. CD. Berkeley, Calif.: Fantasy Records.

McManus, Megan. 2000. "Some Notions of Folklore, History and Museum Interpretation: A Time for Reappraisal?" In *From Corrib to Cultra: Folklife Essays in Honour of Alan Gailey*, ed. Trefor M. Owen, 18–28. Belfast: Institute of Irish Studies.

Mechling, Jay. 1987. "The Alligator." In *American Wildlife in Symbol and Story*, ed. Angus K. Gillespie and Jay Mechling, 73–98. Knoxville: University of Tennessee Press.

———. 1989. "'Banana Cannon' and Other Folk Traditions between Human and Nonhuman Animals." *Western Folklore* 48:312–23.

———. 1991. "From Archy to Archy, Why Cockroaches Are Good to Think." *Southern Folklore* 48:121–40.

———. 2001. *On My Honor: Boy Scouts and the Making of American Youth*. Chicago: University of Chicago Press.

———. 2005. "The Folklore of Mother-Raised Boys." In *Manly Traditions: The Folk Roots of American Masculinities*, ed. Simon J. Bronner, 211–27. Bloomington: Indiana University Press.

Mechling, Jay, and David Scofield Wilson. 1988. "Organizational Festivals and the Uses of Ambiguity: The Case of Picnic Day at Davis." In *Inside Organizations: Understanding the Human Dimension*, ed. Michael Owen Jones, Michael Dane Moore, and Richard Christopher Snyder, 303–18. Newbury Park, Calif.: Sage.

Meyer, Melissa L. 2005. *Thicker than Water: The Origins of Blood as Symbol and Ritual*. New York: Routledge.

Miami Valley Outdoor Media. 2008. "Outdoor Kids Club Magazine." http://www.outdoorkidsclub.com/ (accessed February 9, 2008).

Midgley, Mary. 1983. *Animals and Why They Matter: A Journey around the Species Barrier*. New York: Penguin.

Mieder, Wolfgang. 1992. *A Dictionary of American Proverbs*. New York: Oxford University Press.

———. 1993. *Howl Like a Wolf: Animal Proverbs*. Shelburne, Vt.: New England Press.

Mignot, Suzanne Le. 2006. "Local Quail Hunter Weighs in on Cheney Accident." *CBS2Chicago.com*. http://cbs2chicago.com/topstories/local_story_045223206.html (accessed July 20, 2007).

Miller, Sunlen. 2008. "Obama Fires Back at Clinton; 'Shame on Her.'" *ABC News*, April 13. http://blogs.abcnews.com/politicalradar/2008/04/obama-fires-back.html (accessed June 2, 2008).

Milner, Neal. 1989. "The Denigration of Rights and the Persistence of Rights Talk: A Cultural Portrait." *Law and Social Inquiry* 14:631–75.

Mione, Christopher. 1991. "Deercamp Folklore." Archives of Pennsylvania Folklore and Ethnography, Center for Pennsylvania Culture Studies, Pennsylvania State University, Harrisburg.

Mitchell, Carol. 1985. "Some Differences in Male and Female Joke-Telling." In *Women's Folklore, Women's Culture*, ed. Rosan A. Jordan and Susan J. Kalčik, 163–86. Philadelphia: University of Pennsylvania Press.

Morella, Connie. 1998. "Animal Violence, Youth Violence and Domestic Violence: A Deadly Progression." *Animal Guardian* 11:6–7.

Morgan, David. 1998. *Visual Piety: A History and Theory of Popular Religious Images*. Berkeley: University of California Press.

Morris, Hillary. 1996. "A Perspective on Hegins Pigeon Shoot, 1996." AnimalConcerns.Org. http://articles.animalconcerns.org/ar-voices/archive/hegins_perspective.html.

Morrison, Hugh. 1952. "'Shavetail' Again." *American Speech* 27:230–31.

Moyer, Ben. 2007. "Hunting: Number of Hunters Is Dropping, but Not Public Support for Those Who Hunt." *Pittsburgh Post-Gazette*, July 1. http://www.post-gazette.com/pg/07182/798452–358.stm (accessed July 16, 2007).

Muth, Robert M., and Wesley V. Jamison. 2000. "On the Destiny of Deer Camps and Duck Blinds: The Rise of the Animal Rights Movement and the Future of Wildlife Conservation." *Wildlife Society Bulletin* 28:841–51.

Myerhoff, Barbara. 1982. "Rites of Passage: Process and Paradox." In *Celebration: Studies in Festivity and Ritual*, ed. Victor Turner, 109–35. Washington, D.C.: Smithsonian Institution Press.

"A National Disgrace." 1873. *New York Times*, August 30, 4.

National Society for the Abolition of Cruel Sports. 1968. *A Foul Sport: Facts about Hare Coursing, a Brutal and Indefensible Pastime*. London: National Society for the Abolition of Cruel Sports.

National Wild Turkey Federation. 2003. "Hunting Heritage: The Important Things in Hunting Never Change." http://www.nwtf.org/toolkit-2003-Thanskgiving/z_content/Features/HuntTraditions.html (accessed July 9, 2007).

Newall, Venetia. 1971. *Discovering the Folklore of Birds and Beasts*. Tring, England: Shire Publications.

———. 1983. "The Unspeakable in Pursuit of the Uneatable: Some Comments on Fox-Hunting." *Folklore* 94:86–90.

Nibert, David. 2003. "Help Build Our New ASA Section." *Animals and Society* 3 (May): 1.

Nugent, Ted. 2000. *God, Guns, & Rock 'N' Roll*. Washington, D.C.: Regnery.

Nye, Russel B. 1966. *This Almost Chosen People: Essays in the History of American Ideas*. East Lansing: Michigan State University Press.

Odato, Meredith A. 2005. "Why I'm the Future of Hunting." *Sunday Patriot-News* (Harrisburg, Pa.), March 13, 40.

Opie, Iona, and Peter Opie. 1969. *Children's Games in Street and Playground*. Oxford: Oxford University Press.

Opie, Iona, and Moira Tatem, eds. 1989. *A Dictionary of Superstitions*. Oxford: Oxford University Press.

Oring, Elliott, ed. 1986. *Folk Groups and Folklore Genres*. Logan: Utah State University Press.

Ortega, José y Gasset. 1995. *Meditations on Hunting*, trans. Howard B. Wescott. Belgrade, Mont.: Wilderness Adventures Press.

Ó Súilleabháin, Seán. 1942. *A Handbook of Irish Folklore*. Dublin: Educational Company of Ireland for the Folklore of Ireland Society.

Owen, Trefor M. 1959. *Welsh Folk Customs*. Llandysul, Wales: Gwasg Gomer.

———. 1981. "Folk Life Studies: Some Problems and Perspectives." *Folk Life* 19:5–16.

Oxford English Dictionary. 1971. Oxford: Oxford University Press.

Palmer, Roy. 1991. *Britain's Living Folklore*. London: David and Charles.

Partridge, Eric. 1961. *A Dictionary of the Underworld: British and American*. New York: Bonanza Books.

———. 1970. *A Dictionary of Slang and Unconventional English*. New York: Macmillan.

Patterson, Charles. 2002. *Eternal Treblinka: Our Treatment of Animals and the Holocaust*. New York: Lantern Books.

Peate, Iorwerth C. 1959. "The Study of Folk Life; and Its Part in the Defence of Civilization." *Gwerin* 2:97–109.

Pelikan, Jaroslav. 1992. *Sacred Writings, Judaism: The Tanakh*. New York: Quality Paperback Book Club.

Pennsylvania State Data Center. 2000. "Hunting Is Big Business in Pennsylvania." *Research Brief* press release, December 7.

———. 2002. "2002 Deer Season to Begin Statewide on December 2nd." *Research Brief* press release, November 22.

Pentikäinen, Juha. 1997. "Ritual." In *Folklore: An Encyclopedia of Beliefs, Customs, Tales, Music, and Art*, 2 vols., ed. Thomas A. Green, 733–36. Santa Barbara, Calif.: ABC-CLIO.

PETA (People for the Ethical Treatment of Animals). 2005. "About PETA." http://www.peta.org/about (accessed May 27, 2005).

Phelps, Norm. 2002. *The Dominion of Love: Animal Rights According to the Bible*. New York: Lantern Books.

————. 2007. *The Longest Struggle: Animal Advocacy from Pythagoras to PETA*. New York: Lantern Books.

"Pigeon Shooting." 1872. *New York Times*, January 1, 4.

Pine, Leslie. 1966. *After Their Blood: A Survey of Blood Sports in Britain*. London: William Kimber.

Plank, Dave. 1995. "Why the Caged Bird Stings: Nobody to Be Prosecuted for Role in Illegal 'Hunt.'" *Phoenix New Times*, August 17–23. http://www.urbanwildlifesociety.org/pigeons/NTWPijShoot.html (accessed July 9, 2007).

"Plans of the Trap Shooters." 1893. *New York Times*, July 3, 8.

Pollack, William. 1998. *Real Boys: Rescuing Our Sons from the Myths of Boyhood*. New York: Random House.

Poole, Steven. 2000. *Trigger Happy: The Inner Life of Videogames*. London: Fourth Estate.

Posewitz, Jim. 1994. *Beyond Fair Chase: The Ethic and Tradition of Hunting*. Guilford, Conn.: Globe Pequot Press.

Poulsen, Richard C. 1974. "Mules as Venison: Or the Fecundity of Utah's Oral Tradition." *Western Folklore* 33:326–31.

Prescott, Heidi. 1995. "How Hunters Make My Job Easy." Address to the Fourth Annual Governor's Symposium on North America's Hunting Heritage, Green Bay, Wis., August.

————. 1998. Letter to Jodi Anderson, March 31.

Prescott, Sir Mark. 1984. "Hare Coursing." In *The British Sporting Heritage*, 54–56. London: Sotheby's.

————. 2006. "Madness, Mad-Madness." *National Coursing Club News*. http://www.nationalcoursingclub.org/maintain/news.htm (accessed May 2, 2006).

Primatt, Humphry. 1992 [1776]. *The Duty of Mercy and the Sin of Cruelty to Brute Animals*. London: Centaur.

"Puritans' Feast Day: How the City Gave Thanks and Cause for Thanks." 1882. *New York Times*, December 1, 8.

Rachels, James. 1990. *Created from Animals: The Moral Implications of Darwinism*. Oxford: Oxford University Press.

Radner, Joan N., and Susan S. Lanser. 1987. "The Feminist Voice: Strategies of Coding in Folklore and Literature." *Journal of American Folklore* 100:412–25.

Randolph, Vance. 1951. *We Always Lie to Strangers: Tall Tales from the Ozarks*. New York: Columbia University Press.

————. 1952. *Who Blowed up the Church House? And Other Ozark Folk Tales*. Notes by Herbert Halpert. New York: Columbia University Press.

————. 1976. *Pissing in the Snow and Other Ozark Folktales.* Annotations by Frank A. Hoffmann. Urbana: University of Illinois Press.

————. 1992. *Roll Me in Your Arms: "Unprintable" Ozark Folksongs and Folklore,* ed. G. Legman. Fayetteville: University of Arkansas Press.

Raphael, Ray. 1988. *The Men from the Boys: Rites of Passage in Male America.* Lincoln: University of Nebraska Press.

Rappaport, Roy A. 1992. "Ritual." In *Folklore, Cultural Performances, and Popular Entertainments: A Communications-Centered Handbook,* ed. Richard Bauman, 249–60. New York: Oxford University Press.

————. 1996 [1979]. "The Obvious Aspects of Ritual." In *Readings in Ritual Studies,* ed. Ronald L. Grimes, 427–40. Upper Saddle River, N.J.: Prentice-Hall.

Ravitch, Diane. 2002. "Education after the Culture Wars." *Daedalus: Journal of the American Academy of Arts and Sciences* 131:5–21.

"Readers Love to Pass on Heritage." 2008. *Sunday Patriot-News* (Harrisburg, Pa.), February 10, Sports 31.

Reaver, J. Russell. 1972. "From Reality to Fantasy: Opening-Closing Formulas in the Structures of American Tall Tales." *Southern Folklore Quarterly* 36:369–82.

Regan, Tom. 2001 [1983]. *Defending Animal Rights.* Urbana: University of Illinois Press.

————. 2004. "The Case for Animal Rights." In *The Animal Ethics Reader,* ed. Susan J. Armstrong and Richard G. Botzler, 17–24. New York: Routledge.

Regan, Tom, and Peter Singer, eds. 1976. *Animal Rights and Human Obligations.* Englewood Cliffs, N.J.: Prentice-Hall.

Reik, Theodor. [1931]. "Couvade and the Psychogenesis of the Fear of Retaliation." In *Ritual: Psycho-Analytic Studies,* trans. Douglas Bryan. New York: W. W. Norton.

Renteln, Alison Dundes. 2004. *The Cultural Defense.* Oxford: Oxford University Press.

Renteln, Alison, and Alan Dundes, eds. 1994. *Folk Law: Essays in the Theory and Practice of Lex Non Scripta,* 2 vols. Madison: University of Wisconsin Press.

Richardson, Charles. 1903. "Coursing the Hare." In *The Hare,* 109–41. London: Longmans, Green.

Rickaby, Joseph. 1976. "Of the So-called Rights of Animals." In *Animal Rights and Human Obligations,* ed. Tom Regan and Peter Singer, 179–80. Englewood Cliffs, N.J.: Prentice-Hall.

Riney-Kehrberg, Pamela. 2005. *Childhood on the Farm: Work, Play, and Coming of Age in the Midwest.* Lawrence: University Press of Kansas.

Ritchie, D. G. 1976. "Why Animals Do Not Have Rights." In *Animal Rights and Human Obligations*, ed. Tom Regan and Peter Singer, 181–84. Englewood Cliffs, N.J.: Prentice-Hall.

Robbins, Kyle. 2007. "My Outdoor Experiences Helped Me through It All and Enabled Me to Grow Smarter and Stronger." U.S. Army advertisement. *Field and Stream* (October): 20.

Roberts, Leonard W. 1955. *South from Hell-fer-Sartin: Kentucky Mountain Folk Tales*. Lexington: University of Kentucky Press.

Roberts, Richard. 1990. *Save the Whales*. San Aneselmo, Calif.: Vernal Equinox Press.

Robinson, Kayne. 2007. "Raising Kayne for Hunters" *Gone Huntin'*, 7.

Robinson, Mairi, ed. 1985. *The Concise Scots Dictionary*. Aberdeen, Scotland: Aberdeen University Press.

Rollin, Bernard E. 1981. *Animal Rights and Human Morality*. Buffalo, N.Y.: Prometheus Books.

Roman, Joe. 2006. *Whale*. London: Reaktion.

Rotundo, E. Anthony. 1993. *American Manhood: Transformations in Masculinity from the Revolution to the Modern Era*. New York: Basic Books.

Russell, Ian. 2002. "The Hunt's Up? Rural Community, Song, and Politics." *Acta Ethnographica Hungarica* 47:127–41.

Ryder, Richard D. 1989. *Animal Revolution: Changing Attitudes toward Speciesism*. Oxford: Basil Blackwell.

Saad, Lydia. 2007. "Americans Rate the Morality of 16 Social Issues." Gallup poll Web site, May 31. http://www.galluppoll.com/content/default.aspx?ci=27757&pg=2 (accessed July 19, 2007).

Sackett, S. J., and William E. Koch, eds. 1961. *Kansas Folklore*. Lincoln: University of Nebraska Press.

Salmon, M. H. Dutch. 1977. *Gazehounds and Coursing: The History, Art and Sport of Hunting with Sighthounds*. Silver City, N.M.: High-Lonesome Books.

Salt, Henry S., ed. 1915. *Killing for Sport*. London: G. Bell and Sons.

Samuelson, Sue. 1982. "Folklore and the Legal System: The Expert Witness." *Western Folklore* 41:139–44.

Sandys, Ed W. 1894. "Rod and Gun." *Outing: An Illustrated Monthly Magazine of Recreation* 23 (January): 80–81.

Schlereth, Thomas J. 1989. "Country Stores, County Fairs, and Mail-Order Catalogues: Consumption in Rural America." In *Consuming Visions: Accumulation and Display of Goods in America, 1880–1920*, ed. Simon J. Bronner, 339–75. New York: W. W. Norton.

Schneck, Marcus. 1998. "Oh Shoot—Hunting's on Decline: Symposium Considers Strategies to Increase Interest." *Patriot-News* (Harrisburg, Pa.), August 13, A1, 16.

———. 1999. "A Hunt for Memories—Opening Day Isn't Just Deer: It's about Forming Kinships that Transcend Generations." *Patriot-News* (Harrisburg, Pa.), November 28, A1, 20.

———. 2001a. "Deer Hunters Harvest Tradition." *Patriot-News* (Harrisburg, Pa.), November 25, A1, 24.

———. 2001b. "Sparking More Interest in Young Hunters a Key Goal." *Patriot-News* (Harrisburg, Pa.), October 11, C5.

———. 2007. "Mentored Hunters Create Memories." *Patriot-News* (Harrisburg, Pa.), December 2, Sports 35.

———. 2008. "Free Tickets, New Products for Show." *Sunday Patriot-News* (Harrisburg, Pa.), January 27, Sports 31.

Schorger, A. W. 1973 [1955]. *The Passenger Pigeon: Its Natural History and Extinction.* Norman: University of Oklahoma Press.

Schwartz, Jane. 1989. "Up on the Roof: Pigeon Flyers and City Skies." *Folklife Annual 1988–1989*, ed. James Hardin and Alan Jaboour, 34–45. Washington, D.C.: Library of Congress.

Scully, Matthew. 2002. *Dominion: The Power of Man, the Suffering of Animals, and the Call to Mercy.* New York: St. Martin's Press.

Seward, John. 2005. "Big Outdoor Retailers Fight for Market Share." ESPN.com: Hunting Web site. http://sports.espn.go.com/outdoors/hunting/news/story?id=2075457 (accessed July 20, 2007).

Shapiro, Kenneth J. 1993. "Introduction to Society and Animals." *Society and Animals* 1:1–4.

Shaw, George Bernard. 1915. "Preface." In *Killing for Sport*, ed. Henry S. Salt, xi–xxxiv. London: G. Bell.

Sheldon, Joann. 2004. "Time Together." Letter to the editor, *Patriot-News* (Harrisburg, Pa.), December 10, A17.

Shepard, Paul. 1973. *The Tender Carnivore and the Sacred Game.* Athens: University of Georgia Press.

Sheppard, Vera. 1979. *My Head against the Wall: A Decade in the Fight against Blood Sports.* Bradford-on-Avon, England: Moonraker Press.

Shoemaker, Henry W. 1992 [1912]. *Pennsylvania Deer and Their Horns.* Baltimore: Gateway Press.

———. 1993 [1917]. *Extinct Pennsylvania Animals, Parts I and II.* Baltimore: Gateway Press.

Sikes, Wirt. 1880. *British Goblins: Welsh Folk-lore, Fairy Mythology, Legends and Traditions.* London: Sampson Low, Marston, Searle, and Rivington.

Simons, Hi. 1933. "A Prison Dictionary." *American Speech* 8:22–33.

Simpson, Caroline M. 2004. "Disgusting Photo." Letter to the editor, *Patriot-News* (Harrisburg, Pa.), December 3, A13.

Simpson, Jacqueline, and Steve Roud. 2000. *A Dictionary of English Folklore*. Oxford: Oxford University Press.

Singer, Peter. 1990 [1975]. *Animal Liberation*. Rev. ed. New York: Avon.

Sirius. 1876. "Coursing: The Waterloo Cup." *Baily's Magazine of Sports and Pastimes* 28:210–20.

Slinsky, Jim. 1999. "Is Banning Pigeon Shoot Beginning of End for Hunting?" *Pottsville Republican*, October 28. http://archives.pottsville.com/archives/1999/Oct/28/A2182330.htm.

Slotkin, Richard. 2000 [1973]. *Regeneration through Violence: The Mythology of the American Frontier*. Norman: University of Oklahoma Press.

Smedley, Lauren. 1990. "Hunting Rabbits, Squirrels, and Little Girls." *Feminists for Animal Rights Newsletter* 5 (1–2): 9.

Smith, Henry Nash. 1970 [1950]. *Virgin Land: The American West as Symbol and Myth*. Twentieth Anniversary Printing. Cambridge, Mass.: Harvard University Press.

Smith, Johnson. 1935. *Humorous Recitations*. Detroit: Johnson Smith.

Smith, Kathryn C. 1978. "The Role of Animals in Witchcraft and Popular Magic." In *Animals in Folklore*, ed. J. R. Porter and W. M. S. Russell, 96–110. Ipswich: D. S. Brewer.

Snyder, Yolanda K. 1987. "Butcher's Bull: A Study in Occupational Folklore." *Mid-America Folklore* 15:1–13.

Sommers, Christina Hoff. 2000. *The War against Boys: How Misguided Feminism Is Harming Our Young Men*. New York: Touchstone.

Song, S. Hoon. 2000a. "The Great Pigeon Massacre: The Bestiary Biopolitics of Whiteness in a Deindustrializing America." PhD diss., University of Chicago.

———. 2000b. "The Great Pigeon Massacre in a Deindustrializing American Region." In *Natural Enemies: People-Wildlife Conflicts in Anthropological Perspective*, ed. John Knight, 212–28. London: Routledge.

Sontag, Susan. 2003. *Regarding the Pain of Others*. New York: Farrar, Straus and Giroux.

Spiegel, Marjorie. 1996. *The Dreaded Comparison: Human and Animal Slavery*. Rev. and expanded ed. New York: Mirror Books.

Spinelli, Jerry. 1997. *Wringer*. New York: HarperCollins.

Spradley, James P., and Brenda J. Mann. 1975. *The Cocktail Waitress: Woman's Work in a Man's World*. New York: McGraw-Hill.

Stange, Mary Zeiss. 1997. *Woman the Hunter*. Boston: Beacon Press.

———. 1999. "Arms and the Woman: A Feminist Reappraisal." In *Guns in America: A Reader*, ed. Jan E. Dizard, Robert Merrill Muth, and Stephen P. Andrews Jr., 351–87. New York: New York University Press.

Stange, Mary Zeiss, and Carol K. Oyster. 2000. *Gun Women: Firearms and*

Feminism in Contemporary America. New York: New York University Press.

Steele, Darren. 1998. "The Bucks Stop Here in Pa. Hunting Season." *Weekly Collegian* (State College, Pa.), December 9, 14.

Stein, Max. N.d. *Comic Songs, Funny Stories and Recitations.* Chicago: Max Stein Publishing House.

Stein, Ralph, and Harry Brown. 1943. *It's a Cinch, Private Finch!* New York: McGraw-Hill.

Steiner, Rudolf. 1997 [1907]. *Occult Significance of Blood.* Kila, Mont.: Kessinger.

Sterba, Richard. 1947. "Some Psychological Factors in Negro Race Hatred and in Anti-Negro Riots." In *Psychoanalysis and the Social Sciences*, vol. 1, ed. Géza Róheim, 411–27. New York: International Universities Press.

Stratton, Rev. J. 1915. "Clay-Pigeon versus Live Pigeon." In *Killing for Sport*, ed. Henry S. Salt, 166–68. London: G. Bell and Sons.

Suarez, Fernando. 2008. "Clinton's Hunting History." *CBS News*, February 18. http://www.cbsnews.com/blogs/2008/02/18/politics/fromtheroad/entry3842857.shtml (accessed June 2, 2008).

Sullivan, Robert. 2000. *A Whale Hunt: How a Native American Village Did What No One Thought It Could.* New York: Simon and Schuster.

Sutton-Smith, Brian. 1972. *The Folkgames of Children.* Austin: University of Texas Press.

———. 1997. *The Ambiguity of Play.* Cambridge, Mass.: Harvard University Press.

Swan, James A. 1995. *In Defense of Hunting.* New York: HarperSanFrancisco.

———. 1999. *The Sacred Art of Hunting: Myths, Legends and the Modern Mythos.* Minocqua, Wis.: Willow Creek Press.

———. 2003. "A Countryside up in Arms." *National Review Online*, May 15. http://www.nationalreview.com/swan/swan051503.asp (accessed July 9, 2007).

Sweterlitsch, Richard. 1997. "Custom." In *Folklore: An Encyclopedia of Beliefs, Customs, Tales, Music, and Art*, 2 vols., ed. Thomas A. Green, 168–72. Santa Barbara, Calif.: ABC-CLIO.

Sykes, Christopher. 1960. "Summing up with Some Memories." In *In Praise of Hunting: A Symposium*, ed. David James and Wilson Stephens, 203–31. London: Hollis and Carter.

Taksel, Rebecca. 1992. "Feminists in the Making: Women Activists in the Animal Rights Movement." *Feminists for Animal Rights Newsletter* 6 (3–4): 4–5.

Telleen, Maurice. 2003. "The Mind-set of Agrarianism . . . New and Old." In *The Essential Agrarian Reader: The Future of Culture, Community, and the Land*, ed. Norman Wirzba, 52–61. Lexington: University Press of Kentucky.

Terwilliger, Vicki. 1999a. "Concern, Celebration: Shoot Winners Express Fears for Their Rights." *Pottsville Republican*, August 19. http://archives.pottsville.com/archives/1999/Aug/19/E255676.htm (accessed July 9, 2007).

———. 1999b. "Decision Surprises Hegins People: Supporters Hate to See Event Halted." *Pottsville Republican*, August 18. http://archives.pottsville.com/archives/1999/Aug/18/E253035.htm (accessed July 9, 2007).

Thigpen, Kenneth, and George Hornbein. 1984. *Buck Season at Bear Meadows Sunset*. State College, Pa.: Documentary Resource Center. Original 16mm format available at http://www.folkstreams.net/film,100 (accessed February 8, 2008).

Thomas, Richard B. 1983. *The Politics of Hunting*. Aldershot, England: Gower.

Thompson, Stith. 1975. *Motif-Index of Folk-Literature*, 6 vols. Rev. and enlarged ed. Bloomington: Indiana University Press.

"Timeline: Hunting Row." 2005. BBC News, February 17. http://news.bbc.co.uk/1/hi/uk___politics/1846577.stm (accessed July 4, 2006).

TLC. 1999. *Fanmail*. CD. New York: La Face.

"To Prohibit Pigeon Shooting: The Slater Measure Passed by the Senate after Some Debate." 1901. *New York Times*, April 20, 6.

Toelken, Barre. 1996. *The Dynamics of Folklore*. Rev. ed. Logan: Utah State University Press.

Trapshooting Hall of Fame. 2004. "Live Bird Grands: The First Ten Grand Americans." http://www.traphof.org/live_bird_GAH_history.htm (accessed July 9, 2007).

Trijicon. 2008. "You're at the Top of the Food Chain, So Enjoy the View." Advertisement. *Field and Stream* (June): 6.

Turner, Victor W. 1967. *The Forest of Symbols: Aspects of Ndembu Ritual*. Ithaca, N.Y.: Cornell University Press.

———. 1969. *The Ritual Process: Structure and Anti-Structure*. Chicago: University of Chicago Press.

Underwood, Lamar, ed. 2003. *Classic Hunting Stories*. Guilford, Conn.: Lyons Press.

Updike, John. 1962. *Pigeon Feathers and Other Stories*. New York: Alfred A. Knopf.

Urban Dictionary. 2008. "Shavetail." http://www.urbandictionary.com/define.php?term=shavetail (accessed January 30, 2008).

U.S. Department of the Interior, Fish and Wildlife Service, and U.S. Department of Commerce, Bureau of the Census. 1993. *1991 National Survey of Fishing, Hunting, and Wildlife-Associated Recreation: Pennsylvania.* Washington, D.C.: U.S. Fish and Wildlife Service.

———. 1998. *1996 National Survey of Fishing, Hunting, and Wildlife-Associated Recreation: Pennsylvania.* Washington, D.C.: U.S. Fish and Wildlife Service.

———. 2003. *2001 National Survey of Fishing, Hunting, and Wildlife-Associated Recreation: Pennsylvania.* Washington, D.C.: U.S. Fish and Wildlife Service.

Uther, Hans-Jörg. 2004. *The Types of International Folktales: A Classification and Bibliography,* 3 vols. Helsinki: Suomalainen Tiedeakatemia.

Van Gennep, Arnold. 1961. *Rites of Passage.* Chicago: University of Chicago Press.

Van Putten, Mark, and Sterling D. Miller. 1999. "Prairie Dogs: The Case for Listing." *Wildlife Society Bulletin* 27:1113–20.

Various NAHC Members. 1999. "Deer Camp Traditions." In *Hunting Camp Almanac: A Compendium of Stories, Tips, Tidbits, Old-Time Folklore and Humor of Interest to Hunters,* ed. Teresa Marrone, 18–19. Minnetonka, Minn.: North American Hunting Club.

Vermont Folklife Center. 2006. *Deer Stories.* Transcription of radio broadcast. Middlebury: Vermont Folklife Center Media.

Video Game Critic. 2008. "The Video Game Critic's Atari 2600 Reviews." http://www.videogamecritic.net/2600ss.htm#Save_The_Whales (accessed January 30, 2008).

War Department Bureau of Public Relations—Radio Branch. 1943. "Army Chuckles." *Behind the Headlines in Our Army* 83 (January 12): 4.

"The Way Ahead." 2006. *National Coursing Club News.* National Coursing Club Web site. http://www.nationalcoursingclub.org/maintain/news.htm (accessed July 9, 2006).

Weaver, William Woys. 1983. *Sauerkraut Yankees: Pennsylvania-German Foods and Foodways.* Philadelphia: University of Pennsylvania Press.

———. 1993. *Pennsylvania Dutch Country Cooking.* New York: Abbeville Press.

Wegner, Robert. 1984. *Deer and Deer Hunting: The Serious Hunter's Guide.* Harrisburg, Pa.: Stackpole.

———. 1987. *Deer and Deer Hunting Book 2: Strategies and Tactics for the Advanced Hunter.* Harrisburg, Pa.: Stackpole.

Weimer, Orpha. 1993. "North Manchester Airport Provided Flying Opportunities for Residents in 1930s and 40s." *North Manchester Historical Society Newsletter* (November). http://mcs.k12.in.us/histsoc/nov93.htm#anchor5383812.

Weinbaum, Matthew. 2004. "Makah Native Americans vs. Animal Rights Activists." Environmental Justice Case Studies Web site, University of Michigan. http://www.umich.edu/~snre492/Jones/makah.htm#table (accessed July 22, 2007).

Wentworth, Harold, and Stuart Berg Flexner, eds. 1967. *Dictionary of American Slang.* New York: Thomas Y. Crowell.

Weston, Coe. 2002. "Ten Facts about Live Pigeon Competition Shooting." *Trafalgar Times* 7 (summer). http://www.tafalgar-mlc.fsnet.co.uk/journal/summer-2002.htm (accessed July 9, 2007).

White, Richard. 1997. "The Current Weirdness in the West." *Western Historical Quarterly* 28:5–16.

White Sands Missile Range. 2008. "Missiles in Missile Park." http://www.wsmr.army.mil/pao/FactSheets/mispark.htm (accessed June 30, 2008).

Whiting, Bartlett Jere. 1977. *Early American Proverbs and Proverbial Phrases.* Cambridge, Mass.: Belknap Press of Harvard University Press.

Wicklund, Freeman. 1998. "Direct Action: Progress, Peril, or Both?" *Animals' Agenda* 18 (July/August): 23–27.

Williams, Raymond. 1973. *The Country and the City.* London: Chatto and Windus.

Windeatt, Philip. 1982. *The Hunt and the Anti-Hunt.* London: Pluto Press.

Wiscount, Joe. 1989. "Pennsylvania Dutch Pigeon Matches and Shoots." Manuscript, Center for Pennsylvania Culture Studies, Penn State Harrisburg, Middletown, Pa.

Wise, Steven M. 2000. *Rattling the Cage: Toward Legal Rights for Animals.* Cambridge, Mass.: Perseus.

Wolf, Tania E. 2004. "Horrifying Image." Letter to the editor, *Patriot-News* (Harrisburg, Pa.), December 6, A11.

Wolfe, Cary. 2003. *Animal Rites: American Culture, the Discourse of Species, and Posthumanist Theory.* Chicago: University of Chicago Press.

Wolgemuth, Rachel. 2000. "How Do I Bear This Heartache? Pet Cemeteries in American Culture." Master's thesis, Pennsylvania State University.

"The World According to Ted Nugent: Quotes and Stories from Ted's Writings and Interviews." 2000. No Compromise Web site, July 31. http://www.nocompromise.org/news/000731c.html (accessed July 22, 2007).

Yeager, Chuck. 2001. "Introduction." In *Cabela's, World's Foremost Outfitters: A History* by David Cabela, xiii–xv. Forest Dale, Vt.: Paul S. Eriksson.

"Young Hunters Excel at Safety." 2005. *Sunday Patriot-News* (Harrisburg, Pa.), February 20, 40.

Zemencik, Rebecca. 2003. "The Duchess of the Hegins Valley." *Citizen-Standard* (Valley View, Pa.), May 14. http://newsitem.com/cgi-bin/citizen/articles (accessed July 9, 2007).

Zukin, Sharon. 2005. *Point of Purchase: How Shopping Changed American Culture.* New York: Routledge.

Index